INDIGENOUS INTERFACES

Critical Issues in Indigenous Studies

Jeffrey P. Shepherd and Myla Vicenti Carpio
SERIES EDITORS

INDIGENOUS INTERFACES

SPACES, TECHNOLOGY, AND SOCIAL NETWORKS IN MEXICO AND CENTRAL AMERICA

JENNIFER GÓMEZ MENJÍVAR AND
GLORIA ELIZABETH CHACÓN
FOREWORD BY **ARTURO ARIAS**

THE UNIVERSITY OF
ARIZONA PRESS
TUCSON

The University of Arizona Press
www.uapress.arizona.edu

© 2019 by The Arizona Board of Regents
All rights reserved. Published 2019

ISBN-13: 978-0-8165-3800-3 (paper)

Cover design by Leigh McDonald
Cover art adapted from *Weaving Loom 2* by Mike Russell

Library of Congress Cataloging-in-Publication Data are available at the Library of Congress.

Printed in the United States of America
♾ This paper meets the requirements of ANSI/NISO Z39.48-1992 (Permanence of Paper).

For my abuelita Janda (1920–2014). J. G. M.

For Nawal. G. E. C.

CONTENTS

FOREWORD

Indigenous Subjects and the Mastering of Science

It suffices to read the table of contents of this volume to ascertain the impressive depth of topics being explored. Yet it is not only a matter of topics. It is about cutting-edge technology being implemented by Indigenous subjects. In our times, this is breaking news. It may seem surprising to some, however, that Indigenous subjects—not only subalternized and racialized but derided throughout the Western Hemisphere as nonsubjects coexisting and intermingling with modernity or as beings excluded from conventional discourse—should suddenly give the impression that they just now mastered cutting-edge technology. Needless to say, those surprised by what they may perceive as a sudden turn of events can never escape the sense of ignoring much about Indigenous cultures. They might have never put themselves in the subject position of another, or they might have simply absorbed the simplified version of events as written by both Christopher Columbus upon his accidental arrival at what was for Europeans a New Word and Hernando Cortés, the leader of the Spanish invasion of Mexico in 1519, who justified a military occupation that directly or indirectly killed 90 percent of the population. Cortés's account distorted forever the understanding of the destruction of sophisticated cultures that were more advanced than Europe's in the fifteenth century CE, except in armament and military strategy. Cortés's version described Mexicas as guilty of human sacrifice and cannibalism. The legend was crafted to exploit Mesoamerica's wealth for economic and political gain.

This volume's introduction already points out the compulsion to perceive Indigenous peoples as located outside of technology's purview. However, this was not the case prior to the arrival of Europeans in what they called "the New World." Let us first remember Columbus's stance on this matter. Columbus returned from his first trip with enslaved Indigenous subjects that were later paraded through the streets of Barcelona and Seville. Columbus's actions were the beginning of settler colonialism in the hemisphere.[1] Under his orders, the Spanish attacked the Tainos, reducing Hispaniola's Taino population, estimated at two million in 1492, to near extinction within thirty years. Needing labor to replace the rapidly declining Tainos, the Spanish introduced African slaves to Hispaniola in 1502. By 1510, the slave trade was of critical importance to the Caribbean economy. Columbus bears responsibility for the first global Holocaust, a term used by historian David. E. Stannard in his text *American Holocaust: The Conquest of the New World* (1992), of which Indigenous and African peoples were the primary victims.

Given this established preconception, it should not be surprising that from the very beginning of his contact with the Mexicas in Tenochtitlan on November 8, 1519, Hernando Cortés belittled the Huey Tlahtoani Moteuctzomatzin Xocoyotzin while ennobling himself. At first, Cortés did paint the Huey Tlahtoani as a disciplined, thoughtful, curious, and impeccably courteous man. It was only after the Noche Triste—June 30, 1520, "The Night of Sorrows" in English, though literally meaning "The Sad Night," the night when the invading Spaniards' army was thrown out of Tenochtitlan and only managed to survive because the Tlaxcaltecs rescued them—that the Spanish commander wrote his newer version of events, the one that went on to become a myth of Western supremacy. Cortés disguised the unpremeditated attack of his second-in-command Pedro de Alvarado's forces on civilian revelers celebrating the festival of Tóxcatl, a horrific massacre where estimates have claimed that up to ten thousand Mexicas were killed, as an attempt to prevent mass sacrifice in the name of the Christian faith. He mainly skipped the outraged Mexica reaction, one leading to their swiftly surrounding the city to prevent the Spaniards' escape, and did not mention that he pressed ahead and, crossing the Mixcoatechialtitlan canal, reached dry land while the rest of the expedition was left to fend for itself. Cortés glosses over the battered condition in which the Spanish survivors were left, and that they literally were physically carried all the way back to Tlaxcallān, where they arrived five days later.

In *When Montezuma Met Cortés* (2018), Matthew Restall points out how as early as March 1521 news had reached Europe of how Cortés understood Mexica culture, their city, and their leader (36).[2] Never once did the myths he advanced contemplate appreciation of cultural or scientific achievements. They were based almost exclusively on religious prejudice. Spaniards, and most Europeans, assumed that Christianity was the only true and valid religion. In sixteenth-century European understanding, Indigenous religious practices were idolatrous. At the same time, Indigenous subjects lacked, in their eyes, the rationality to understand that their idols were possessed by the devil, practiced human sacrifice, ate human flesh, and, as if all that were not enough, were sodomites, as Restall notes (77–85). In this logic, and in a European world that itself had not discovered science, the issue of local knowledges was moot. Let us not forget that, after the ascendancy of Protestantism and the emergence of Enlightenment thinking in the eighteenth century, Spaniards themselves were considered lacking scientific knowledge, a trope that monopolized modernity among Northern European—primarily Protestant—nation-states.

For most Europeans, Indigenous religions were, and have remained, indecipherable. They are so because they cannot be explained rationally, any more than Christianity and the ritual of transubstantiation can be for those who do not partake of the Christian faith. Religions—Indigenous or not—struggle when expressing the interplay of absolute and relative truths and the fundamental nondualism of their teachings. In Eurocentric thinking, as in Indigenous knowledges, we have a major breach between knowledge and belief. Because of this, Eurocentric scientific knowledge tried to differentiate itself from Christianity since at least the end of the seventeenth century. Its practitioners enacted specific methodological and epistemological grounds on which reality could be investigated. They codified when any given scholarship could be regarded as deploying technical insights, quantitative data, and warranted "universal" validation anchored in institutional origins and moorings, so that it could be labeled as following a scientific method to reach its conclusions. Yet when individuals sidestep the religious issue, much as anthropologist E. N. Anderson does, the nature of scientific knowledge surfaces. Anderson (2000) states: "Yucatec Maya ethnobiology agrees with contemporary international biological science in many respects, almost all of them highly specific, pragmatic and observational. It differs in many other respects, most of them highly inferential and cosmological" (129). Anderson's description would be of a similar nature were we differentiating Eurocentric science from Christian faith.

While Europe underwent its own religious wars in the seventeenth century, and these were followed by the gradual emergence of Enlightenment thinking, Indigenous knowledges largely disappeared from the map because of the first global Holocaust. Despite Henry F. Dobyns's polemical contention in his seminal article "An Appraisal of Techniques with a New Hemispheric Estimate" (1966) that the Indigenous population of the Americas totaled about one hundred million people in 1492—an assertion that nevertheless changed the demographic field—most scholars estimate that the Indigenous population of the Americas hovered at around fifty to seventy million by 1492 (Taylor 2001, 40; Thornton 1990, 11). An estimated 80 to 90 percent of this population—that is, a minimum of forty million people—were dead fifty years after Columbus's arrival, according to Stannard and other scholars reworking new data during the last twenty-five years, even if the high number was not the exclusive result of military violence, racism, and enslavement. To a large degree, diseases brought to the New World by white Europeans played a key role.[3] Despite their differences, Indigenous peoples of the Americas share the common history of this Holocaust, one of haunting legacies, "things [pasts] hard to recount or even remember, the results of a violence that holds an unrelenting grip on memory yet is deemed unspeakable" (Schwab 2010, 1). At the same time, as Anderson has explained, Indigenous scientific knowledge was associated with their cosmological thinking. Thus, these practices were forbidden, labeled witchcraft, and persecuted by Spain's Holy Inquisition.

In 1550 and 1551, Friar Bartolomé de las Casas participated in a series of debates with the Spanish royal historian Juan Ginés de Sepúlveda before the Council of the Indies in Valladolid on the putative humanity or inhumanity of Indigenous peoples. As stated in previous writings of mine, David Theo Goldberg has argued in *The Racial State* (2002) that this was the true beginning of the concept of race. Despite Las Casas's spirited defense of Indigenous peoples, the Spanish colonial order, rooted in racism and segregation, and upheld through violence and antagonism, prevailed. Criollo historian Francisco Antonio de Fuentes y Guzmán's *Recordación Florida* (1690) consolidated the subalternization and racialization of Indigenous peoples in Central America (which at the time included Chiapas) by portraying them as "those miserable, blind and savagely hopeless, primitive Indians of this Kingdom of Goathemala" (16). Yet despite such small inklings of hope, in the Yucatecan town of Máani' the infamous Franciscan friar Diego de Landa (1524–79) conducted an auto-da-fé on July 12, 1562, in which Maya codices and approximately twenty thousand Maya cult images were burned.[4]

After the Spaniards' arrival, Mayas had suffered massive deaths in the Yucatan Peninsula, primarily due to smallpox, for which they had no antibodies. They turned to their medicine and what we could very well call scientific knowledge to find solutions to the problem. Doing so, of course, implied spiritual practices as well. Gerardo Aldana (2007) adds that "Maya priests in and around the major cities of northern Yucatán strove to preserve Indigenous knowledge in the face of Christian persecution" (192). When in May 1562 the Franciscans discovered these practices in Maya communities, they reacted with rage and a brutal degree of violence. Torture was applied to those who confessed, as well as to those who did not. As Clendinnen (1987) states, no records were kept, and the Franciscans had no authority to inflict physical punishments (75). When Diego de Landa, arrived at Máani,' he was even fiercer. In his mind, these practices had nothing to do with furthering medical knowledge and a lot with devil worshipping. For three months, he kept the procedures of mass arrests and "savage unselective torture" (75). Landa extended these proceedings to two adjacent provinces, where the treatment of Mayas was even worse. More than 4,500 Mayas were tortured during this period and, according to the few records found, 158 died during their interrogations. Many committed suicide or disappeared. Hundreds were left crippled, "their shoulder muscles irreparably torn, their hands paralyzed" (76). Historian John F. Chuchiak (2005) illuminates this Indigenous cultural ruination: "With one single bonfire, centuries of Maya culture and religion perished forever. Landa himself later wrote, 'Finding in these books nothing more than the deceit of the devil, we had them burned. . . .' This auto-da-fé and the subsequent destruction of Maya religious implements made Landa infamous, securing him a polemical place in history" (615). Given the evidence of medical and botanical knowledge that has survived in colonial texts such as the *Books of Chilam Balam* or *Rituals of the Bacabs*, we can presume that a great deal of scientific knowledge went up in flames in this gigantic bonfire that crippled one of the greatest of humanity's ancient cultures. More will be said later about these books.

Landa's inquisitorial gestures shocked Mayas then living on the peninsula.[5] Even other authority figures in the Catholic Church, such as Landa's predecessor, Bishop Francisco de Toral, viewed this behavior as excessive and made it known (Chuchiak 2005, 616). Landa was so unusually violent for his time that many Mayas fled into the forests to escape his grip (Chuchiak 2005, 628). Even the Spanish governor was troubled by his proclivity for torture. This reviled man created the peninsula's precedents for racialized cultural genocide. Indeed, the emblematic date of the burning of the Maya classical codices is akin to contemporary Taliban destruction in Afghanistan. And yet, ironically, after destroying the codices, Landa recorded many of the glyphs of Maya writing in *Relación de las cosas de Yucatán* (1566).

Under the circumstances previously described, from Columbus's own arrival to the present-day Caribbean islands, to Landa's auto-da-fé in Yucatan—all within the span of seventy-five years—the sophistication that the Spaniards encountered in the Americas in the sixteenth century was quickly forgotten, if ever recognized or understood. It has also been forgotten that Europeans had no science either at the time—certainly not what we came to understand as "science" as of the eighteenth-century European Enlightenment. In this regard, it is important to consider how Aldana defines science in premodern worlds (whether pre-Enlightenment Europe or pre-Hispanic America):

> When considering premodern cultures, science generally has referred to areas of knowledge that maintain historical trajectories with bodies of contemporary "scientific" knowledge. Healing traditions, for example, can be considered premedical sciences, natural philosophy as pre-physical science, and even alchemy as early/pre-chemistry. For non-cMd cultures, then, *sciences* are those analogues to these pre-modern sciences. . . . A more interesting alternative is to appeal to recent studies of modern science. In many of these studies, it is not the specific subject matter that defines *science* but rather the approach. . . . *Science* is thus defined by the combination of a community of practitioners, a common specialized language with a quantitative basis, a collectively maintained and produced repository of knowledge, and a collectively agreed upon quantifiable phenomenon (or set of phenomena) suitable for investigation. (2007, 198)

When following definitions such as these, while also noting that complex cultures in pre-Hispanic America not only fit this conceptualization but also had a specialized quantitative language that required the adoption of methodological conventions enabling individuals to apply the mathematical language being used to approach unfamiliar problems, we cannot deny that science, and scientific minds, existed in the region.

Before the turn of the century, Walter Mignolo had already documented in *The Darker Side of the Renaissance* (1995) the intellectual assumptions that Europeans carried with them in their voyages to the "New World." Of the various paradigms or frameworks of knowledge with which these adventurers made sense of what they encountered (or heard about), Mignolo focused on the Spaniards' claim that Indigenous people were "illiterate." Not recognizing forms of literacy other than their own (most Spaniards who came to the Americas in the sixteenth century were themselves illiterate), they concluded that Indigenous peoples were "illiterate." Europeans instrumentalized this notion to conceptualize the complex societies they found as "savage," as being on a much inferior level to the progress exemplified by Europe. This prejudice was instrumentalized to deny any recognition of achievements or sophistication of any sort ("denial of coevalness," Johannes Fabian in Mignolo 1995, xii) to those cultures encountered, in their descriptions of their social and scientific practices.

Spaniards claims notwithstanding, most Mesoamerican Indigenous cultures had written literature and science, not only prior to the arrival of Spaniards but also during the colonial period. We know that writing developed in Mesoamerica since what archaeologists have labeled the Preclassic period, extending from 1500 BCE to 300 CE, and was generalized throughout the region. The calligraphic style and pictorial complexity of Maya glyphs are like no other writing system, as epigrapher David Stuart has made evident.[6] All pre-Hispanic Maya words were formed from various combinations of nearly eight hundred signs, in which each sign represented a syllable. British scholar Gordon Brotherston (1992) proffers these examples: ". . . we see text as a framed composition, with its own integrity, an 'author-ized' example of discourse, which has its own inner structure and capacity to reflect upon itself while forming part of a larger literary system" (46).

Nathan C. Henne (2016) has explained how Mayas' transition to the Latin alphabet was difficult for sixteenth-century Maya writers because it was the combination of the pictograph with the phonetic sound in their glyphs what created meaning for them. Without the visual symbol in question, they came to depend heavily on couplets to attempt to achieve a similar meaning (Knowlton labels them "kennings" elsewhere), offering "pairs of slightly different words that work discursively to identify another concept in the space that exists between them" (Henne 2016, 38). Henne then explains how this works in the *Popol Wuj*.[7]

Maya K'iches in Guatemala wrote the first Maya text using the Latin alphabet in the 1540s. It constitutes a grand cosmogony and history. Not accidentally, Brotherston has labeled it "an unrivaled point of reference for cosmogonical texts from cultures to west and east" (215). Yukatek Mayas responded to the Spanish invasion in analogous fashion. The *Books of Chilam Balam* were first written early in the seventeenth century, though most appeared in the eighteenth. The title uses the plural *Books* because nine of them are known, all different, though all claim to be the mouthpiece of, or to have been written by, a legendary author called, or labeled with the name of, Chilam Balam. Aldana claims that "these books contain compendia of records initiated by a translation of a hieroglyphic codex into the Latin script" (192).

Brotherston and Tedlock offer fragments they consider significant from the *Book of Chilam Balam of Chumayel*, a text that Timothy W. Knowlton informs us was penned by a compiler through "what he called *u kahlay cab tu kinil* ('the world history of the era')" (2010, 1).[8] In Brotherston's understanding, to capture this text's magnitude, we must know that "two different, if complementary, metaphysical orientations" existed in pre-Hispanic Maya civilization. Knowlton submits:

> By the Late Classic period, ancient Maya civilization had developed one of the richest humanistic traditions in the world. Its logosyllabic writing system communicated the sound and meaning of human speech in beautiful calligraphy. Its painters and sculptors signed their subtle and elaborate carvings, murals, and painted vases by name. Its historians chronicled changing political fortunes of their city-states and traced royal genealogies back to the dawn of the present era. Its astronomers tracked and mathematically predicted the movements of the heavenly bodies and correlated them with the seasonal phenomena into tables, calculating recurring celestial cycles from time immemorial far into the future. (18)

Given the depth of these accomplishments, a good part of this humanistic tradition survived the Spanish invasion. Among them were included both metaphysical orientations that Knowlton analyzed. The first system is the mathematical one employed "to interpret all phenomena as interconnected" with time (Knowlton, 19). It explicates the prevalence of calendars to obtain "the knowledge necessary to harmonize human activity with the temporal rhythm of the cosmos" (Knowlton, 19). The second, in Knowlton's terms, "perceives phenomena as composed of dualities: day and night, sky and earth, cloud and rain, female and male. Other phenomena are the effects of these fundamental pairings. This metaphysics corresponds to a widespread and enduring Mesoamerican literary device, the couplet metaphor or diphrastic kenning" (21).

By "diphrastic kenning," Knowlton understands "a metaphorical term, or pair of terms, substituting for a noun" (31). These "pairs of complementary metonyms create a meaning for which there is no individual Maya noun" (31).

The "flint and shield" not only are physical objects but also signify the abstract concept of military efficiency (22). "Mat and throne" refer to political authority, and "land and well" mean an inhabited territory in this same logic. Knowlton documents their earliest use to the lowland Maya hieroglyphic texts from the Classic period. Both metaphysical orientations suffered their own transformations during the colonial period, but they are present in the *Books of Chilam Balam.* In his conclusions, Knowlton turns to Smith and Berdan's affirmation that Postclassical Mesoamerica was, in effect, a "world system" (182) and raises the possibility that Yucatecan textualities were written "in dialogue not just with Christian missionary works . . . but with . . . Indigenous ethnic and linguistic groups elsewhere throughout the sphere of the Postclassic Mesoamerican world system" (182). This is, doubtlessly, a tantalizing hypothesis that ought not to be easily tossed aside when examining the overall production of Indigenous scientific knowledge. Those like myself who are interested in tracing the evidence of sophistication and advanced comprehension of data and mathematical calculations that enable the argument that during most of history, all the way to the fifteenth century, complex societies in the Americas were more advanced than European ones, including in the sciences, must examine not only the evidence provided by scholars such as Knowlton but also especially the evidence of complex mathematical use.

In this latter sense, it must be assumed that among the material destroyed by Landa were many codices we could have called "scientific" nowadays. This, because Aldana has documented the sophisticated use of mathematics in classical Maya astronomical observations in *The Apotheosis of Janaab' Pakal: Science, History, and Religion at Classic Maya Palenque* (2007), as well as in his recent article "Discovering Discovery: Chich'en Itza, the Dresden Codex Venus Table and 10th Century Mayan Astronomical Innovation" (2016). Aldana makes the case in this latter article for a remarkable innovation in mathematics and astronomy made by a Maya scientist at the city of Chich'en Itza (Chi'ch'èen Itsa' in contemporary Yukateko Maya) around 875–900 CE. This anonymous astronomer figured out a correction for Venus's irregular cycle of 583.92 days—much like the Earth's leap year—to chart the dates when Venus would appear on the Earth's horizon over time. This information was valuable for the city's ritual cycles, much like Copernicus did in 1543 when he discovered the heliocentric nature of the solar system while trying to figure out the predictions for future dates of Easter. We cannot but admit the achievement of discovering Venus's irregular cycle is indeed a classic scientific discovery of Copernican and Galilean magnitude. Yet we should consider that this event took place nearly seven hundred years before the European scientists made analogous achievements.

Aldana, who was an engineer before becoming an archaeologist, also figured out the extensive hieroglyphic corpus on astronomical calculations composed in Palenque (its real name being B'akaal, as hieroglyphs have evidenced) during the reigns of Janaab' Pakal (615–683 CE), his son K'inich Kan B'ahlam (684–702 CE), and his grandson K'inich Akal Mo' Naab' (722–741 CE). These astronomical calculations enabled Palenque to tower over their city-state's rivals Calakmul and Toniná because astronomical knowledge gave them an ample advantage in both agriculture and war. Aldana recognizes that other scientists, such as John Teeple, had already found elements of lunar astronomy in the inscriptions from the Kan B'ahlam Triad Group (155). Aldana claims that scientific knowledge of this nature reveal "the nuances of Classic Maya political and elite religious thought" and "betray a *longue-durée* Maya conceptualization of Creation" (155). He adds that astronumerology played "a very practical function in the composition of official history" (156). Ultimately, for Aldana, ". . . the astronumerology of Palenque grew out of a grand vision. . . . The presence of these learned scholars in the maintenance of the astronumerological language speaks to a continuity with the tradition recovered from the *Books of Chilam Balam* and maintained by the Yucatec choirmasters . . . a unique historical context and a new perspective brought from the history of science permits us to retrieve not only Maya application of astronomical knowledge but also the social function it held within Classical Maya Culture" (2007, 194–96).

Scientific knowledge was not solely the purview of pre-Hispanic Mesoamerica. Carlos Milla Villena (Wayra Katari) has crafted in *Génesis de la cultura andina* (2011; *Genesis of Andean Culture*) an in-depth study of the sacred Chakana or Andean Cross. He argues that four thousand years ago there was an Andean world with a geometric system of measurements, based on the concept of π, or Pi. For him, "the Andean Cultural Revolution happened as a result of the discovery of geometry, and the use of an Operative System of Measurements created as a result of the first" (that is, from geometry; 27). Represented in the geometric formula of the Squared Cross (Chakana; similar to the Maya cross in Mesoamerica), Wayra Katari claims that this knowledge resulted from the ancient cult of the Southern Cross constellation. As we know, this constellation is shaped in the form of a cross, with invisible lines uniting all four points. Katari argues that ancient Andeans calculated the geometrical proportions of the Southern Cross at their peak, when the longer axis of the constellation is found at its highest point and is positioned in a vertical line in relation to the zenith, the point in the sky directly above an observer (36). This phenomenon usually happens in the Andean region on the night of May 2–3. The geometrical calculations of the Southern Cross became the modular element of their mathematical system, thus instrumentalizing the importance of both squares and diagonal figures in the Andean region (30). In their effort to reconfigure the shape of the cosmos on Earth, Andean cultures used analogous geometrical calculations for the development of their architecture.

This archeoastronomical evidence is analogous to factors documented for Mesoamerica. Dutch ethnohistorian Ruud van Akkeren (2012) has shown that in this region the cosmological role that was played in the Andean region by the Southern Cross was instead done with the constellation of Orion, given that the Southern Cross is not visible in Mesoamerica, and neither is the North Star (184). Van Akkeren places the origins of these sophisticated mathematical calculations in Teotihuacan (188–89). Yet in both the Northern and Southern Hemispheres the phenomenon is nearly identical. In Wayra Katari's understanding, the discovery of the geoglyphs (the figures configured by the Nazca lines) and their comparison with other archaeological evidence on the Peruvian coast, such as at the temple of Paramonga in Chan Chan, the capital of the Chimú civilization that lasted from AD 850 to around 1470, confirm his hypothesis.

Katari makes a reference to Anthony Aveni (1997) in his study. Aveni is the founder of archeoastronomy in the Western world. In his classic text, *Stairways to the Stars*, he argues that Inka culture rested on the foundation of the rich tradition of Huari, Chimu, and Nazca for its developments on cosmology. Using the diagram of Cuzco's Coricancha—the Temple of the Ancestors—made by chronicler Joan Santa Cruz Pachacuti Yamqui, Aveni claims that the document in question "attests to the importance of Incaic constellations as well as to the central role of the Coricancha temple in astronomical endeavors" (151). In his understanding, throughout the Americas and elsewhere in ancient cultures of the planet, "astronomical knowledge is expressed via sight lines connecting the place of appearance of sunrise and sunset on important days in the calendar" (154).

John C. Earls and Gabriela Cervantes (2015) argue as well that Inka culture had systematic astronomy and a coherent calendar kept by specialized functionaries (122). They also explain the sophistication of the Inka use of the high mountain macroclimate—"the most diverse, per unit area, of any known in the world" (131)—through a very complex creation of sophisticated agricultural technology that carved terraces of different extension according to microclimate variability (132). To build this vast system, Inkas created a model at Moray that enabled them to artificially articulate microclimatic engineering by incorporating mechanisms that converted the information that farmers provided at a local level into large-scale experimental models (136). According to them: "For example, an unusual spate of flash floods (Quechua *huayco*) might damage the local fields and irrigation canals to such a degree that their reparation is beyond the capabilities of the traditionally employed communal work procedures, and thus expected yields are significantly reduced. The pertinent information (date of occurrence, types of crops, quantity lost, offerings made to the *apu*, etc.) would be channeled up the administrative hierarchy and cross-checked with the relevant *khipu* registers concerning the state of the storage silos (*qollqa*), climate forecasters, and the like, for other areas" (137). Earls and Cervantes conclude that the climatic and astronomical information evidenced by the Moray site as a small-scale model of the Inka agricultural system evidences very sophisticated engineering and mass agricultural projects developed by Inka technology (143). They add that many other Moray-like structures have been accidentally observed, and many remain unreported. They presuppose that many of these may have played analogous roles for different ecoclimactic conditions, thus evidencing an extremely sophisticated network of agricultural engineering throughout the Andes.

It is also in this logic of *science* as defined by Aldana that historian Restall has documented the sophistication of the Mexicas' zoos and botanical gardens, which were unparalleled in European history at the time. Restall says: "The Aztec emperor's palaces, gardens and zoos were so extensive, well ordered, intensely maintained, aesthetically impressive, and—in foreign eyes—exotic and strange, that they drew immediate interest in Europe" (2018, 119). He adds that plants were organized in subcategories. However, the most important were the herbal and medicine gardens, whose properties were studied by Mexica physicians and applied to all the sick (123). In Restall's opinion, Mexicas were "dedicated ornithologists" (123).

Indeed, significant advances were made in many areas of the sciences by Mexicas. As final examples, let me simply mention in passing Mandujano Valdez and Izazola Álvarez's 1987 publication on stomatology and dental science in pre-Hispanic Mexico, concluding that they were more advanced at that stage in history than Europeans. Dentistry was indeed advanced, agrees Joseph E. Sanfilippo (1990) in an article of his own. He argues that dental practices in the new world in the sixteenth century were different from the ones done in Europe at that time when it came to their ornamental nature, but most were curative. French odontologists Cadot and Miguel (1990) add in this respect that the technology of dental inlays and the cement employed for these purposes were of the highest quality, outdoing European dental work of the same period.

To conclude this foreword, let me add that even in the West there has been a great deal of debate about the ability to master science. After all, we should remember that quantum mechanics was polemical in the West in the 1920s, and the debate extended itself throughout the twentieth century. The West has never been exempted from polemics on this and other topics. Nonetheless, the issue of Indigenous subjects and the sciences has been, more than polemical, merely nonexistent. The lack of coevalness previously mentioned pretty much took care of that. Never acknowledged as equals, premodern beings, according to Western public opinion, could never handle, let alone succeed, in dominating what represented the prime example of Eurocentric superiority: modern science. Yet these reductive racist stereotypes merely evidence a lack of historical knowledge as well. Indeed, during close to two thousand years, pre-Hispanic complex societies were superior to European ones in the development of scientific knowledges, as Aldana has defined them. Reduced to 10 percent of their original numbers after the sixteenth-century Holocaust, and enslaved, malnourished, and prevented from having access to European knowledge for hundreds of years, it is not surprising that their scientific knowledge production was systematically repressed.

Educational barriers in the hemisphere, of course, were not limited to Indigenous populations. Until the 1960s, most nation-states had but one national university and a private Catholic one in their capital city except for larger nations such as Mexico, Brazil, Argentina, and Colombia. It was only after significant migrations from the countryside to the city began to take place during the 1950s that Indigenous subjects began to enroll in urban public schools. It would take a few more decades for the most advanced Indigenous students to enter institutions of higher education. Some endured in the process a significant amount of public scorn and humiliation from mestizo students and faculty, as has been narrated in numerous novels and testimonies. Intercultural Argentinian scholar Daniel Mato (2016)—who developed most of his work in Venezuela—argues that Indigenous peoples have long fought for educational rights "in order to successfully advance projects of social, economic, political, institutional, and/or legal reforms" (211). He adds:

The historical struggle of Indigenous peoples around the world, along with the actions of other social agents with overlapping agendas, resulted in the establishment of several international instruments in the 1960s that have been helpful in advancing the recognition of their rights. The adoption of the International Convention on the Elimination of All Forms of Racial Discrimination (1965) was a first step, followed by the formulation of several other international instruments that have been invaluable in this regard. It is generally accepted that the Indigenous and Tribal Peoples Convention, established by the International Labour Organization (ILO) in 1989, and known as "ILO Convention 169" has been the most influential among them; at least until the adoption of the United Nations Declaration on the Rights of Indigenous Peoples in 2007. (214)

This tendency has grown in the last forty or so years. As Mato documents, this has happened in the hemisphere's conventional universities, as well as in intercultural ones, a euphemism to designate new institutions created in the last decades to favor an overall Indigenous curriculum specifically designed for them. These have either been established by state agencies, as in the Mexican case, by "conventional" universities as in Iximuleu, or else by groups of professors in collaboration with Indigenous organizations, activists, and intellectuals, as in many cases in the Andean countries. In some, Indigenous peoples also manage these institutions.

Chilean scholar Claudia Zapata Silva (2013) has noted the critical importance of the emergence of Latin American Indigenous intellectuals since the 1970s. She documents a segment of Indigenous professionals formed at the university that exercise many more critical functions in their respective societies as time moves on, eager for social and scientific legitimation. This sector emerged around the 1970s, as a product of the expansion of educational systems during the twentieth century in the continent. Given this history, it should be less of a surprise that university-trained Indigenous subjects are booming, by a quirk of history, just as digital technologies are doing so as well. Their path has accidentally joined at their present juncture, dumping into the dustbin of history the old cliché that held that Indigenous peoples were outside technology. As we can see, configurations of otherness emerged from, and were intricately conditioned, by the dark side of modernity and the Enlightenment. Public education contributed to making them nonviable. In the flux of transformations that has marked the last half-century, perpetual becoming, unexpected encounters of multiplicities, expired differential categories of selves and others, continually reconfigured subjectivities by social transformation and material practices, have become the norm. As a result, in digital technology, as in many other areas, Indigenous thought has unsettled—and continues to unsettle—the taken-for-granted quality of the ancient Spanish colonial enterprise.

Arturo Arias

NOTES

1. The concept of "settler colonialism," in the sense put forth by Patrick Wolfe 2006 has been widely applied to the United States, Canada, Australia, and New Zealand. There are emerging debates with regard to its applicability to Abiayala.

2. Restall 2018 adds that stories circulated in Europe already in the 1490s, claiming that Columbus had found islands full of cannibals (77). These tall tales persisted for centuries. Further stories imagined "Indigenous orgies of idolatry, sacrificial slaughter, and cannibalism" (78) that furthered a "European imagination of satanic horror in the Americas" (78).

3. See Eric Hinderaker and Rebecca Horn's "Territorial Crossings: Histories and Historiographies of the Early Americas" (2010). Also, *American Indian Holocaust and Survival: A Population History Since 1492* by Rusell Thornton (1990), as well as Thornton's article "Population History of Native North Americans" (2000) and Herbert C. Northcott and Donna M. Wilson's *Dying and Death in Canada* (2008), among others.

4. See John F. Chuchiak's "In Servitio Dei" (2005).

5. In a controversial article titled "Mayan Ethnogenesis" (2004), Matthew Restall argues that inhabitants of the peninsula did not call themselves "Mayas" in the sixteenth century, and that Spaniards did not call them so, but rather *indios* or *naturales*. However, Maya scholar Juan Castillo Cocom replied to him that, whereas it is indeed important to demystify the essentialist notion of "Maya" (2004, 180), Restall's argument is just an inversion of Landa's position. Landa called them Mayas because of the name of the city of Màayapáan. Restall argues that only the inhabitants of Màayapáan were called Maya (180). Castillo Cocom also points out problems with the concept of territory, and the fact that Restall limited his analysis of the word exclusively to its presence or absence in colonial archives (182). See Castillo Cocom's "Lost in Maya Land" (2004). In a personal communication on Friday, March 14, 2014, Maya anthropologist Ana Rosa Duarte Duarte also disagreed strongly with Restall, with whose article she was very familiar. She states that Restall uses the name of *macegual* to define colonial Mayas, without ever stating in his article that *macegual* is a Nahua term employed in the Central Valley of Mexico by both pre-Hispanic Toltecs and Mexicas. She thus corroborates the Toltec arrival—whether peaceful or military—to the Yucatan Peninsula, which Restall denies as having taking place. Restall's attitude evidences the equivocal-

ness of archival labels for local populations when research is limited to archival documentation written by bureaucrats working for colonial authorities, who were often detached from how local racialized subjects reconfigured their identities and subjectivities in the give-and-take with colonizing authorities.

6. See *Maya Decipherment*.
7. See "A Cartography of the Uncertain: The Maya Textual Exile" (2016).
8. See Knowlton 2010.

REFERENCES

Aldana, Gerardo. 2007. *The Apotheosis of Janaab' Pakal: Science, History, and Religion at Classic Maya Palenque*. Boulder: University Press of Colorado.

Aldana, Gerardo. 2016. "Discovering Discovery: Chich'en Itza, the Dresden Codex Venus Table and 10th Century Mayan Astronomical Innovation." *Journal of Astronomy in Culture* 1 (1): 57–76. https://escholarship.org/uc/item/6cr1s6jd.

Anderson, E. N. 2000. "Maya Knowledge and 'Science Wars.'" *Journal of Ethnobiology* 20 (2): 129–58.

Anonymous. 1941. *Chilam Balam of Chumayel*. México D.F.: UNAM.

Aveni, Anthony. 1997. *Stairways to the Stars: Skywatching in Three Great Ancient Cultures*. New York: John Wiley.

Brotherston, Gordon. 1992. *Book of the Fourth World: Reading the Native Americas Through Their Literature*. Cambridge: Cambridge University Press.

Cadot, S., and J. L. Miguel. 1990. "Descriptive and Technical Study of Dental Inlays in Pre-Columbian Mexico." *Odonto-Stomatologie Tropicale* 13 (2): 41–51.

Castillo Cocom, Juan. 2004. "Lost in Maya Land." *The Journal of Latin American Anthropology* 9 (1): 179–98.

Chuchiak, John F. 2005. "In Servitio Dei: Fray Diego de Landa, the Franciscan Order, and the Return of the Extirpation of Idolatry in the Colonial Diocese of Yucatán, 1573–1579." *The Americas* 61 (4): 611–46.

Clendinnen, Inga. 1987. *Ambivalent Conquests: Maya and Spaniard in Yucatan, 1517–1570*. Cambridge: Cambridge University Press.

Dobyns, Henry F. 1966. "An Appraisal of Techniques with a New Hemispheric Estimate." *Current Anthropology* 7 (4): 395–416.

Earls, John C., and Gabriela Cervantes. 2015. "Inka Cosmology in Moray: Astronomy, Agriculture, and Pilgrimage." In *The Inka Empire: A Multidisciplinary Approach*, edited by Izumi Shimada, 121–47. Austin: University of Texas Press.

Fuentes y Guzmán, Francisco Antonio de. 1883. *Recordación Florida*. Madrid: Luis Navarro [1690].

Goldberg, David Theo. 2002. *The Racial State*. Oxford: Blackwell.

Henne, Nathan C. 2016. "A Cartography of the Uncertain: The Maya Textual Exile." In *Cartographies of Exile: A New Spatial Literacy*, edited by Karen Elizabeth Bishop, 25–43. New York: Routledge.

Hinderaker, Eric, and Rebecca Horn. 2010. "Territorial Crossings: Histories and Historiographies of the Early Americas." *The William and Mary Quarterly* 67 (3): 395–432.

Knowlton, Timothy W. 2010. *Maya Creation Myths: Words and Worlds of the Chilam Balam*. Boulder: University Press of Colorado.

Mandujano Valdez, M. E., and J. J. Izazola Álvarez. 1987. "Estomatología y ciencia dental en el México prehispánico." *Práctica Odontológica* 8 (3): 18–22.

Mato, Daniel. 2016. "Indigenous People in Latin America: Movements and Universities. Achievements, Challenges, and Intercultural Conflicts." *Journal of Intercultural Studies* 37 (3): 211–33.

Mignolo, Walter. 1995. *The Darker Side of the Renaissance: Literacy, Territoriality, & Colonization*. Ann Arbor: University of Michigan Press.

Milla Villena, Carlos (Wayra Katari). 2011. *Génesis de la cultura andina*. Lima: Amary Wayra.

Northcott, Herbert C., and Donna M. Wilson. 2008. *Dying and Death in Canada*. 2nd. ed. Peterborough, Ontario: Broadview Press.

Restall, Matthew. 2004. "Mayan Ethnogenesis." *The Journal of Latin American Anthropology* 9 (1): 179–98.

Restall, Matthew. 2018. *When Montezuma Met Cortés: The True Story of the Meeting that Changed History*. New York: HarperCollins.

Sanfilippo, Joseph E. 1990. "Esthetic Dentistry in the Prehispanic World." *Practical Odontology* 11 (5): 45–50.

Schwab, Gabriele. 2010. *Haunting Legacies: Violent Histories and Transgenerational Trauma*. New York: Columbia University Press.

Stannard, David. E. 1992. *American Holocaust: The Conquest of the New World*. New York: Oxford University Press.

Stuart, David. 2013. "Leaf Glyphs: Spellings with yo and YOP." *Maya Decipherment: A Weblog on the Ancient Maya Script*. Last modified March 6, 2013. http://decipherment .wordpress.com/2013/03/06/leaf-glyphs-spellings-with-yo-and-yop.

Taylor, Alan. 2001. *American Colonies*. New York: Viking.

Tedlock, Dennis. 2010. *2000 Years of Mayan Literature*. Berkeley: University of California Press.

Thornton, Russell. 1990. *American Indian Holocaust and Survival: A Population History Since 1492*. Norman: University of Oklahoma Press.

Thornton, Russell. 2000. "Population History of Native North Americans." In *A Population History of North America*, edited Michael R. Haines and Richard Hall Steckel, 9–50. Cambridge: Cambridge University Press.

Van Akkeren, Ruud. 2012. *Xib'alb'a y el nacimiento del nuevo sol: Una visión posclásica del colapso maya*. Guatemala: Piedra Santa.

Wolfe, Patrick. 2006. "Settler Colonialism and the Elimination of the Native." *Journal of Genocide Research* 8 (4): 387–409.

Zapata Silva, Claudia. 2013. *Intelectuales indígenas en Ecuador, Bolivia y Chile: Diferencia, colonialismo y anticolonialismo*. Quito: Abya Yala.

ACKNOWLEDGMENTS

This volume grew out of a project funded by a Global Spotlight International Research Seed Grant through the University of Minnesota system that sought to examine the strategic use of cyberspace in Maya communities in Guatemala. The project led to conversations with the chapters' authors, whose research expanded the geographic scope of the inquiry to include Mexico and Central America. We are honored to have had the opportunity to work with the contributors and we hope that the pieces lead to more scholarship on technology and Indigenous peoples. Working together on this project has been incredibly energizing and fruitful, and we look forward to this work's reception.

Several colleagues assisted us at various stages of the process, and we wish to thank William Noel Salmon, Meghan Armstrong, Bianet Castellanos, Jill Doerfler, Ricardo Lima-Soto, and Maureen Tobin Stanley in particular for their eminently helpful suggestions. We are grateful to Arturo Arias for accepting the invitation to write the foreword to this anthology. We have long admired his contributions to the field and value his generosity; it is a great honor to have him present the first words of this volume. Special thanks to Alexis Elder for brilliantly pointing out the historical connection between weaving, looms, and computers, and to Melisa Gómez for remarking upon the special relationship between Indigenous languages and binary en/coding. We thank our editor at University of Arizona Press, Kristen Buckles, for answering our initial email inquiry within minutes and for sharing our enthusiasm for this volume.

Indigenous Interfaces went through a round of peer review at the proposal stage and another at the manuscript stage, and at each phase of the project Buckles placed our work with carefully chosen anonymous reviewers. Those five readers provided us and our contributors with insightful comments, and we thank them for the critical reflections that resulted in a much sharper anthology.

Finally, we would like to thank the University of Minnesota system, especially the Global Programs and Strategy Alliance, the Office of the Vice-President for Research, and the Institute for Diversity, Equity and Advocacy, for providing financial support for this project. We also express our gratitude to the College of Liberal Arts at the University of Minnesota Duluth for a generous contribution that resulted in this volume being financially accessible to scholars across a wide range of institutions. At the University of California, San Diego, we would like to thank the Office of Research Affairs for its financial contribution to the making of this book. We would also like to thank Yingjin Zhang, chair of the Literature Deparment at UC San Diego, for his support.

INDIGENOUS INTERFACES

INTRODUCTION

NO STATIC

Re-Indigenizing Technology

JENNIFER GÓMEZ MENJÍVAR AND
GLORIA ELIZABETH CHACÓN

For the first time, native people are on the breaking edge of information technology in terms of computer systems and the Internet, which means that we are going back to an old tradition, the oral visual representation and the storyteller's credibility.
—PAUL DEMAIN, QTD. IN *THE NEW MEDIA NATION*, 2010

Generations ago, Mayan ancestors learned a language, assembled a set of tools, and carved meaning into a rock face. Generations later, their granddaughters learned to program, assembled a series of laptops and radio equipment, and carved meaning into the airwaves flowing from the mountaintops of Chiapas to homes in Chicago, Mexico City, and Los Angeles.
—MARISA ELENA DUARTE, *NETWORK SOVEREIGNTY*, 2017

In 1994, when the first Zapatista emails from deep within the jungles of Chiapas, Mexico, circulated in cyberspace, many people expressed awe that a heavily Indigenous movement would strategically use the Internet to popularize their struggle. Characterized as a "war of ink and Internet" by then Mexican Secretary of Foreign Affairs José Ángel Gurria and described as a "struggle over symbols" by then Zapatista Army of National Liberation (EZLN) Subcommander Marcos, the emails from Chiapas signaled that the association between technology and indigeneity in Mesoamerica demanded a recalibration of the dominant narrative.[1] The EZLN strategically identified the territory of symbols as an occupied landscape, particularly those related to Mexico's national story: "Upon entering the landscape of language, of symbols, one must enter it fighting in order to take up a space within it. . . . This language begins to find its own battlegrounds, the terrain of the press, of symbols, and occupies whatever spaces materialize. One new space, cutting-edge, so new that no one thought a guerrilla could resort to it, is the information superhighway, the Internet. It was a space that no other forces occupied" (Marcos and Le Bot 1997, 348–49).[2] The circulation of the EZLN's communiques and reports via listservs and websites began to dismantle the myth that technology and the Global North represented an exclusive unit. It also unraveled the myth of "authentic" indigeneity as an experience excised from ever-evolving modes of communication. The "electronic fabric of struggle," to use Harry Cleaver's (1998) term, that the EZLN wove in the 1990s extended into a wider practice by political agents using the Internet to build transnational networks and demand Indigenous self-governance. The EZLN capitalized early on the Internet because they recognized it, as Mark Poster (1997), Linda Harasim (2003), Thomas Olesen (2005), and other scholars would ascertain years later, as not just an improvement on earlier forms of communication but as a medium with the potential for creating social space. Consequently, communication rights were central to the objectives of the EZLN. In fact, part of the San Andrés Accords (1996) stipulated the right for Indigenous communities to autonomous media. This historical agreement could not have happened fifteen years earlier, as the Internet had not yet transformed communication flows between the Global North and the Global South, or in and across the Indigenous nations therein. By the time the Accords were signed, however, the meticulous tending to social networks, the vivid storytelling, and the vital meaning-making that have long been associated with Indigenous cultures had transferred smoothly into the Internet.

The ever-widening use of new media among Indigenous communities across the United States, Canada, Australia, and New Zealand since the 1990s generated numerous critical theorizations that link indigeneity to technology from the critical lenses of various disciplines, ranging from information studies to ethnic studies. At the macro level, indigeneity and technology scholarship reflects an important historical, intellectual, and political genealogy traceable to the "Fourth World Movement," which inspired the concept of "New Media Nation" (Alia 2010, 1–20).[3] The latter reflects a key paradigm in thinking about Indigenous people's increasing use of digital platforms globally. As an imagined community rather than a geographically bounded group of peoples, this New Media Nation is, according to Alia, "linked to the explosion of Indigenous news media information technology, film, music, and other artistic and cultural developments" (7). The Fourth World Movement and the New Media Nation ascribe Indigenous peoples with a potency to establish a sense of belonging across local and international spheres. Akin to what we find in Jürgen Habermas's writings on the public sphere and the role of a citizenry in devising its dynamic formation and reconfiguration, or in Benedict Anderson's notable work on the role of newspapers and other print material in the formation of national consciousness in Latin American countries, Indigenous peoples shape and reshape ideas about citizenship, culture, language, and geography within their respective nations, but also contribute to a transnational Indigenous imaginary. Alia asserts that George Manuel argued that "language and communication help to engineer and maintain the oppression of Indigenous Peoples" (13). Hence, the control of content as well as autonomously formed and freely developed subjective and affective expression within Indigenous communities has transformative potential. In fact, as Alia indicates, "while it may be subject to state regulations and control, in a broader sense, the New Media Nation [. . .] exists outside the control of any particular nation-state and enables its creators and users to network and engage in transcultural and transnational lobbying, and access information that might otherwise be inaccessible within state borders" (8). For that reason, the last decade has seen an increase in a number of local manifestations by Indigenous peoples responding to social and political injustices via digital activism within their respective nation-states (see Coon's and Spears-Rico's contributions in the third section of this volume). While it is beyond the scope of this introduction to describe them all in detail, we wish to highlight, of course, the #Idlenomore campaign launched by four women in Saskatchewan, Canada, in 2012 as one of the most high-profile actions in the Americas since 1994.[4]

In tandem with the rise of Indigenous participation in virtual spaces, the number of Native and non-Native critics generating a body of work focused on the use of social media in political protests by Indigenous communities has likewise increased in the last decade. A recent addition to this new scholarship is Yaqui scholar Marisa Elena Duarte's *Network Sovereignty* (2017), which provides a timely analysis of broadband access and use on tribal lands. She discusses how Native American and Indigenous peoples "leverage information and technology to subvert the legacies and processes of colonization as it manifests over time across communities in many forms" (15). She contributes to an empirical understanding of networks, and in particular, both symbolic and material exclusion (15–17). For Duarte, it is clear that the use of digital devices and systems by Native American and Indigenous peoples to resist and subvert colonizing systems "is not an unexpected practice; it is becoming a technique of Indigenous praxis" (18). The use of the Internet is pervasive among Indigenous and Native American groups, who have historically been excised from nation-formation processes and denied a voice in the public sphere. Their online presence is extensive in various platforms. They exercise agency by building networks within and beyond the local, an activity that carries with it the potential to subvert the narratives of the disappearing Indian and the perennially prehistoric Native community. This subtext to the practice of indigenizing technology transforms new media into a tool for survival and, more specifically, into a survivance story. As generations of scholars in Native American studies, most notably Anishinaabe scholar and writer Gerald Vizenor, have demonstrated: "Native survivance is an active sense of presence over absence, deracination, and oblivion; survivance is the continuance of native stories, not just a reaction, however pertinent, of the mere right of a survivable name. Survivance stories are renunciations of dominance, detractions, obtrusions, the unbearable sentiments of tragedy, and the literary legacy of dominance and victimry" (Vizenor 2007, 13). Throughout the New Media Nation, Indigenous users are enacting an active sense of presence as storytellers of their own and their communities' pasts, present, and future—all of which are themes that the contributors in the present volume tackle in their pieces. Of course, this dynamic is not beyond critique.

While it is the subversive potential of new media that the present volume underscores, we are keenly aware that there are real obstacles to complete freedom. We would be remiss to omit Internet access inequality, the end of net neutrality, and the misuse of information circulating in cyberspace—three of the most critical issues that have transformed the web from the democratic tool it was considered to be in the 1990s to what is now increasingly perceived as an affront to privacy (Flew 2014).[5] In the same vein, we heed some of the risks that information technology may present for Indigenous cultures through GIS mapping, surveillance, and resource extraction (Gómez-Barris 2017). Furthermore, some Indigenous nations, particularly in the Amazon, reject technology, echoing Spanish researcher Antonio García Gutiérrez's (2016) position that the very act of purchasing a smartphone buys into a particular ideology: "digital capitalism." We therefore don't overlook the ideological and political implications in glibly embracing digital technologies and concur with critics that digital technology could indeed inflict symbolic violence on Indigenous communities by enforcing and inviting cultural homogeneity. However, we don't necessarily share García Gutiérrez's view that digital technology "dilutes Indigenous cultures." Though issues of access are still at play in many rural areas, projects such as Ik'ta K'op—constituted by Tseltal high schoolers in Ocosingo, Chiapas, who built seven antennas to provide Internet access to 40 percent of the population—are valued by Indigenous users. Even in the most recondite Indigenous communities, the use of technology cannot be dismissed simply as deleterious to culture. Ultimately, the relationship between technology and society is best summarized by Melvin Kranzberg's First Law of Technology (1986), cited in the first volume of Manuel Castell's groundbreaking trilogy, *The Rise of the Network Society* (1996): "Technology is neither good nor bad, nor is it neutral. It is indeed *a force*, probably more than ever under the current technological paradigm that penetrates the core of life and mind" (65, emphasis ours). Indigenous peoples are increasingly interfacing with this new force and their cyber-mediated practices alter cultural practices, indeed, but not always to their detriment. Mexican researcher Maria de Lourdes de León Pasquel's (2018) study of smartphone use among Tsotsiles in Chiapas, for example, reveals that Indigenous youth are using apps to relate to one another romantically, an unprecedented activity given that matchmaking is in a parents' domain in some communities in the highlands of Chiapas. Access to applications such as Whatsapp are, in effect, opening up new concepts of romantic love and offering youth more personal autonomy than they might have enjoyed in the past. From linguistic and cultural perspectives, the use of this app is creating a space wherein the advantage of using the Maya Tsotsil language is recognized and validated by youth in the Indigenous community. These unforeseen outcomes raise the prestige of Indigenous languages and can contribute to increased language use and long-term language maintenance. As we demonstrate with this volume, Mesoamericans are at the forefront of devising new ways of strengthening networks and developing strategies for increasing cultural and linguistic vitality (see Lillehaugen's and Cruz and Robles's contributions to this volume).

The present volume seeks to complement and add to Pamela Wilson and Michelle Stewart's *Global Indigenous Media* (2008) and Alia's *The New Media Nation* (2010), both groundbreaking volumes that take a comprehensive approach to the Indigenous-technology interface. Their work signals the ease with which Indigenous communities worldwide have made use of a wide range of media in order to ensure the longevity of their communities, cultures, and languages. As we noted with the case of the EZLN emails from the Lacandón Jungle in Chiapas at the outset of this introduction, "control of media representation and of cultural self-definition asserts and signifies cultural and political sovereignty itself. As such, Indigenous media are the first line of negotiation of sovereignty issues as well as a discursive locus for issues of control over land and territory, subjugation, and dispossession under colonization, cultural distinctiveness and the question of ethnic and minority status, questions of local and traditional knowledge, self-identification and recognition by others, and notions of Indigeneity and Indigenism themselves" (Wilson and Stewart 2008, 5). This networked indigeneity, so to speak, has bolstered the recognition of a technological legacy within Indigenous communities. As Paul DeMain and Marisa Elena Duarte signal in the epigraphs to this introduction, technology is old and it is something that we have inherited from our ancestors. We thus invite readers to see indigeneity in conversation with technology as it takes place in Mesoamerica with fresh eyes and a knowing heart.

STATE OF THE QUESTION: MEDIA ECOLOGIES IN ABIAYALA/LATIN AMERICA

Why are indigeneity and technology widely seen as incompatible? As we hope to make clear, the specter of incompatibility that haunts the question of indigeneity and technology has to do with the colonialism, nation-state formation, and the subsequent marginalization of Indigenous communities. These processes have historically aligned to reinforce and justify the concentration of Indigenous peoples in rural areas, and of mestizos and ladinos in predominantly urban areas. The concentration of both financial and social capital in urban areas remained consistent even as the republics passed from being colonies to sovereign nation-states.[6] As a result, these power-centralizing processes denied Indigenous peoples' own technology and have historically precluded them from having access to the latest technological innovations. In this section, we turn to the scholarly state of the question with respect to indigeneity and technology in Abiayala/Latin America.[7]

The compulsion to perceive Indigenous peoples as benighted has deep historical roots and begins, as Arturo Arias reminds us in the foreword to this volume, in the colonial period. The edifices, goldsmithing and silversmithing, horological and astrophysical records, and literatures they produced, however, are just a handful of the many materials that provide quantifiable evidence to Indigenous technological innovation pre-Spanish invasion in 1492. Even the earliest Iberian accounts confirmed that the Western Hemisphere was, in fact, an "Old World before it was New," to borrow Miller's (2007) description. Despite these primary documents, however, the violence of genocide and colonization by Spanish invaders and subsequent European intruders was quickly masked by tales of superior European technology in the form of metal armor and gunpowder—itself appropriated from China. While discussing the complex reasons leading up to the defeat of the most powerful Indigenous nations in Mesoamerica is beyond the scope of this introduction, we underscore that Indigenous technologies were not "less advanced" at the time of the invasion of Indigenous nations by Western European monarchies. It was, nonetheless, the teleology of the nation-formation period in what had been Abiayala that cemented the perception of Indigenous peoples in opposition to technology.

Supported by ideologies of positivism and environmental determinism circulating in Abiayala/Latin America during the process of nation-building, criollos created a deeply entrenched narrative that technology, and its attendant themes—progress, innovation, freedom, equality, and modernity—originated across the Atlantic. As the increasing use of fossil fuels gave way to the Industrial Revolution, elites in the region literally moved mountains to clear the way for industrial technology on their side of the hemisphere, countering the Indigenous ideologies of the synchronic relationship between technology and the natural landscape (Miller 2007, 136–66). Seen as alien to technology at best and as purgeable impediments to technology at worst throughout the nineteenth and twentieth centuries, Indigenous peoples today interrogate and challenge the grand narratives that have claimed that technology is outside of Indigenous peoples' ken.

At the root of this claim is what Johannes Fabian calls "the denial of coevalness," or the "persistent and systematic tendency to place the referent(s) of anthropology in a Time other than the present of the producer of anthropological discourse" (1983, 31). While Fabian focuses on anthropological research, the problem surfaces across many disciplines and it is likewise found in the framing of the national discourses of the newly independent nation-states superimposed on Abiayala. The denial of coevalness represents a fallacy leading to erroneous conjectures about the "Indigenous experience" as outside Christian time and modernity; these speculations underlie the rhetoric used to nationalize Indigenous communities in Abiayala/Latin America. As a result, even the best scholarship on the global flow of goods and communication technologies in Abiayala/Latin America has stemmed from an erroneous point of departure.

Scholars in Abiayala/Latin America began to examine the rise of mass media and popular cultures upon the demise of authoritarian regimes in the Southern Cone, placing close scrutiny to the television and advertising techniques that bolstered them.[8] As questions of governance met with questions of mass media communication, scholars turned to analyses of culture as a resource. Yet with the exception of Juan Francisco Salazar's trailblazing work on communication rights and use of information technology in Mapuche communities in Chile and Antarctica, few scholars, to date, have delved into the question of media ecology and Indigenous experience in the Americas.[9] "Media ecology," as Neil Postman reminds us, is the study of media environments, including their structure, content, and impact on people in their daily lives (Postman, qtd. in Ott and Mack 2010, 266). Following Postman's vast contributions, we believe that media ecology's goal of studying the interaction between people and their communications technology must become a part of Mesoamerican studies. If media ecology looks into the matter of how media affect human perception, understanding, feeling, and value, as well as how our interaction with media facilitates or impedes our chances of survival, this volume is all the more urgent. Even as the concept of "communicative sovereignty" (Reilly 2016, inter alia) has surfaced in political and academic spheres across Abiayala/Latin America, analyses of information technology have centered on non-Indigenous sectors in the nation-states of the region. Specialists on new media have omitted contemporary Indigenous experience from their studies of digital theory and media ecology.[10]

TECH-SAVVY NETWORKED NATIVES

In response to these recurring discourses, we deconstruct the presentism involved in thinking of technology in Abiayala/Latin America. Etymologically, the term "technology" comes from the Greek to describe skill in arts. In both its original meaning and in the contemporary sense of the term describing human-made implements, technology has never been peripheral to Indigenous communities—a position that Worley and Palacios explore further in the first chapter to this volume. Cultural, political, and social theoretical positions vary in their approach to technology and indigeneity. Nonetheless, in certain academic fields, "modernity is seen as foreign and detrimental to Indigenous cultures," particularly for those in Mesoamerica (Pitarch and Orobitg 2012, 10). This same line of thinking tags "Indigenous modernities" as Westernized, implying an incompatibility between Indigenous experience and contemporary societies. Aníbal Quijano (2007) and Walter Mignolo (2011) make clear that coloniality is the other side of modernity and that both operate as simultaneous subjections. And, while we cannot lose sight of the real perils of cultural homogenization that digital technology can impose on Indigenous communities, the use of cyber technology in many Indigenous nations can best be understood as a creative and empowering tool to combat language death, raise political awareness, and ingeniously create Indigenous networks across various geographies. As Māori scholar Linda Tuhiwai-Smith indicates, kinships and networks are central to Indigenous communities: "relationships constitute the very fabric of reality: without relations, there is no world or life" (qtd. in Blaser et al. 2011, 8). Far from the alienation captured in Eurocentric existentialist theories of self or deconstructivist theories of fragmentation, Indigenous theories of experience have relationships as their basis. In other words, "Indigenous knowledges are built upon relationships—with oneself; with one's family, community, or nation; with other nations; and with other nations; and with the other-than-human" (Blaser et al., 8). The ontological centrality of relationships is transmitted to the cyberspace technology and, specifically, new media, providing Indigenous peoples with a toolkit to strengthen relationships and networks that allows for the continuity of these practices over new platforms.

Despite the tensions inherent in using the word "new," we use the term "new media" to refer to the tools developed within and through cyberspace to facilitate the diffusion of knowledge and communication between peoples in different geographic points. Terry Flew (2014) cautions against conflating the novel with the new and adds that we must understand that "new media" are not just those which have been recently developed. "New media" are instead—like electrical technologies in the nineteenth century—factors in wider social change that become quickly embedded in the social context. The term "new media," argues Flew, takes into account "the wider transformations in work, lifestyle, identity and culture, as well as politics, global affairs, and forms of interaction" that leads us to consider the magnitude of its social impact (Flew 2014, 2). Flew notes that important changes occurred in the new media environment in the 1990s and the 2000s around the concept of Web 2.0, a term that was understood as a shift to the Internet as a platform upon which services could be delivered, collective intelligence could be harnessed, and open source development practices would lead users to drive innovation and invent new purposes to the platform (Flew 13–14). The fastest growing websites of the 2000s—Wikipedia, YouTube, Blogger,

WordPress, Instagram, Pinterest, Facebook, Google, and Twitter—were all based on Web 2.0 principles. These, along with the proliferation of digital devices and the growing array of digital media, have led to a cycle of ubiquitous use of user-created content and user-led innovation of new media. Criticized by some and lauded by others, it is nonetheless certain that convergence, understood as "the interlinking of computing and IT, communications networks, media content enabled by digital technologies, and the convergent products, services, and activities that have emerged as a result" (Flew 19), does not only occur in North America, nor is it only manifest among non-Indigenous peoples.[11] If research agendas on Mesoamerica are indeed to serve Indigenous communities, they must account for new media's impact on multiple discursive arenas.

As will become evident through the contributions in this volume, the use of new media in Indigenous communities does not focus on greater efficiency in stock trades or on counting the number of steps the user takes in a day. Indigenous interests are distinct, for they "involve the conquest and expropriation of territories; massive loss of life through war, forced labor, and disease; erasure of or marginalization of languages; and the redefinition of a process of violent conquest as 'inevitable' because of supposed differences in levels of 'civilization'" (Mallón qtd. in Arias 2018, 21). We observe that Indigenous peoples interface with new media as a means to ensure network building/maintenance and cultural preservation. In doing so, they *do* bring their culture into the use of technology. In the same way that counting steps reflects a cultural concern in the Global North with regard to the diminishing amount of physical activity as a consequence of the prevalence of sedentary lifestyles, a key driving force behind Indigenous interfacing with cyber technology is to advance the process of decoloniality and its attendant nationalist manifestations. This is not to say that there are not any parallels between users in the Fourth World/New Media Nation and users in the Global North. It is substantially clear, however, that interfacing with technology is not an end in itself but rather a means by which Indigenous people across generations can connect and build networks in the face of the onslaught of colonial and national pressures to lose culture.

NEW MEDIA IN MESOAMERICAN MILLENNIAL CULTURES

We have made overtures to the global and the local, the First World and the Fourth World, the transnational and the national, and in this section we shift now from the macro focus on Abiayala/Latin America to Mesoamerica in order to underscore its significance as a vibrant and significant geopolitical unit whose media ecologies merit special attention.

Colonization and genocide began with the arrival of the first Spaniards in the Caribbean, but it was only after Moctezuma was deposed in Tenochtitlan (the great Aztec capital that marked the inception of Mesoamerica as a socio-politically connected geographic area) that coloniality's tentacles entrenched fully into the social fabric of the hemisphere. Mesoamerica's first peoples were the first on the mainland to become what Brazilian anthropologist Darcy Ribeiro (2004) calls "testimonial peoples," representatives of the old autochthonous civilizations that European imperialism demolished. As survivors of the destroyed cities and empires, they became the plundered peoples of history whose identities were a result of the sociocultural factors that shaped their subjectivity after Spanish invasion: "centuries of subjugation or of direct or indirect domination have deformed them, pauperizing their peoples and traumatizing their whole cultural life" (2004, 73). Studies of colonialism and coloniality, postcolonialism and subalternity, postmodernity, and cultural factors in the northern and southern reaches of the hemisphere have touched on the creative technologies of Indigenous survival from the sixteenth to the twenty-first centuries in Mesoamerica and elsewhere in the Americas.[12] Despite the decades of scholarly debates over methodologies and practices related to Indigenous peoples, however, the deployment of new media by Indigenous users in Mesoamerica as a creative strategy of survival and resistance appears for the first time in this anthology. In the twenty-first century, the perception of Indigenous peoples in Mesoamerica as innocent bystanders or stricken victims of an increasingly dynamic cyberspace is shifting—as the chapters in this anthology demonstrate—precisely due to their increased use of new media.

Our volume seeks to open up the field of scholarship on traditional literature and cyberspatial possibilities, which has proceeded without attention to the Indigenous-new media interface for Mesoamerica.[13] We have many reasons to highlight the use of new media among Indigenous peoples in twenty-first century Mesoamerica. First, the sheer number of ethnolinguistic communities concentrated in the countries that comprise it make questions of language and culture pressing. Perhaps the second most critical factor is the increasing migration of Indigenous peoples from Mexico and Central America to the United States, giving rise to the thickening of technology-based networks established by communities, who have defied colonialism, nation-state borders, and now neoliberalism. Mesoamerican communities have always established networks across ethnic and geopolitical boundaries using period-specific technology, whether it be the letters, photographs, cassettes, and videos of the past or the Facebook, Instagram, YouTube, and Twitter of today. All of these factors draw our attention to Mesoamerica. This geographic area is a cradle of linguistic diversity and is heir to some of the most prodigious advances in math, astronomy, and writing, and a recording of time that continues to be more accurate than the Gregorian calendar commonly used today. In this century, Indigenous women and youth have become increasingly active in the public sphere, making their voices heard in both analog and cyber platforms. Two issues—the fate of mother tongues and cultural/environmental sustainability—have become paramount in Mesoamerican Indigenous movements since the mid-1990s (Gómez Menjívar and Salmon 2018). The number of Indigenous linguists and writers continues to grow, giving rise to a Mesoamerican literary movement that has taken Indigenous writing out of the annals of history and into the twentieth and twenty-first centuries (Chacón 2018).

Truly, Mesoamerican socioeconomic networks are much different today than those that Sol Tax (1953) discussed in his study of Maya communities, *Penny Capitalism*. While being rooted in a community remains a critical concern for Mesoamerican Indigenous peoples, the globalization of society, politics, and the economy has irrevocably altered Indigenous peoples' ways of living and their communication networks. Indigenous communities today are ever more conscious of their identities, as well as the political and economic ramifications of using them (Little 2004, 14). Projects like Tevé Tz'inkin (Tz'inkin TV) or the Maya Leaders of Southern Belize Facebook page are examples of media produced by and for Indigenous peoples that exist alongside the national media industries of Guatemala and Belize, respectively. The use of new media has increased Mesoamerica's Indigenous peoples' contacts beyond national borders, which in itself challenges the crushing isolation and paternalistic discourses that have denied Indigenous peoples coevalness and dynamism. New media functions as a refurbished tool to achieve an objective that has been important to ancestors and their descendants: strategic network building with the purpose of remaining connected to land and kin in order to ensure cultural survival. While Indigenous languages and textiles have accomplished the task since time immemorial, new media is the primary toolkit that today facilitates preservation goals.

Resiliency and the ability to continue crafting culture in the face of colonialism and, most recently in Mesoamerica, genocide, are nothing short of remarkable. Though Indigenous peoples have been bound by national borders since the nineteenth century, today they use cell phones and Facebook to cross virtual and analog divides. They continue to use their mother tongues in both analog and virtual communication, contributing to the vitality of Indigenous languages by using emoticons and acronyms suited to the orthography and phonology of their languages. Mesoamerican indigeneity is dynamic and has always been shaped by sociohistorical processes and media ecologies, including the cyberspatial and transnational virtual networks in vogue today. As the chapters in *Indigenous Interfaces* illustrate, Mesoamerican Indigenous peoples live in fast-paced communities with local and global connections.

The loss of land, language, and identity—and, most recently, the comodification of all three—are constant threats. Yet new media emerges as a means of prompting and intensifying the virtual networks used to give continuity to threatened lives and traditions. In effect, new media allows Indigenous communities to establish virtual connections and transport goods, languages, and ideas across cybernetic and national spaces. As Manuel Castells reminds us, "the ability or inability of societies to master technology, and particularly technologies that are strategically decisive in each historical period, largely shapes their destiny, to the point where we could say that while technology per se does not determine the historical evolution or social change, technology (or the lack of it) embodies the capacity of societies to transform themselves, as well as the uses to which societies, always in a conflictive process, decide to put their technological potential" (1996, 7). While Indigenous communities in Mexico and Central America were already destined to change as a result of the geopolitical shifts and transformations of the twenty-first century, new media is the force with which they are moving toward a change that they themselves direct with hands firmly on the reins, or perhaps more appropriately, with fingers on keyboards and touch screens.

INDIGENOUS THOUGHT AND CYBERPRACTICES IN MESOAMERICA

We do not directly discuss issues of sovereignty and autonomy, but acknowledge they represent some of the most pressing concepts in Indigenous political thought. Sovereignty can be associated with governance, decision-making over resources, and rights of Indigenous peoples in contexts where they are governed by groups descended from invaders and settlers. Autonomy has dimensions beyond policy and focuses specifically on the community's ability to develop without intrusion of the nation-state. We note with Randel Hanson (2004) that the concept of self-determination as a right not only of states but also of peoples challenged the notion of state sovereignty and with it the legality and morality of its domestic practices with respect to Indigenous peoples (289–93). These ideas of Indigenous self-governance, sociopolitical laissez-faire, crowd-sourcing resourcefulness are fundamental to decolonization, and what we would call denationalization efforts, across Mesoamerica. Both concepts resonate and mark the various chapters in this book. Our position is that cyberpractices and, specifically, the use of new media in Indigenous communities support the goals of autonomy and sovereignty.

The informal economy is one space that is by definition unregulated, but so is cyberspace to a great extent. What transpires in this space when it is at the behest of Mesoamerican communities with a history of creative practices that spans millennia is innovatively and critically explored in this volume. Although it is possible to argue that Mesoamerican Indigenous individuals' access to media is limited, the steady rise in cell and smartphone use, the communal use of Wi-Fi and devices, and the plethora of digital projects in Indigenous languages signal the rise of communal networked access to new media. The cutting-edge contributions we present here transgress the dividing lines of various disciplines and make fresh interventions across theoretical and methodological approaches. While the non-Indigenous elites in Mesoamerica continue to determine the direction of their nation-states and encroach upon the self-determination of Indigenous communities, there is a growing number of Indigenous users and techies involved in achieving a rearrangement of social dynamics in cyberspace. Cyberpractices, both within Indigenous communities and across the north/south boundaries, are fundamental for any engagement with twenty-first-century Indigenous thought across multiple platforms. In taking this stance, we are reminded of Duarte's poignant observation: "Weaving broadband infrastructures into Indian Country is not just for general purposes of education, enterprise, or entertainment but is also about educating younger generations in Native, Indigenous, and tribal ways of knowing, supporting tribal enterprise, and encouraging the creativity of Native peoples in spite of colonization" (2017, 144). As the contributions in this volume indicate, Indigenous peoples in Mexico and Central America are using new media, and in particular social media sites and apps, in creative ways in order to promote the visibility, economic viability, and cultural continuity of their communities. Eschewing the tendency in academia to examine indigeneity in crisis, our volume provides thoughtful analyses of the interface between indigeneity and technology and the impact/reception of new media on/by Indigenous communities, without which the current Indigenous experience in Mexico and Central America cannot be adequately understood, documented, and analyzed. Our contributors respond to the following interrelated questions: What divides are blurred by cyberspace and what possibilities for autonomy can be imagined by virtual social networks? How does the intensification of this interface alter, enhance, and contribute to (self)representations of indigeneity in Mesoamerica? How are these media tools used for language and cultural preservation?

PART I: PROBLEMATIZING TECHNOLOGY

The chapters in the first section problematize the hegemonic definition of technology as a Western cultural product rooted in the use of scientific knowledge for practical purposes. They remind us that technology is neither new in Mesoamerica nor the result of machinery and equipment serving industry in the Global North. Textiles are presented as one of the oldest forms of inscription of knowledge, of the dissemination of knowledge, and of that knowledge moving across time and space. Beset with the threat of losing knowledge encoded in Indigenous languages themselves, textiles remind readers that cybertechnology is an implement among the many inherited from ancestors to preserve ancient ways of knowing and telling. Facing the dictum that technology, modernity, and modernization are synonymous, they straightforwardly and eloquently counter that they are indeed not new practices in Mesoamerica.

In "(Re)Technologizing the Word: Recording, Knowledge, and the Decolonial Aesthetics of Maya Ts'íib," Paul M. Worley and Rita M. Palacios provide an innovative theoretical approach to Mayan cultural productions as *ts'íib*—a capacious Mayan term closely related to the notion of inscription that encompasses phonetic writing as well as other means of representing discourse, including textiles. They propose reading these discursive formats as enduring and flexible technologies linked to particular social networks. Worley and Palacios argue that their forms simultaneously embody performance and archive information. They further problematize the separation of textiles from cybernetic/industrial technology and from the notion of networks. Their piece invites readers to rethink digital technology as a precondition for social networking, as these virtual connections are neither Western nor a direct result of the rise of the Internet. Worley and Palacios propose that we approach textiles as platforms of encoded knowledge that have, like the web, been the means of social networking for many Mayan communities in Mexico. In so doing, they lead us to question the definition of technology as a novel application of scientific knowledge in service to the diffusion of information across borders and boundaries. They thus challenge the oft taken-for-granted machinery premises of technology, reminding us that platforms for encoding information need not take a digital form.

The discussion of textiles continues in the second chapter, "Dule Molas: The Counterpoint-Counterplot Practice of the Traversable Cloth in (Non)-Digital Realms" by Sue P. Haglund (Dule). The chapter's objectives are manifold. First, it takes into consideration the identities and lived experiences of Dule communities in Panama for whom mola textiles are important sources of ancestral, cultural, and environmental memory. Second, the chapter discusses Panamanian national appropriation of molas but also delineates the type of encoded knowledge that circulates between Panamanian-based Dule and Dule outside of Panama, as they construct similar networks to those discussed in the preceding chapter. The third and most compelling intervention is Haglund's theorization of the mola as space, as aesthetic body and fluidity that negotiates a number of physical and digital platforms. The mola thus moves back and forth from clothing proper to a virtual text that reproduces Dule ontologies and beliefs—physically and cybernetically.

Just as the first two chapters present a critical perspective of Indigenous textiles as technologies, the third chapter, "Using Technology to Revitalize Endangered Languages: Mixe and Chatino Case Studies" by Emiliana Cruz (Chatino) and Tajëëw Robles (Mixe), cautions the reader to avoid the temptation of seeing the Internet as an inexhaustible opportunity for saving languages. They argue that although long-term linguistic vitality cannot be guaranteed, information technology provides one platform among many at the disposal of Indigenous peoples for language use and language maintenance, particularly among youth. Cruz and Robles focus on the irony that despite changes in Mexico's constitution that acknowledge Indigenous rights and embrace of the Declaration of Linguistic Rights, Mixe and Chatino languages continue to be under the threat of extinction. They urge readers to consider the need to support other technologies that are instrumental in preserving Indigenous languages—such as radio, television, and print literature—that do not receive federal funding. Ultimately,

Cruz and Robles see the future of language maintenance less in the technologies themselves than in the networking of Indigenous youth engaged in both digital and analog forms of activism.

PART II: CYBERSPATIAL NATION BUILDING

The second section beckons us to focus on the role that new technologies have in establishing affective relationships within and across national borders. The chapters in this section allow us to problematize nation-state reception of indigeneity across cyberspace and to dispute national boundaries. Collectively, they critically assess national nostalgia for decontextualized Indigenous pasts and demonstrate how cyberspace becomes a platform for discussion and critical interpretation of indigeneity by Indigenous people themselves. Harkening back to Habermas's idea of a public sphere, these chapters allude to a "new" public sphere wherein Indigenous subjects-to-the-nation in fact subject the nation to scrutiny as they build networks across boundaries in cyberspace. More than focusing on the national space or Indigenous community in question, we ask readers to think here about the types of media where these dynamics and conversations take place. Poignantly, the contributions illustrate the ways that technologies allow Indigenous nations autonomy over self-fashioning their identities in this New Media Nation.

In "YouTubing Maya Rock: B'itzma Sobrevivencia's Aural Memory of Survival," Alicia Ivonne Estrada discusses the development of Maya music, a genre that has found an outlet in cyberspace, given its isolation in the Guatemalan national music industry. These Mayan productions—which became prolific after 1996—created a space for Indigenous people to develop and respond to philosophies about indigeneity and its implications for national, regional, and local identity (building). Estrada traces the production and distribution of the genre to YouTube, which represented a no-cost, prolific, and effective way for Mayan artists to reach their audiences. She focuses on the hybrid music style and its digital format to point to the creativity driving many of these Mayan music projects. Profiling groups such as Sobrevivencia, Estrada notes how this tool also allows fans to co-create the band's YouTube video. Furthermore, the chapter brings us to consider Indigenous diasporas outside of Guatemala and the types of networks that can be built through cyberspace as a communicative and dialogical tool between subjects with shared experiences of deterritorialized identities. The chapter makes overtures to Mayanness abroad as a focal point for national belonging.

The second chapter in this cluster, Debra A. Castillo's "Trafficked Babies, Exploded Futures: Jayro Bustamante's *Ixcanul*," discusses the complex forums created in cyberspace for Indigenous people to examine their national and Indigenous identities. By taking this feature film—the first to involve Kaqchikel protagonists and acted out entirely in this Mayan language—as a point of departure, Castillo brings readers to consider issues of representation and appropriation at the production level, and how these then become segmented at the moment of reception. *Ixcanul* led Indigenous audiences to turn to social media online to highlight the Ladino-informed interpretation of Maya experience in Guatemala and, importantly, to discuss linguistic variation across Kaqchikel communities (an issue hitherto unexplored in the academic literature). Through hashtagged articles and comments sections, Maya viewers thus presented critical assessments of a film that they far from accepted as an "accurate" representation of their reality. Moving beyond the indigenista tropes of the film and the events that inspired it, Castillo discusses the protagonist's pregnancy and the implications of the child's birth/death. The chapter thus chillingly brings to center the differential impacts of modernity via new biotechnological practices and the dark period in Guatemala's history of Maya child trafficking.

In the last chapter of part 2, "Joysticks and Jaguars: Bribri-Inspired Games in Neoliberal Costa Rica," Mauricio Espinoza examines the production and distribution of Indigenous-inspired video games in contemporary Costa Rica. His chapter engages with the history of Bribri communities in the country, presenting a discussion of their invisibility in the Central American region as well as in his country. Costa Rica, which has long fashioned a "white" identity for itself, has been considering the discourse of multiculturalism in the last decades. The reservations designated for Indigenous communities in Costa Rica have now become reservoirs for "ethnic" material from which the Costa Rican government can dress itself. In the midst of this, Bribri-inspired video games have begun to be developed by non-Indigenous techies. Programmers consulted with Indigenous players of the video games, and the second generation of the games display a more powerful way of interfacing with technology that appeals to its Indigenous users. While Costa Rica has had neoliberal reasons for its "use" of indigeneity, gaming represents an area where indigeneity can serve as an affirmation of identity among the Indigenous youth it interpellates. This chapter raises ethical and political questions about indigeneity, cultural appropriation in new media, and national belonging. Assessing the thin line between cultural appropriation and educational possibilities for non-Indigenous Costa Ricans, the chapter concludes that the country's turn to Indigenous content in new media will have a critical impact on the relationship between Indigenous communities and future Costa Rican national agendas.

PART III: INDIGENIZING SOCIAL MEDIA

The third part reflects on the various ways Indigenous peoples have indigenized social media. The chapters invite us to think about what kind of "value added" element does the use of social media have for practices that have a long-standing presence in Indigenous communities? What is their perceived utility in Indigenous communities? Social media has without a doubt become the means par excellence through which Indigenous peoples interface with new media. In gauging their appeal, the authors in this final section highlight social media's power as a space for that which Mexico and Central America have not apportioned to their Indigenous people: rights to cultivate their languages, venerate the ancestors, and live with dignity.

In the first chapter, "Digitizing Ancestral Memory: Garifuna Settlement Day in the Americas and in Cyberspace," Paul Joseph López Oro (Garifuna) examines the role of Facebook and Twitter in connecting the Garifuna community in New York with the ancestral realm. With a nuanced discussion of Garifuna peoples at the crossroads of Central American, African American, and Indigenous identities as his point of departure, López Oro delves into the social, cultural, and political networks this community has established via social media. The chapter takes a close look at Garifuna Settlement Day, which commemorates the expulsion of Garifuna ancestors by the British from the island of St. Vincent to Central America, as an important identity marker for the transnational Garifuna community. As López Oro explains, Facebook and Twitter play an important role in shaping the planning and execution of the event, and they have likewise led multiple generations of Garifuna to commemorate ancestors. Drawing from digital resources and interviews with members of the Garifuna diaspora in the United States, Belize, and Honduras, López Oro puts forth a critical study of the new media's role in bridging the great divides of age, language, and distance affecting one the most often discounted Indigenous communities in Central America.

Continuing with the discussion of ancestors in spiritual realms, Gabriela Spears-Rico (P'urhépecha/Matlatzinca) focuses on the lingering presence of Indigenous souls in her chapter "In a Time of War and Hashtags: Rehumanizing Indigeneity in the Digital Landscape." Taking a hemispheric approach in her theoretical framing of Indigenous death and its social haunting in Mexico, Spears-Rico moves into a discussion of the impact of the Drug War on Indigenous communities. Although they face execution and forced disappearance by different state entities for protecting their land and people, some Indigenous communities have been active in creating hashtag campaigns that denounce violence and call for justice for Indigenous victims, thus raising the visibility of the toll of the Drug War on Mexico's first peoples. In a context where mainstream media sources mock Indigenous victims, and even go so far as justifying the murder of Indigenous activists, new media has become an alternative outlet used by and for Indigenous peoples. As Spears-Rico makes clear, the hashtag campaigns of today continue the work initiated by the EZLN in 1994 when it took to the Internet to denounce NAFTA and centuries of Indigenous exclusion in Mexico and beyond. Hashtags, in particular, challenge the prevailing concept of disposable Indigenous lives and provide an international forum through which Indigenous people can denounce the Mexican government's crimes against its first peoples.

In the third contribution, "Tweeting in Zapotec: Social Media as a Tool for Language Activism," Brook Danielle Lillehaugen continues the discussion of what social networking provides its Indigenous users. She discusses the history of digital language activism and focuses on the Voces del Valle project and the #UsaTuVoz hashtag used on Twitter. Through these innovative language revitalization projects, speakers of Zapotec, especially young people, began to tweet for the first time in languages that hitherto were solely perceived to be spoken languages. Lillehaugen brings the reader to think of Twitter as an archive that contains rich examples of speakers of Zapotec discussing topics as varied as their favorite wrestlers, delicious turkey legs, and pride in using their mother tongue on social media for the first time. The chapter also opens a discussion—which we hope will promote further research—into the use of emoticons for strengthening Indigenous identity. Twitter offers an environment in which speakers of Zapotec can create a space for their languages, something that is not available in national Mexican media outlets. The chapter highlights the use of digital tools to expand the number of domains in which Indigenous languages are used, while noting that Indigenous communities determine for themselves the course they will follow as they assess the future of their languages.

The last chapter in the cluster, Adam Coon's "From Facebook to *Ixamoxtli*: Nahua Activism through Social Networking," examines the multilayered content of Mardonio Carvallo's *Las horas perdidas* and his Facebook profile. Carvallo used this social media platform to denounce the Mexican government's complicity in the disappearance of Ayotzinapa's Forty-Three and to vindicate Indigenous language rights in Mexico. Coon's chapter, written at the crossroads of literature, music, and online content, brings the reader to think about the ways that these distinct textual forms intersect in cyberspace. As Coon explains, Carvallo layers his literary persona in this space by alternating between posts about traditional Indigenous cuisine, his hometown, his political opinions and grassroots activism, and his prolific career as a singer. In doing so, Carvallo excels in his efforts to keep his hometown Nahua networks connected to his professional and activist endeavors.

MOVING FORWARD: CYBER-INSPIRED

These writings emerge from distinct contexts across Mesoamerica, bringing to the table the experiences of Indigenous communities across Mexico and Central America who continue to assert technological agency and innovation. They shine a light on Indigenous interpretations of new media, including the ways in which Indigenous individuals have reset modes of communication and redirected the flow of information to lay claim to autonomous and sovereign ways of being Indigenous in the twenty-first century. The rise of cyberspatial projects employing virtual reality as a tool used in conjunction with those inherited by ancestors continues to grow, fomenting the sense of new media as a collective right for Indigenous peoples in Mesoamerica and beyond.

Social media is, as of this writing, leading to the increasing development and use of apps designed by and for Indigenous users. Emerging platforms such as Kernaia, for example, have the express purpose of establishing an "ecosystem of digital content for Indigenous languages."[14] Access to digital information platforms and increasingly diverse virtual content and cross-generational participation in the New Media Nation will indeed have critical implications for the vitality of Indigenous communities in this millennium and the hereafter. For us, as co-editors with Indigenous and Afro-descendant roots deep in the borderlands of Central America but raised in Los Angeles, being connected to other *indígenas* and their digital activism empowers us to theorize indigeneity beyond its land-based definition, inspiring our ongoing commitment to make Mesoamerican issues central to our scholarship and political imaginaries. Adaptability—to earthquake rumbles and volcanic eruptions, to colonial invasion, to nation-formation, to the extraction of natural resources, to loss of language, to displacement, and to the new tools that are needed to overcome these situations—is the mode we have inherited from our ancestors. We thus move forward in the twenty-first century, cyber-inspired.

NOTES

1. The original phrase in Spanish is "guerra de papel y de Internet" and is known as "War of Ink and Internet" in English. The translation comes from Froehling 1997.

2. Our translation. The extended version in Spanish reads: "Entonces, cuando aparece el EZLN tiene que disputar al Estado mexicano ciertos símbolos de la historia nacional. El terreno de los símbolos es un terreno ocupado, sobre todo en lo que es historia de México. A la hora en que entran en el terreno del lenguaje, del símbolo, es un terreno al que uno tiene que entrar combatiendo para ocupar un lugar. [. . .] Este lenguaje empieza a buscar sus propios terrenos de lucha, el terreno de la prensa, de los símbolos, y ocupa los espacios que aparecen. Un espacio nuevo, novedoso, que era tan nuevo que nadie pensaba que una guerrilla pudiera acudir a él, es la superautopista informativa, el Internet. Era un terreno no ocupado por ninguna fuerza."

3. According to Alia 2010: "[George] Manuel used the term to clarify the position of Indigenous Peoples in relation to the layers of dominance and subordination, and centrality and marginalization of peoples within political power structures in the relatively privileged 'First' and 'Second' worlds and the 'Developing' or 'Third' world [. . .]. Peoples of the 'Fourth World' cannot be confined within national or state borders. [. . .] Manuel framed the Fourth World not as a place, but as a global highway. 'The Fourth World is not . . . a destination. It is the right to travel freely, not only on our own road but in our own vehicles'" (13–14).

4. For more on #Idlenomore, please see Coates 2015. As Coates makes clear, this hashtag call to action was a protest against generations of injustice, the separation of families through boarding schools and forced adoptions during the Sixties Scoop, and a rallying cry for survival in which elders, families, and young people all participated. In another notable study on the use of hashtags, Carlson et al. 2017 underline the efficacy of Indigenous dads using hashtags to counter racial stereotypes against Indigenous fatherhood in Australia. The authors coin the term "shared recognition" to theorize a collective anger and frustration triggered by ongoing colonialism manifested in the public domain by a racial and gendered vilification of Indigenous Australians.

5. According to Rheingold 2000, the democratic potential of new media lay in the decentralized nature of the networked communication it enabled. Throughout that decade, the Internet was perceived as a democratizing force for six prin-

cipal reasons: the Internet enabled horizontal, peer-to-peer and many-to-many communication, in contrast to the top-down transmission of print and broadcast communication; users could access, share, and independently verify information at little to no cost from multiple sources around the globe; there was a relative lack of governmental control over the Internet, as opposed to the laws and regulations over print and broadcast media; the ability to form virtual communities or online communities of shared interest across great distances; the capacity to have a voice through the dissemination and debate on current issues; and the potential to access unfiltered political information and new forms of electronically based democratic political organization. For more, please see Flew 2014, in addition to Hague and Loader 1999, Coleman and Gøtze 2001, and Couldry 2010.

6. In her introduction to *Global Networks: Linked Cities*, Sassen 2002 describes this phenomenon as it applies to cities in the twenty-first century: "National and global markets are where the work of globalization gets done. Finance and advanced corporate services are industries producing the organizational commodities necessary for the implementation and management of global economic systems. Cities are preferred sites for the production of these services, particularly the most innovative, speculative, internationalized service sectors" (8). Parnreiter, in the same volume, examines the case of Mexico City's "global embeddedness" (2002, 145–79). Along with other scholars on the region, we see Mesoamerica as a region that became globally embedded from the colonial period forward, and we find these analyses useful in furthering our understanding of the centralization of power and capitals in Mesoamerican cities throughout its history.

7. While for some readers the term Abiayala may be unfamiliar, it is part of a profound epistemological decolonial undoing to rename the continent with an Indigenous name. Abiayala means land in maturation or land of eternal spring in the Guna language. The proposal to name the continent "AbiaYala" came from the Aymara leader Takir Mamani. Mamani argued that "placing foreign names on our towns, cities and continents is tantamount to subjecting our identity to the will of our invaders and their heirs" (qtd. in Albó 1993, 33). Also see Emilio del Valle Escalante 2014 for the renaming as an intellectual project.

8. See the following: Barbero 1987, Richard 1994 and 1998, García Canclini 1990 and 1995, Sarlo 2001 and 2004, and Yúdice 2003. Together they represent some of the landmark Latin American texts on the rise of mass media and popular cultures in the Hispanophone contexts of the Western Hemisphere. Latin America. Notably, the feature film *No* (2012) examined how groups opposing Augusto Pinochet used the media to forge a counter campaign during the plebiscite that was held to determine if the Chilean dictator should remain in office. The fourteen-minute television spot that was granted to the opposition to present its platform can be found here: https://www.youtube.com/watch?v=MUNB_PxP6i8&feature=related.

9. Chilean scholar Juan Francisco Salazar has carried out decades of fieldwork on communication rights and information technology among Mapuche communities. We direct the reader to his article "Self-Determination in Practice: The Critical

Making of Indigenous Media" (2009) and his professional website for a full list of contributions to this area of inquiry. https://www.westernsydney.edu.au/ics/people/researchers/juan_francisco_salazar#publications.

10. For further reading on the Abiayala/Latin American experience with information technology, see Guerrero 2015, Correa-Díaz and Weintraub 2016, and Azor, Grijalva Maza, and Gómez Rossi 2016.

11. Flew 2014 cites statistics from Internet World Stats (2012) that indicate that there was a 1,179 percent growth in the number of Internet users worldwide between 1995 and 2000. The rate of growth in the number of Internet users worldwide between 2000 and 2006 and between 2006 and 2012 was 298 percent and 223 percent, respectively. The highest rate of growth of Internet users was observed in Africa (3,606.7 percent growth), followed by the Middle East (2,639 percent growth), and Latin America and the Caribbean (1,310.8 percent growth).

12. Abiayala/Latin American intellectual history comprises hundreds of years of intellectual interventions that are far too numerous to include here. We direct the reader to consult Quijano 1992, Mallon 1995, and Mignolo 2012 for more on colonialism and coloniality in the region. For discussions of postcolonialism and subalternity, see Beverley 1999, Rodríguez 2001, and Rabasa, Sanjines, and Carr 1994. Further readings on modernity and postmodernity, see Beverley and Oviedo 1993 and Hopenhayn 2001. For more on the Latin American cultural studies tradition, see Moreiras 2001 and del Sarto, Ríos, and Trigo 2004.

13. For more on literature and cyberspace, see Soldán and Castillo 2001 and Burns 2015. Notably, Debra A. Castillo returns to the question of technology/cultural production in this volume to examine media ecology and Maya experience in Guatemala.

14. The Kernaia website asks its visitors to imagine: "an ecosystem of digital content for Indigenous languages, collectively created by communities, artists and authors all integrated in a platform for its distribution and global commercialization." For more on the Indigenous language projects that use Kernaia as a platform, see http://kernaia.com/en. Last accessed October 21, 2018.

REFERENCES

Albó, Xavier. 1993. "Our Identity Starting with Pluralism at the Base." In *The Postmodernism Debate in Latin-America*, edited by John Bevereley and José Oviedo, 18–33. Durham: Duke University Press.

Alia, Valerie. 2010. *The New Media Nation: Indigenous Peoples and Global Communication*. New York: Berghahn Books.

Arias, Arturo. 2018. *Recovering the Lost Footprints, Volume 1*. Albany: SUNY Press.

Azor, Ileana, Luisa Fernanda Grijalva Maza, and Alfonso Adolfo Rodolfo Gómez Rossi. 2016. *Más allá del texto: cultura digital y nuevas epistemologías*. Puebla: Universidad de las Américas.

Barbero, Jesús Martín. 1987. *De los medios a las mediaciones*. Barcelona: Ediciones Gili.

Beverley, John. 1999. *Subalternity and Representation: Arguments in Cultural Theory*. Durham: Duke University Press.

Beverley, John, and José Oviedo. 1993. *The Postmodernism Debate in Latin-America*. Durham: Duke University Press.

Blaser, Mario, Ravi De Costa, Deborah McGregor, and William D. Coleman. 2011. *Indigenous Peoples and Autonomy: Insights for a Global Age*. Vancouver: University of British Columbia Press.

Burns, John. 2015. *Contemporary Hispanic Poets: Cultural Production in the Global, Digital Age*. Amherst: Cambria Press.

Carlson, Bronwyn Lee, Lani V. Jones, Michelle Harris, Nelia Quezada, and Ryan Frazer. 2017. "Trauma, Shared Recognition and Indigenous Resistance on Social media." *Australasian Journal of Information Systems* 21: 1–18. http://journal.acs.org.au/index.php/ajis/article/view/1570/775.

Castells, Manuel. 1996. *The Rise of the Network Society, Volume 1* (The Information Age: Economy, Society and Culture). Malden: Blackwell.

Chacón, Gloria Elizabeth. 2018. *Indigenous Cosmolectics: Kab'awil and the Making of Maya and Zapotec Literatures*. Chapel Hill: University of North Carolina Press.

Cleaver, Harry. 1998. "The Zapatistas and the Electronic Fabric of Struggle." In *Zapatista! Reinventing Revolution in Mexico*, edited by John Holloway and Eloína Peláez, 81–103. London: Pluto Press.

Coates, Ken. 2015. *#Idlenomore: And the Remaking of Canada*. Regina: University of Regina Press.

Coleman, Stephen, and John Gøtze. 2001. *Bowling Together: Online Public Engagement in Policy Deliberation*. London: Hansard Society.

Correa-Díaz, Luis, and Scott Weintraub. 2016. *Poesía y poéticas digitales/electrónicas/tecnos/New-Media en América Latina*. Bogota: Editorial Universidad Central.

Couldry, Nick. 2010. *Why Voice Matters: Culture and Politics After Neoliberalism*. London: Sage.

de León Pasquel, Maria de Lourdes. 2018. "Entre el mensaje romántico y el etnorock en YouTube: repertorios identitarios en los paisajes virtuales de jóvenes mayas tsotsiles." *LiminaR. Estudios Sociales y Humanísticos* 16 (1): 40–55.

del Sarto, Ana, Alicia Ríos, and Abril Trigo. 2004. *The Latin American Cultural Studies Reader*. Durham: Duke University Press.

del Valle Escalante, Emilio. 2014. "Self-Determination: A Perspective from Abya-Yala." In *Restoring Indigenous Self-Determination: Theoretical and Practical Approaches*, edited by Marc Woons, 101–9. Bristol: E-International Relations.

Duarte, Marisa Elena. 2017. *Network Sovereignty: Building the Internet Across Indian Country*. Seattle: University of Washington Press.

Fabian, Johannes. 1983. *Time and the Other: How Anthropology Makes its Object*. New York: Columbia University Press.

Flew, Terry. 2014. *New Media*. South Melbourne: Oxford University Press.

Froehling, Oliver. 1997. "The Cyberspace 'War of Ink and Internet' in Chiapas, Mexico." *The Geographical Review* 87 (2): 291–307.

García Canclini, Néstor. 1990. *Culturas híbridas. Estrategias para salir y entrar de la modernidad.* Mexico City: Editorial Grijalbo.

García Canclini, Néstor. 1995. *Consumidores y ciudadanos: conflictos multiculturales de la globalización.* Mexico City: Editorial Grijalbo.

García Gutiérrez, Antonio. 2016. *Frentes digitales: Totalitarismo tecnológico y transcultural.* Salamanca: Comunicación Social Ediciones y Publicaciones.

Gómez-Barris, Macarena. 2017. *The Extractive Zone: Social Ecologies and Decolonial Perspectives.* Durham: Duke University Press.

Gómez Menjívar, Jennifer Carolina, and William Noel Salmon. 2018. *Tropical Tongues: Language Ideologies, Endangerment, and Minority Languages in Belize.* Chapel Hill: University of North Carolina Press.

Guerrero, Manuel Alejandro. 2015. *Conexión pública: consumo mediático y construcción cívica en la vida cotidiana.* Mexico City: Niamh.

Hague, Barry N., and Brian D. Loader. 1999. *Digital Democracy and Decision Making in the Information Age.* London and New York: Routledge.

Hanson, Randel. 2004. "Contemporary Globalization and Tribal Sovereignty." In *A Companion to the Anthropology of American Indians,* edited by Thomas Biolsi, 204–303. Malden and Oxford: Blackwell Publishing.

Harasim, Linda Marie. 2003. *Global Networks: Computers and International Communication.* Cambridge, Mass: MIT Press.

Hopenhayn, Martín. 2001. *No Apocalypse, No Integration: Modernism and Postmodernism in Latin America.* Durham: Duke University Press.

Little, Walter E. 2004. *Mayas in the Marketplace: Tourism, Globalization and Cultural Identity.* Austin: University of Texas Press.

Mallon, Florencia E. 1995. *Peasant and Nation: The Making of Postcolonial Mexico and Peru.* Berkeley: University of California Press.

Mignolo, Walter. 2011. *The Darker Side of Western Modernity: Global Futures, Decolonial Options.* Durham: Duke University Press.

Mignolo, Walter. 2012. *Local Histories/Global Designs.* Princeton: Princeton University Press.

Miller, Shawn William. 2007. *An Environmental History of Latin America.* Cambridge: Cambridge University Press.

Moreiras, Alberto. 2001. *The Exhaustion of Difference: The Politics of Latin American Cultural Studies.* Durham: Duke University Press.

Olesen, Thomas. 2005. *International Zapatismo: The Construction of Solidarity in the Age of Globalization.* London: Zed Books.

Ott, Brian L., and Robert L. Mack. 2010. *Critical Media Studies.* Hoboken: Wiley-Blackwell.

Parnreiter, Christoph. 2002. "Mexico: The Making of a Global City." In *Global Networks: Linked Cities,* edited by Saskia Sassen, 145–82. New York and London: Routledge.

Paz-Soldán, Edmundo, and Debra A. Castillo. 2001. *Latin American Literature and Mass Media.* New York and London: Garland Publishing.

Pitarch, Pedro, and Gemma Orobitg. 2012. *Modernidades indígenas.* Madrid: Iberoamericana.

Poster, Mark. 1997. "Cyberdemocracy: Internet and Public Sphere." In *Internet Culture*, edited by David Porter, 201–18. London and New York: Routledge.

Quijano, Aníbal. 1992. "Colonialidad y modernidad/racionalidad." *Perú indígena* 13 (29): 11–20.

Quijano, Aníbal. 2007. "Coloniality and Modernity/Rationality." *Cultural Studies* 21 (2–3): 168–78.

Rabasa, José, C. Javier Sanjines, and Robert Carr. 1994. Special Issue: Subaltern Studies in the Americas. *Dispositio* 19 (46).

Reilly, Katherine. 2016. "Communicative Sovereignty in Latin America: The Case of Radio Mundo Real." *Journal of Alternative and Community Media* 1: 97–113.

Rheingold, Howard. 2000. *The Virtual Community: Homesteading on the Electronic Frontier*. Cambridge, Mass., and London: MIT Press.

Ribeiro, Darcy. 2004. "Excerpts from *The Americas and Civilization*." In *The Latin American Cultural Studies Reader*, edited by Ana del Sarto, Alicia Ríos, and Abril Trigo, 58–82. Durham: Duke University Press.

Richard, Nelly. 1994. *La insubordinación de los signos: cambio político, transformaciones culturales y poéticas de la crisis*. Buenos Aires: Editorial Cuarto Propio.

Richard, Nelly. 1998. *Residuos y metáforas: ensayos de crítica cultural sobre el Chile de la transición*. Buenos Aires: Editorial Cuarto Propio.

Rodríguez, Ileana. 2001. *The Latin American Subaltern Studies Reader*. Durham: Duke University Press.

Salazar, Juan Francisco. 2009. "Self-Determination in Practice: The Critical Making of Indigenous Media." *Development in Practice* 19 (4–5): 504–13.

Sarlo, Beatriz. 2001. *Tiempo presente: notas sobre el cambio de una cultura. Siglo veintiuno editores Argentina*. Buenos Aires: Siglo Veintiuno Editores.

Sarlo, Beatriz. 2004. *Escenas de la vida posmoderna*. Barcelona: Editorial Seix Barral.

Sassen, Saskia. 2002. "Introduction: Locating Cities on Global Circuits." In *Global Networks: Linked Cities*, edited by Saskia Sassen, 27–43. New York and London: Routledge.

Subcomandante Marcos and Yvon Le Bot. 1997. *El sueño Zapatista*. Barcelona: Plaza y Janés.

Tax, Sol. 1953. *Penny Capitalism: A Guatemalan Indian Economy*. Washington, D.C.: U.S. Government Printing Office.

Vizenor, Gerald. 2007. *Literary Chance: Essays on Native American Survivance*. Valencia: Publicacions de la Universitat de València.

Wilson, Pamela, and Michelle Stewart. 2008. *Global Indigenous Media: Cultures, Poetics, and Politics*. Durham: Duke University Press.

Yúdice, George. 2003. *The Expediency of Culture: Uses of Culture in the Global Era*. Durham: Duke University Press.

PART I

PROBLEMATIZING TECHNOLOGY

1

\

(RE)TECHNOLOGIZING THE WORD

Recording, Knowledge, and the Decolonial Aesthetics
of Maya Ts'íib

PAUL M. WORLEY AND RITA M. PALACIOS

*América es un continente analfabeta de lo indígena. (On a continental level, the
Americas are illiterate with regard to Indigenous ways of writing.)*
—HUGO JAMIOY, QTD. IN *PALABRAS MAYORES,*
PALABRAS VIVAS, 2012

While Western perspectives often emphasize the novelty of digitized social
networks that have accompanied the rise of the Internet as an aspect of daily
life in a global environment, these interpretations of virtual human interaction begin with a series of assumptions concerning text and textuality. In other
words, despite the oft-cited democratizing or universalizing tendencies of such
networks and their ability to bring people together, their apparent privileging
of certain kinds of media (video, writing in Latin script) over others (embodied
performance, texts in non-Western languages) would seem to reproduce many
of the fundamental inequalities of the global status quo.

In a historical moment when such technologies are frequently said to be
accelerating language shift and cultural loss, how Indigenous peoples engage
with and, indeed, "indigenize" these tools become important questions with
regard to the production and reproduction of indigeneity in the twenty-first
century. In turn, when we recognize that writing, and "especially alphabetic
writing," is itself, as observed by Walter J. Ong, its own form of technology
requiring its own specialized tools, whether these be the pen or the computer
(1982, 80), we grasp that Indigenous peoples have actually confronted these

difficulties before, and that these questions are simply the latest chapter in struggles going back more than five hundred years. Rather than beginning from the question of Western technology, however, this chapter explores these questions from Maya notions of *ts'íib* in order to demonstrate how Maya orientations toward the recording and production of knowledge have always comprised a kind of social network such that Western technologies like the Internet and the global interventions it offers fit comfortably within Maya philosophies.[1] Although frequently translated as "writing," ts'íib, as a category of aesthetic production, expands upon Western notions of writing to include diversity media such as stone, wood, ceramics, textiles, and even the natural world. In order to ground its examples of contemporary Maya aesthetic practices within traditions of ts'íib, the present chapter will focus on textiles as a site of recording knowledge, as well as how these have circulated as socially networked text for more than one thousand years, providing the reader with a nuanced appreciation on the relationship between technology and the recording of knowledge.

TS'ÍIB AS A MULTIMODAL MAYA TEXTUALITY

Our turn toward Maya notions of ts'íib situates this chapter within the growing corpus of scholarship in Native American and Indigenous studies that recognizes that Latin script is, to paraphrase Chadwick Allen, a single option among many for the recording and retrieval of knowledge (2012, xxii–xxiii). This shift away from alphabetic literacy as a universal standard of reading, transcribing, and recording knowledge, and toward Indigenous and Native conceptualizations of how these activities transpire, exposes that fact the Western binary orality/literacy designates a colonial cultural hierarchy more so than a meaningful distinction among peoples (Worley 2013, 8–12). In colonial contexts, non-Western, nonalphabetic literacies are frequently ignored or discounted as legitimate knowledge (Smith 1999, 32; Brander Rasmussen 2012, 3). In line with Arturo Arias's recent *Recuperando las huellas perdidas* (2016, 9), the present seeks to denormalize the standard vocabulary of Western literary criticism and, as part of a broader decolonial process, revindicate Indigenous knowledges in the Americas. Moreover, in using ts'íib as a point of departure for literary criticism written in English, we quite consciously respond to the positions of Indigenous and Native American intellectuals who maintain, quite correctly in our view, that criticism of Indigenous texts must begin originating from Indigenous perspectives and through Indigenous categories.[2] In sum, our introduction of ts'íib into the critical lexicon is a profoundly decolonial move that not only privileges Maya ways of understanding the world but also underscores the difficulty, if not impossibility, of using traditional literary terminologies when discussing non-Western verbal aesthetic production. For example, in *Orality and Literacy* Walter J. Ong acknowledges not only that in the Western tradition the term "text" comes from "a root meaning 'to weave,'" but that supposedly oral cultures from the time of the Greeks have generally conceived of utterance as "weaving or stitching" (1982, 13). "Textuality" in this ancient sense, then, may be the closest we can come to translating ts'íib into English, particularly insofar as it recognizes an affiliation between weaving and writing; and yet as we shall see "textuality" as a term falls well short of encompassing ts'íib's expansiveness. Further, if we depart from the notion that Maya thought, "Es más bien una concepción holística, praxiológica y relativista que obedece a contextos coyunturales y culturales" (Rocché 2013, 169), we see how a broadly understood "intertextuality" as the "*intersection of textual surfaces* rather than a point (a fixed meaning) as a dialogue among several writings" (Kristeva 1980, 65, cited in Allen 2011, 38) is one of ts'íib's defining features. In other words, and as we shall explore further down, in the manner of particle physics and fractals, everything is already "intertextual" and always a "citation" of the world around it, as the smallest parts of ts'íib reflect the structure of the universe as a whole and vice versa.[3]

In this regard, ts'íib is an example of the kind of writing and non-Western sense of the "literary" described by Miguel Rocha Vivas when he says that, rather than imposing this Western category, we must better pay attention "to how the words are put together, how they interact, are organized, and express ideas according to the norms and aesthetics of individual languages" (2012, 74). Maya intellectuals writing about ts'íib note its flexibility, understanding it as an aesthetic practice that produces meanings not bound by the written word or by sharply defined categories of art. In his important work on the topic, which is appropriately enough entitled *Kotz'ib': Nuestra literatura maya*, the Q'anjob'al Maya writer and intellectual Gaspar Pedro González states that ts'íib "etymologically can be said to refer to anything that is painted or engraved on a surface," going on to include a graphic of various textile designs as also including "other forms of ts'íib" (1997, 35–36).[4] Similarly, Kaqchikel Maya scholar Irma Otzoy notes that in all contemporary Maya languages, save Huastec, "the verb root *tz'ib'* ('to write,' alphabetically or hieroglyphically) encompasses other forms of 'writing' such as painting or drawing" (1996, 151). As with González above, she includes weaving as a form of ts'íib and goes on to explain how the *käqpo't*-style huipil of Comalapa is both written (bottom-top on a backstrap loom) and read (top-bottom while on the body of a woman) (Otzoy 1996, 148). For the Yucatec Maya intellectual and writer Pedro Uc Be, as a category of aesthetic production, ts'íib is expansive enough to include even the pattern that a farmer makes when planting his *milpa*, the traditional Maya corn garden (2015). In a more expansive sense, ts'íib could even be said to refer to "apparent presence of pattern, not to medium," and include "the striped pattern on the body of a snake" or "an angry pattern of bug bites across a person's back" (Herring 2005, 73).

Barbara and Dennis Tedlock sum up ts'íib's implications of what we would call intertextual production in their explication of the opening lines of the K'iche'Maya *Popol Vuh*, specifically the juxtaposition of the narrative voices that "shall inscribe" and "shall implant" the text in question (1985, 63). The Tedlocks make explicit the relation between weaving and writing in Maya cosmovision, evidencing the complexity and multiplicity of ts'íib: not only do the verbs stems "-tz'iba-" and "-tiqui-" refer to writing/painting and the transplanting/inter-planting of crops, respectively, but "[t]he actions referred to by the stem–tz'iba-include the creation of designs by means or weaving, while those referred to by–tiqui- include brocading, the principle technique by which highland Maya textile designs were (and are) actually realized" (1985, 126). The reach of ts'íib as a multimodal site of cultural production (textile, textual, architectural, divinatory, or agricultural) is understood by the Tedlocks as a "Quiché intertextuality," that is a category that encompasses different media and operates in different domains (Tedlock and Tedlock 1985, 141).

While the Tedlocks amply demonstrate that these relationships are inter-textual, we contend that they are ultimately performatic[5] and, hence, social.[6] In many ways, ts'íib transcends the categories of archive and repertoire described by Diana Taylor in her illuminating work on performance. Acknowledging the overlap between the two, Taylor identifies the archive as hard, easily identifiable textual documents, "all those items supposedly resistant to change," and the repertoire as involving one who "enacts embodied memory . . . [through] acts usually thought of as ephemeral, nonreproducible knowledge" (2003, 19–20). Maya cultural production, particularly literature, has been typically studied with an approach that privileges static texts but glosses over the dynamic forces that activate the repertoire's "embodied knowledge." Yet, as Walter J. Ong observes, writing and print (that is, archival documents) tend to isolate the reading subject from her peers, such that even if a "speaker asks the audience to read a handout provided for them, as each reader enters into his or her own private reading world, the unity of the audience is shattered, to be re-established only when the oral speech begins again" (1982, 73). Framing Ong through Taylor's terminology, we see that even though the performance of accessing the archive may be conceived of as an act that links one with members of a larger community,[7] the process of reading itself is nonetheless one that immediately isolates the reader from those around her. By comparison, and as we shall explore in the specific context of textiles, the production and reception of ts'íib require a performance based in a sense of citationality[8] that demonstrates both the producer's and the reader's membership within a given community. Although we cannot fully explore the concept here due to space limitations, this is the lens through which we view Genner Llanes Ortiz's (2015) theoretical intervention where he proposes that the term *cha'anil* be used to reflect a specifically Maya understanding of performance, particularly regarding contemporary Maya literary movements in the Yucatan, where the viewer/listener can appreciate Maya language and the spectacle of the event even if she does not speak Maya. Moreover, implicit in Llanes Ortiz's notion of cha'anil is the fact that literary texts are not ends in themselves but pretexts for later oral performance. That is, if Latin script tends to isolate in the immediacy of its reception because of how we perform reading, on some level, one of ts'íib's primary tendencies would be to congregate as it entails acts of reading being performed as cha'anil.

TS'ÍIB AS SOCIAL NETWORK

Within this context, then, what is ts'íib, and how does it anticipate if not encompass notions of "social network" and the twenty-first-century technologies implied by the term "social media"? Digital technologies present us with unique challenges, Diana Taylor reflects, as they shift the ways in which knowledge is traditionally stored and transmitted (2010, 3). Accessing and producing knowledge in these virtual and digital worlds defy notions of authorship and authority among other things, going as far as "offer[ing] the updated Marxist promise for the twenty-first century: that we—individual users—now control the means of production, distribution, and access to information, communities, and online worlds" (Taylor 2010, 5). As more recent research has shown, however, the recent and overpowering shift of Internet communities from peer-to-peer sharing networks to sponsored media platforms may in turn be reproducing long-standing colonialist practices as "algorithmic gatekeeping" most likely disproportionately impacts the promotion of Indigenous communities, knowledges, and other communities outside of dominant global cultures (Gasparotto 2016). But what of existing technologies that have long challenged or resisted Western repositories of knowledge, or, in many cases, been cast aside for their supposed illegitimacy? What can these technologies tell us of "new" digital ones? Ts'íib is such a technology, reliant on and reflecting social networks and straddling the widely accepted categories of archive and repertoire employed in discussions of memory and knowledge.

This Maya concept of artistic creation escapes direct translation and evades equivalencies as it presents a unique way of thinking that views the production of knowledge and its dissemination much differently than we do in the West. In fact, the issues with which critics often grapple when confronting Maya cultural production, both ancient and recent, echo those that arise in the study of digital technologies and their relation to the processes of storing, accessing, and authoring knowledge. We are not suggesting that ts'íib and digital technologies are one and the same; rather, we part from the notion that the challenges and opportunities of digital technologies that we perceive as entirely new and unique are indeed compatible with long-existing ways of thinking that are not limited by the primacy of the written word. Put another way, the apprehensions that arise when dealing with a medium that appears to be fast, unpredictable, and unauthored are the same ones that manifest themselves when the authority and stability of the written word (and the systems that sustain it) are questioned. As Taylor herself remarks, at present in the West, we find ourselves in a moment of transition, as we have before, that sees us move from "the era of the archive" into a new realm where our approaches to memory and knowledge are being altered (2010, 2).

As we argue in *Unwriting Maya Literature: Ts'íib as Recorded Knowledge* (Worley and Palacios 2019) traditional literary analysis ignores the complexity of Maya cultural production, particularly because it marks the beginning of Maya literature with the movement from orality to writing, understanding it as a twentieth-century phenomenon. Reframing our analyses from a ts'íib perspective allows us to initiate the process of unearthing that complexity and understanding cultural production as an intricate web of interactions that occurs on and off the text, with and without the author, here and now, there and then. Ts'íib is a dialogue of different modalities that does not privilege one over another, and that sees the processes of storing and producing knowledge as fluid, collective, and cyclic.[9] When we take into account the ephemeral nature of performance and the fixedness of the archive, a host of meanings that would otherwise remain concealed are revealed. However, these categories are not sufficient for the study of texts/utterances that do not follow the same patterns or respond to the same aesthetic demands and cultural standards as traditional Western works, particularly as it refers to recording history. Taylor addresses this matter in a later work, "Performance and/as History," where she analyzes a fiesta in Tepoztlán, Mexico, in order to rethink the role of performance: "With the Conquest, (certain) forms of embodied practice were denied validity. Performance practices were forcibly expelled from colonial meaning-making systems when they threatened to transmit native history, values, and claims. If we take a historical look at the tension between performance and history, it becomes clearer that performance is not *un-* or *anti-*historical. On the contrary: it has been strategically positioned outside of history, rendered invalid as a form of cultural transmission, in short *made* un- and anti-historical by conquerors and colonists who wanted to monopolize power" (2006, 70). In the case of the woven textiles that we set out to study, due to the prominence of the social networks upon which they act and are acted upon, performance is not complementary or additional but integral and *archival* in the sense that it fulfills the role of storing and transmitting knowledge.[10] But more than simply recognizing the performatic dimension of woven texts we turn to ts'íib to initiate a multilevel reading of the forces at play that all at once create community, record and tell a history, and delight readers. Ts'íib requires different processes of reading with origins in socially oriented processes of relating to a given text. As nonphonetic writing unmoored from Western logocentrism grounded in the letter, we may use Derrida's formulation to frame ts'íib as a kind of writing that "describes relations and not appellations" (1974, 26).

WEAVING AND/AS SOCIAL NETWORKS

For this section, we borrow Taylor's turn of phrase "Performance and/as History" to point to the apparent slippage of a seemingly trivial activity into a "productive" one. As one manifestation of ts'íib, weaving is a social activity that creates community, records personal and collective histories, and delights. In essence, as media it amply articulates a "social network" when this is defined as "a set of entities . . . and the set of ties that represent a designated type of relationship among them" (Grosser and Borgatti 2013, 594). Moreover, gender is a significant component of this equation given that women comprise the majority of weavers and wearers of woven garments. Owing largely to this and to the marginal status of textiles in what concerns the arts, woven texts are generally ignored as legitimate historical records or repositories of knowledge. Non-Maya scholars have long held that Indigenous textiles, and Maya textiles in particular, are in some sense readable texts that at the very least communicate ideas and values (Pancake 1988, 313). As such, these woven texts possess layers of meaning that can be reproduced, transmitted, and interpreted, but unlike written records these texts demand interactions beyond the apparent passivity and neutrality of the threads that make up their patterns.

Within the context of contemporary practice, the Tedlocks state that for "Quiché weavers textile designs are considered to be ancient, which makes their continuing use something like the quotation of an ancient text" (1985, 126). That is, new weaving by its nature can be said to cite previous practice and older garments in the manner of what we would typically refer to as "intertextuality." Along these lines, Sheldon Annis points out the difficulty inherent in producing these texts, which we can also apply to their reception/reading. In short, he says that "[weavers'] graphic compositions are the shared product of their collective consciousness. Essentially, one either shares that consciousness or doesn't" (1987, 116). And yet Annis also notes that each huipil (and perhaps any woven textile) "is a record of itself, a record of imbued significance," insofar as these are, in fact, a testament to the individual creative decisions that a particular weaver has made in the weaving production of a given piece (1987, 121). In other words, any individual garment simultaneously rigorously responds to weaving traditions as well as constitutes a wholly unique creation. As we shall see, we may also add to these the fact that social events are commemorated through the innovation of different designs, colors are added as they become available or disappear as they fall out of style, and broader economic changes within a given community all further determine the weaver's performance such that, as much as a weaver's choices are recorded, so too is the broader social situation in which she makes those choices. In addition, weaving also records the very body of the weaver through the tension among the threads themselves, as the backstrap loom requires a woman's body to function, while a given weaving's tension or lack thereof speaks directly to factors such as a woman's age. This last observation comes from conversations with weavers from the Tsobol Anzetik weaving cooperative.

In turn, the socially networked status of weaving as ts'íib may be said to operate at least on two levels: that of the process in moments of weaving (that is, the performance) and through the recording of this process in the woven object. The Tedlocks claim that "the ideal context for the work of weaving is a running conversation, and the best place is a spot in a cornfield," citing a passage from Rigoberta Menchú's *testimonio* where the Maya K'iche' activist describes herself doing just that, saying, "[w]e talk and we weave. It's how we enjoy ourselves with our friends" (1985, 126; Menchú and Burgos Debray 1984, 97).[11] Although dealing with the context of CH'ol Mayas in Chiapas, María Mayo Mendoza's work (2015) on the CH'ol *cholel* (the milpa or corn garden) and the concept of *Cholel-päk'äbtyak* (literally milpa-land for planting) can illuminate the social-spatial connections indirectly suggested by the Tedlocks and Menchú.

Work in the cholel is conceived of in terms of complementary dualities (person-nature, man-woman, etc.), and through working there *Cholel-päk'äbtyak*, "es el espacio de enseñanza-aprendizaje que los choles tienen para consolidar la formación del ser en relación con la madre naturaleza," as well as "un proceso fundamental mediante el cual un CH'ol, hombre o mujer, adquiere su *ch'ujlel*, es decir, adquiere conocimientos y conciencia desde su experiencia de vida para la significación del trabajo en el *cholel*" (Mendoza 2015, 23–24). In other words, labor in the cholel plays a pivotal role in the formation of members of the CH'ol ethnic group *as members of that group*. While the milpa itself is typically coded as a masculine space in scholarship and in discourse, the sense of complementary duality here posits that the activities that occur there are more likely to be gendered than the space itself. As seen in the quote from Menchú, the conversations taking place among weavers in the milpa underscore the process of weaving as a social act through which weavers participate in their community and learn how to be appropriate members of it. Similarly, Christine Eber's *testimonio* of the Tzotzil weaver Antonia reveals that the acquisition of knowledge and social standing can perhaps be extended to the ability to weave specific designs, as Antonia's process of becoming a *batz'i antz*, or "true woman," coincides with her formation as a weaver and embroider, and her creating a blouse with the *batz'i luch*, or "true design," on it when she is around twelve years old (2011, 12).

Beyond the process of their creation, however, textiles also serve a broader purpose in the articulation of community as a textile manifests the presence of a given social group and particular individuals immediately within a given space. That is, their symbolic value goes far beyond simply demonstrating one's origins, be it a specific town or a particular linguistic or ethnic group. In the context of Guatemala's Pan-Maya movement, even as the decision not to wear Maya dress (*traje*) does not connote ladinization, *traje* itself is understood as an intentional expression of a Maya identity to Maya and non-Maya alike (Macleod 2004, 681). Within urban environments such as the cities of Mexico or Guatemala, wearing *traje* thus becomes a de facto political statement by the wearer that destabilizes the expectations of city dwellers who commonly associate indigeneity with underdevelopment and a pre-Hispanic past by displaying one of its foremost signs in a space that all too frequently excludes Indigenous subjects. On a more localized level within a particular community, the textile as document may also situate its wearer on different social levels within the town. For example, in her explication of weaving traditions in the Guatemalan town of Comalapa, Linda Asturias de Barrios observes that, among other things, the clothing a woman wears situates her within a number of geographic, economic, and social spheres, including her degree of urbanization, economic status, specific family lineage, age, and personal prestige as a weaver, down to her individual name (1985, 55). As demonstrated by the Tedlocks in their explication of the scene in the *Popol vuh* where the K'iche' Lords receive their cloaks, Maya textiles have held this social orientation for at least six hundred years (1985, 124). In turn, textiles' status as socially networked, readable objects cannot be identified as a colonial imposition[12] and better pertains to Maya conceptualizations of ts'íib that predate European contact.

INNOVATING THE TRADITIONAL: THE BATZI LUCH FROM SAN PEDRO CHENALHÓ

In order to demonstrate how ts'íib implies what we refer to as a social network, let us turn to two concrete examples from Chenalhó, a Tsotsil Maya speaking town in the highlands of Chiapas, Mexico. The two designs—dog's paw and bees—are relatively new and are a good illustration of the types of social interaction that occur in and around them: first, the composition of the designs themselves requires a sociospatial rooting; then, their dissemination and interpretation rely on embodied practice (i.e., performance). Through their juxtaposition, one gains a more nuanced perspective on cha'anil's relevance to how we understand ts'íib, as well as how ts'íib requires a more dedicated social understanding of textual engagement than that typically associated with Latin script.

Among the weavers of Chenalhó, the first of these is known as both *yok tz'i'*, "dog's paw," and *batzi luch*, "true design" (fig. 1.1).[13] As seen here, it comprises the central, repeated design on women's huipils. That said, the production and reproduction of the *batzi luch* is a dynamic process of performance through which individual weavers display both the citationality (Tedlock) and the collective consciousness (Annis) we associated with ts'íib above. *Batzi luch* is derived from a much older design for the universe that remains prevalent in the town of San Andrés Larrainzar (Morris et al. 2011, 70). The inner form, a set of four nested diamonds, is *sjol jtotic*, the head of our father the sun, which is the sun personified as Jesus Christ (Morris 2009, 37). Moving away from the center design, we see four curled lines that extend from the inner form to create the "wings" of the *pepen*, or butterfly, a metaphor for the sun that, according to Morris, is apt insofar as "también se convierte en habitante del inframundo cuando el día cambia a noche" (2009, 42). Finally, the orientation of the pepen-sun follows the cardinal directions of the Maya universe (dictated by the trajectory of the sun) where top/bottom are east/west, and left/right are north/south. Gil Corredor refers to this as a "concepción especial matematizada" that relates to fractal geometry insofar as in fractals each individual design contains the infinite design of the whole, and vice versa (2015, 86–87). In other words, the design oscillates, spiral-like, between the representation of the whole and its individual parts.

FIGURE 1.1. Close-up of the batzi luch /*yok tzi'i'* ("true design" or "dog's paw") design on a contemporary huipil. Photograph by the authors.

While this cosmological significance speaks to the immemorial past, the performance of the weaving of the designs themselves speaks directly to the dynamic production of Maya textiles and textuality in the present. The *batzi luch* design itself is a little more than one hundred years old, originating with a group of women from the town of Tenejapa. Having had a dream in which their patron saint, Saint Lucia, appeared before them requesting that she be clothed in a brocaded huipil, the women had to pilgrimage to the nearby towns where this technique remained in use, Chenalhó and San Andrés. Having learned how to brocade, however, the women were further confronted by the difficulty of the designs of these towns being adapted for use on huipils comprised of three panels (left side, right side, center) instead of two. Accordingly, "they took the designs apart and made them fit into rows that would cross the two rows to pleasing effect. . . . The simplified design looked like a dog's paw print" (Morris et al. 2011, 69–70). In turn, the *batzi luch* design itself migrated from Tenejapá to Chenalhó.[14] Although lacking a story of divine intervention, the now-fashionable raised pile of the design in Chenalhó represents a similar evolutionary exchange of ideas among Maya women. Morris and Karasik trace the introduction of the "running stitch" technique to the 1920s when, in the aftermath of the Mexican Revolution's belated arrival in Chiapas, the *municipio* of Bochil achieved independence from San Andrés Larrainzar. Reflecting their new-found identity as an independent entity, the women of Bochil took up the running stitch as a technique that allowed them to place designs on commercial cloth, which also meant a move away from weaving. From there, over the next eighty years the running stitch moved throughout the highlands, its movement roughly following the patterns of expansion of roads and electricity (Morris and Karasik 2015, 96–109).

A comparison of the contemporary huipil (fig. 1.1) with one that is nearly fifty years old (fig. 1.2) reveals a sense of dynamism in the dramatic shift in emphasis that has taken place over the years in how the designs are woven into the garment. Woven in the late 1970s, the designs in the huipil in figure 1.2 lay flat against the garment, with the spirals projecting out from the design's center being clearly visible. By comparison, the designs on the newer huipil (fig. 1.1) are raised to the point that an outsider can recognize it as the same design only after careful observation. Morris and Karasik write that, influenced by weavers and embroiderers in nearby Tenejapa, women in Chenalhó began imitating the lofted piles on designs from that town around 2005, taking this to such an extreme that their own designs are raised to as much as half an inch, giving them

FIGURE 1.2. Close-up of the *batzi luck/yok tzi'i'* ("true design" or "dog's paw") design on a huipil from the late 1970s. Photograph by the authors.

a 3-D effect (2015, 103–4). Further, the added heft of the design itself goes hand-in-hand with changes in the huipil's color palette. The base colors shift from red and white to purple and black, thereby further obscuring the woven designs that are in turn augmented to some extent by the addition of multicolored or metallic threads.[15] In other words, from a longitudinal perspective unattainable by observation of a single textile, the design's trajectory as cultural production speaks to broader patterns of intellectual exchange and historical events as the fields of production led by women shift around them. As stated above, the choices they make in the process of weaving and embroidering a garment (as performance, or cha'anil) cannot help but record the ebb and flow of these events, underscoring ts'íib's status as a kind of social network.[16]

FORGING NEW SOCIAL NETWORKS: LAS ABEJAS

Despite our emphasis on dynamism and change in Maya textile designs, the example above perhaps overidealizes the sense of continuity found within Maya textiles traditions, and those associated with ts'íib in particular, as not all designs are derived from ancient patterns. There is one constant, however: the understanding that weaving can serve as a form of communication to sustain a dialogue across community, time, and space. In Chenalhó in particular, one need not look too hard among the huipils that women currently wear to find animals, shiny geometric shapes, hearts, and "caracoles" or snails that recall the Zapatista uprising along the borders that frame the batz'i luch. Some of these, no doubt, simply arise out of the individual tastes of particular weavers and embroiderers, and none of them is so complicated that they could not easily be duplicated by another skilled weaver or embroiderer who admired the innovative designs. This does not preclude some of these contemporary designs from carrying highly localized, readily apparent meanings for the women who weave, embroider, or wear them. As an attempt to explore the significations of one such design, in this final section we hone in on one of the members of Chenalhó's *Tsobol Anzetik* weaving cooperative, Pancha Pérez Pérez, and the significance of the bee design she created.

According to Christine Eber, a U.S.-based anthropologist who has been working with the women of Tsobol Anzetik for almost thirty years, the origin of the bee design at first glance appears to be rather mundane. A key part of the context here is that a number of Tsobol Anzetik's members are also members of the Sociedad Civial Las Abejas (The Bees Civil Association), a pacifist-leaning, liberation theology-oriented group formed in the early 1990s.[17] Eber writes that Pérez, a member of both groups, was inspired by bees and their flight: "I noted their shape and their bodies, with their bodies being black and yellow. I thought about how they make honey and have wings. 'It's like that in our organization, The Bees. We do good things and try to fly.' I thought, 'I want people to see these aspects of how we are'" (2001, n.p.).[18] According to Eber, Pérez first embroidered a coin purse with the bee design that same day, placing five designs on the bag: one at each corner and one in the middle (2001, n.p.). In the context of our discussion of ts'íib, writing, and textiles as a social network, Pérez's approach to the design and its apparent meaning is highly significant. Remembering Herring's previously cited observations that ts'íib encompasses naturally occurring patterns (2005, 73), note that alternating colors of the bees' traje is what first catches Pérez's gaze. Her mind then moves to the bees' actions, which she then relates to her organization (Las Abejas) and its goals (good works and trying to fly). Wanting to communicate to others "how we are," she then decides to embroider the bee design. In other words, her idea for the design does not arise from the name of her organization in the fashion of a Western-style logo, but from her association of the bees' color and their embodiment of hard work. The design therefore brings to mind the collective work of bees in general, which she wants people to associate with Las Abejas. In a certain sense, then, the name itself is shown to be insufficient in communicating these values, requiring the presence of the bees as ts'íib to fully communicate what Pérez wants to represent. Bees and beekeeping are an important part of Maya life, both in the past and in the present as it relates to the everyday and the sacred.[19] While the coin purse design that we have discussed here is new, the bee imagery and the insect's connection to the region are not, which brings up the notion of citationality of ts'íib that we previously addressed. For the members of Las Abejas, Pérez's design activates a process of self-identification, of imagining themselves as part of a specific community; for the inhabitants of the region, the association's relation to bees serves as a marker of place, of locality; and finally, for outsiders, the notion of hard, communal work can be easily extracted from the image (see fig. 1.3). Finally, one must also recognize that, despite the straightforward, mimetic qualities of the bee design, the placement of the five bees hearkens back to Maya cosmology and the five cardinal directions.[20] In other words, in some of its earliest iterations this innovative, new design nonetheless took shape squarely within traditional Maya understandings of the universe.

FIGURE 1.3. Photo of the embroidered bee design on two different coin purses. Photograph by the authors.

Otzoy has argued that Maya weaving and embroidery in general "express cultural creativity while symbolizing continuing Maya political resistance" (1996, 151), and despite its innocuous appearance the bee design is no exception. In fact, it resonates with the aftermath of the Zapatista uprising (January 1, 1994) and what is now referred to as the Acteal Massacre.[21] While the state of Chiapas was undoubtedly occupied by the Mexican military as a response to the Zapatista, June Nash notes that this occupation simultaneously produced the militarization of civil society itself, with a number of armed organizations operating as "'parallel armed groups,' that is adjuncts of the military, according to civil society critics" (2001, 192). In San Pedro Chenalhó this militarization exacerbated political tensions among supporters of the PRI, Zapatista supporters, and those caught in between the two, with one of these being the aforementioned Sociedad Civil Las Abejas. Despite their official use of nonviolent means of opposition to the Mexican government, Las Abejas's success as a node of Indigenous opposition made it a focal point of political violence. A series of violent encounters eventually climaxed with the December 22, 1997, murder of forty-five Las Abejas members, children, women, and men, who had gathered at a church for a prayer meeting in the town of Acteal. Mentioning Las Abejas in any medium therefore becomes a politically charged statement. On the one hand, the fact that Pérez adopts the design to "comunicar al mundo más allá de su municipio, su identidad como miembro de Las Abejas" (Eber 2001, n.p.) recalls the uses of ts'íib as a mode of connoting membership in a group to insiders and outsiders alike, something further underscored by the fact that Pérez willingly disseminated the design to other Las Abejas members. On the other, the embroidered insects are but a charming souvenir for tourists who do not know the stories of Las Abejas and Acteal (Eber 2001, n.p.) and even for non-Mayas in Chiapas. In this sense, the design uncovers and masks its message at the same time, a double gesture that is a feature of many contemporary Maya literatures (Worley 2017).

The bee design that we have discussed here, though innocent at first sight, deals with establishing a dialogue on at least two levels. First, in Benedict Anderson's terms, it symbolically coalesces Pérez's organization by imagining a community and giving it an identity (hard-working and determined women as well as members of a group persecuted by the state). Then, it enters the events associated with it (its founding principles, its membership, and its history) in a dynamic record by accessing a long-existing system of knowledge creation and transmission and chronicling the lives (and deaths) of members of Las Abejas, of the people of Chenalhó, and of Mayas living in present-day Mexico.

CONCLUSION

We have argued that ts'íib is a Maya perspective on the recording and transmission of knowledge that occurs on different media, by different actors. As opposed to logocentric notions of text and textuality that privilege alphabetic writing and seek to record "the voice" of an imagined and authorized individual speaker, ts'íib relies heavily on a networked community of interpretation capable of accessing meanings embedded in and around the text.[22] By focusing on two designs from San Pedro Chenalhó, we have demonstrated the flexibility and dynamism of ts'íib that allows for change over time so that the text, its producer, and interpreters can best reflect the conditions of her and her community's reality. Members of the community who enter into a dialogue through ts'íib understand that these texts signify (from the performance [cha'anil] of their creation to the cha'anil of their dissemination) through socially generated processes, and they see themselves not just as members but also as actors. As we have argued, this orientation makes ts'íib a kind of socially networked writing whose texts not only suggest but indeed require specifically Maya acts of performance in order to be read. Remembering that Ong notes that writing in general is a technology that "call(s) for the use of tools and other equipment: styli or brushes or pens, carefully prepared surfaces such as paper, animals skins, strips of wood, as well as inks or paints, and much more" (1982, 80), we realize that the contingency of the word written in Latin script in an electronic environment is just that, a contingency, one that in many ways requires a culturally specific set of reading and writing performances that have more in common with threads and a backstrap loom than one would consider at first gloss. In this sense, ts'íib anticipates participatory social media in its immediacy and multimodal aspects, and even further underscores how we tend to construct textualities from a linear, Western perspective of progress and development. Recalling the epigraph at the beginning of the chapter, literacy campaigns in the Americas should run both ways. As much as Indigenous peoples may need to learn to read and write in Latin script, true interculturality would require non-Indigenous peoples to learn to read and write in Indigenous forms, among them Maya ts'íib.

ACKNOWLEDGMENTS

First and foremost, the authors would like to thank the women of Tsobol Anze-tik for sharing their knowledge of weaving traditions in San Pedro Chenalhó, Chiapas, Mexico, with them, as well as Christine Eber, who not only put them in touch but also supplied us with the picture of the "bees" bag that appears in this chapter. This research was undertaken with a Provost's Internal Seed Money Grant from Western Carolina University, cowritten with Denise Drury-Homewood. The grant supported the participation of Alli Rios and Sara Rincón in speaking with members of Tsobol Anzetik and creating an exhibition of Maya textiles, "The Language of Weaving," during fall 2016 at Western Carolina University.

NOTES

1. Throughout the chapter we will use the term "Maya" as a noun to designate peo-ple and as an adjective. While "Mayan" is a commonly used adjective, it does not exist as a term in any Maya language. Given that the word can function as a noun (úuchben maaya/the ancient Maya) or an adjective (maaya taan/Maya language) in Yucatec Maya, for example, we feel it better to sustain the already dual nature of the term rather than to employ the Anglicism in English.

2. See Sánchez Chan, cited in Lepe Lira 2009, 76; Womack 1999, 12.

3. As Stéfano Varese recently observed at a conference at the Casa de las Américas en la Habana, Cuba, Indigenous ontologies may well be "mas similar a la física quántica que a la física newtoniana" (2016, 22). We would, of course, agree and argue that ts'íib is a physical manifestation of such an ontology given its infinitely relational character.

4. Unless otherwise noted, all translations from Spanish are our own. "En este sen-tido, etimolóicamente puede referirse a todo aquello que es pintado o rallado sobre una superficie" (González 1997, 35).

5. See Taylor 2003, 6.

6. See our discussion of Genner Llanes Ortiz's (2015) recent groundbreaking piece on cha'anil above.

7. See Anderson 1983 and his discussion of how print capitalism aided in the forma-tion of nations as "imagined communities."

8. As explored further down, we are borrowing this term from Tedlock and Tedlock 1985.

9. Consider for a moment the K'iche' Maya *Popol vuh* and the Maya books of the Chilam Balam, which are typically read as Western-style texts in a literary context though the works themselves rebel against such an approach. As Tedlock reflects on his translation of the *Popol vuh*, what we read today is not a direct translation

of an originary glyphic text. Instead, the people writing this text "quote what readers of the ancient book would say when they gave long performances" (1996, 30), with prime examples being those moments where the narrators "seem to be describing pictures, especially when they begin new episodes in narratives" (1996, 28). Similarly, these aspects are also defining features of the *Books of the Chilam Balam* (Worley 2016, 5–6). Moreover, the fact that the *Books of the Chilam Balam* did not (and do not) exist as static texts in the Western sense but as works that were to be performed by the Maya maestros who were responsible for them (Knowlton 2012, 4–5) signals that when we interact with these works we are in the presence of a non-Western sense of textuality.

10. Though associating an ephemeral act, a performance, with the archive, a stable unchangeable "historical" object, might seem contradictory, in "Performance and/ as History" Taylor reflects on acts better classified as repertoire as repositories of knowledge that serve a similar purpose as the written records of the West (2006, 68).

11. Without going too far afield, this situation resonates with Abenaki Lisa Brooks's observations about the kitchen's role among the women in her family as being "where all the stories are made" (2006, 231). There is still a good bit of research to be done on ideologies of complementarity, gendered labor, and the gendering of different spaces.

12. See, for example, claims made by Martínez Peláez in *La patria del criollo* (1994).

13. Design names can vary even within a given community, which problematizes any reading of them that exclusively relies on them in analyzing the meaning of a given design. For example, in his publications Walter Morris and his collaborators refer to the design under discussion here as *yok tz'i'* (2011, 64; 2009, 43), while the women of Tsobol Anzetik call it *batzi luch*. In deference to our collaborators, here we will refer to it as *batzi luch*.

14. Morris recounts several versions of this narrative. Here the source is found on pages 69–70 of Morris et al. 2011.

15. The extent to which weavers themselves correlate changes in the height of the designs with the addition of various colored threads merits further investigation.

16. The extent to which weavers and embroiderers would themselves make these connections is of note and deserves a closer look. By way of a contingent answer, it is highly significant that during our preliminary interviews with weavers and embroiders in Chenalhó and Oxchuc, members of both weaving co-ops directly associated changes in designs and colors with roads and access to technologies. This would confirm Morris and Karasik's (2015) observations recounted here, and indeed underscore the ts'íib in woven garments as historical texts.

17. For one account of the group's formation, see Moksnes 2012, 197–200.

18. "Vi sus formas y su traje, vi que sus trajes tenían dos colores negro y amarillo. Pensé en cómo ellas hacen miel y tienen alas. 'Es lo mismo que en nuestra organización Las Abejas. Nosotros hacemos cosas buenas y tratamos de volar. Quiero que la gente vea cómo somos,' pensé" (Eber 2001, n.p.).

19.   In the pantheon of the Maya, the Bacabs described by Landa are the four deities who held up the sky, positioned in the four corners of the universe and related to bees and bee keeping (Tozzer 1941, 193–94). The Madrid Codex shows bees resting on log hives, a type of apiary that is still used today for the *melipona beeicheii*, also known as *colel-cab* in Yucatan, a type of stingless, domesticated bee unique to the Mesoamerican region (Bassie-Sweet 1991, 98; Crane 1999, 288–95; Waldbauer 2009, 143).

20.   Though this may seem abstract, keep in mind that the square itself is an abstract representation of the cosmos. In Tseltal cosmology, the human body with its four limbs spread represents an idealized square, with each extremity having five digits, which in turn represents the number twenty, the basis for the Maya counting system (Gil Corredor 2015, 89). While this piece is Tsotsil in origin, one observes a similar pattern here.

21.   Scholars and activists have written a good deal on the run-up to the massacre, the massacre itself, and its impact on Indigenous communities throughout the Highlands. For representative examples, see Moksnes (2012, 195–253), Nash (2001, 188–97), and Eber and "Antonia" (2011, 75–80).

22.   Given the previously noted, ancient connections between weaving and writing in the West, this assertion may seem out of place. However, as observed by Ong, common used notions of text and textuality in the West remain moored to alphabetic writing as a means to understand these terms. For example, Ong states that "when literates today use the term 'test' to refer to oral performance, they are thinking of it by analogy with writing. In the literate's vocabulary, the 'text' of a narrative by a person by a person from a primary oral culture represents a back formation: the horse as an automobile without wheels again" (1982, 13). In our view, ts'íib encompasses and transcends these distinctions.

REFERENCES

Allen, Chadwick. 2012. *Trans-Indigenous: Methodologies for Global Native Literary Studies.* Minneapolis: University of Minnesota Press.

Allen, Graham. 2011. *Intertextuality.* 2nd ed. London: Routledge.

Anderson, Benedict. 1983. *Imagined Communities: Reflections on the Origin and Spread of Nationalism.* London: Verso.

Annis, Sheldon. 1987. *God and Production in a Guatemalan Town.* Austin: University of Texas Press.

Arias, Arturo. 2016. *Recuperando las huellas perdidas: El surgimiento de narrativas indígenas contemporáneas en Abya Yala.* Guatemala: Editorial Cultura.

Asturias de Barrios, Linda. 1985. *Comalapa: El traje u su significado.* Guatemala: Museo Ixchel de Traje Indígena.

Bassie-Sweet, Karen. 1991. *From the Mouth of the Dark Cave: Commemorative Sculpture of the Late Classic Maya.* Norman: University of Oklahoma Press.

Brander Rasmussen, Birgit. 2012. *QueeQueg's Coffin: Indigenous Literacies and Early American Literature.* Durham: Duke University Press.

Brooks, Lisa. 2006. "Afterword: At the Gathering Place." In *American Indian Literary Nationalism*, edited by Jace Weaver, Craig S. Womack, and Robert Warrior, 225–52. Albuquerque: University of New Mexico Press.

Crane, Eva. 1999. *The World History of Beekeping and Honey Hunting*. New York: Routledge.

Derrida, Jacques. 1974. *Of Grammatology*. Translated by Gayatri Chakravorty Spivak. Baltimore: Johns Hopkins University Press.

Eber, Christine. 2001. "Rompiendo la vasija de la opresión: Las mujeres y el cambio en San Pedro Chenalhó, Chiapas, México." Latin American Studies Association, Washington, D.C. Lecture delivered September 2001.

Eber, Christine, and "Antonia." 2011. *The Journey of a Tzotzil-Maya Woman of Chiapas, Mexico: Pass Well over the Earth*. Austin: University of Texas Press.

Gasparotto, Melissa. 2016. "Digital Colonization and Virtual Indigeneity: Indigenous Knowledge and Algorithm Bias." Paper submitted to the 2017 Annual Conference of the Seminar on the Acquisition of Latin American Library Materials. Retrieved from doi:10.7282/T3XG9TFG.

Gil Corredor, Claudia Adelaida. 2015. "El arte textile maya en los Altos de Chiapas, Devenir de una práctica cultural." PhD diss. Mexico City: Centro de Cultura Casa Lamm.

González, Gaspar Pedro. 1997. *Kotz'ib': Nuestra literatura maya*. Rancho Palos Verdes, Calif: Yax Te' Foundation.

Grosser, Travis J., and Stephen P. Borgatti. 2013. "Network Theory/Social Network Analysis." In *Theory in Social and Cultural Anthropology: An Encyclopedia*, edited by R. Jon McGee and Richard L. Warms, 594–97. Thousand Oaks: SAGE Publications, Inc.

Herring, Adam. 2005. *Art and Writing in the Maya Cities, A.D.: A Poetics of Line*. Cambridge: Cambridge University Press.

Knowlton, Timothy. 2012. *Maya Creation Myths: Words and Worlds of the Chilam Balam*. Boulder: University of Colorado Press.

Kristeva, Julia. 1980. *Desire in Language: A Semiotic Approach to Literature and Art*. New York: Columbia University Press.

Lepe Lira, Luz. 2009. *Lluvia y viento, puentes de sonido: Literatura indígena y crítica literaria*. Monterrey, Mexico: Universidad Autónoma de Nuevo León.

Llanes Ortiz, Genner. 2015. "Yaan muuk'ich cha'anil/El potencial de Cha'anil: Un concepto maya para la revitalización lingüística." *Ichan Teolotl/La Casa del Tecolote* 26 (301): 28–30.

Macleod, Morna. 2004. "Mayan Dress as Context: Contested Meanings." *Development in Practice* 14 (5): 680–89.

Martínez Peláez, Severo. 1994. *La patria del criollo*. México, D.F.: Ediciones en marcha.

Menchú, Rigoberta, with Elizabeth Burgos Debray. 1984. *I, Rigoberta Menchú: An Indian Woman in Guatemala*. London: Verso.

Mendoza, María Mayo. 2015. *Cholel-päk'äbtyak: Crecer desde el nosotros*. Tuxtla Gutíerrez, Chiapas, Mexico: CELALI.

Moksnes, Heidi. 2012. *Maya Exodus: Indigenous Struggles for Citizenship in Chiapas*. Norman: University of Oklahoma Press.

Morris, Walter, coord. 2009. *Diseño e iconografía Chiapas, Geometrías de la imaginación*. Mexico: Dirección General de Culturas Populares.

Morris, Walter, and Carol Karasik. 2015. *Maya Threads: A Woven History of Chiapas*. Loveland, Colo.: Thrums.

Morris, Walter, et al. 2011. *Guía textil de los Altos de Chiapas/A Textile Guide to the Highlands of Chiapas*. Loveland, Colo: Thrums.

Nash, June C. Maya. 2001. *Visions: The Quest for Autonomy in the Age of Globalization*. New York: Routledge.

Ong, Walter J. 1982. *Orality and Literacy*. New York: Routledge.

Otzoy, Irma. 1996. "Maya Clothing and Identity." In *Maya Cultural Activism in Guatemala*, edited by Edward F. Fischer and R. McKenna Brown, 141–55. Austin: University of Texas Press.

Pancake, Cherri M. 1988. "Nuevos métodos en la interpretación de textos gráficos: aplicaciones de la 'teoría del lenguaje' a los tejidos de Guatemala." *Mesoamérica* 16: 311–34.

Rocché, Domingo Yojcom. 2013. *La epistemología de la matemática maya*. Guatemala: Editorial Maya' Wuj.

Rocha Vivas, Miguel. 2012. *Palabras mayores, palabras vivas: Tradiciones mítico-literarias y escritores indígenas en Colombia*. Bogotá: Taurus.

Smith, Linda Tuhiwai. 1999. *Decolonizing Methodologies: Research and Indigenous Peoples*. London: Zed Books.

Taylor, Diana. 2003. *The Archive and the Repertoire: Performing Cultural Memory in the Americas*. Durham: Duke University Press.

Taylor, Diana. 2006. "Performance and/as History." *The Drama Review* 50 (1): 67–86.

Taylor, Diana. 2010. "Save As . . . Knowledge and Transmission in the Age of Digital Technologies." Keynote address delivered at the Imagining America's 2010 National Conference in Seattle. Retrieved from http://imaginingamerica.org/wp-content/uploads/2015/08/Foreseeable-Futures-10-Taylor.pdf.

Tedlock, Barbara, and Dennis Tedlock. 1985. "Text and Textile: Language and Technology in the Arts of the Quiché Maya." *Journal of Anthropological Research* 41 (2): 121–46.

Tedlock, Dennis, ed. 1985. *Popol Vuh: The Definitive Edition of the Mayan Book of the Dawn of Life and the Glories of Gods and Kings*. Translated by Dennis Tedlock. Rev. ed. New York: Simon and Schuster.

Tedlock, Dennis. 1996. "Introduction." In *Popol Vuh: The Definitive Edition of the Mayan Book of the Dawn of Life and the Glories of Gods and Kings*, edited and translated by Dennis Tedlock, 21–60. New York: Simon and Schuster.

Tozzer, Alfred Marston. 1941. *Landa's Relación De Las Cosas De Yucatan: A Translation*. Cambridge, Mass.: The Peabody Museum.

Uc Be, Pedro. 2015. "La escritura maya: Una muestra de creación. Uts'íibil ts'íib." *Sinfín: Revista Electrónica* 15: 10–12.

Varese, Stéfano. 2016. "Los fundamentos éticos de las cosmologías indígenas." II Coloquio Internacional de Estudios sobre Culturas Originarias de América, Habana, Cuba. Lecture delivered October 2016.

Waldbauer, Gilbert. 2009. *Fireflies, Honey, and Silk*. Berkeley and Los Angeles: University of California Press.

Womack, Craig S. 1999. *Red on Red: Native American Literary Separatism*. Minneapolis: University of Minnesota Press.

Worley, Paul M. 2013. *Telling and Being Told: Storytelling and Cultural Control in Contemporary Yucatec Maya Literatures*. Tucson: University of Arizona Press.

Worley, Paul M. 2016. "Pan-Maya and Trans-Indigenous: The Living Voice of the Chilam Balam in Victor Montejo and Leslie Marmon Silko." *Studies in American Indian Literatures* 28 (1): 1–20.

Worley, Paul M. 2017. "Máseual excluido/Indio permitido: Neoliberal Translation in Waldemar Noh Tzec." *Latin American and Caribbean Ethnic Studies* 12 (3): 290–314.

Worley, Paul M., and Rita M. Palacios. 2019. *Unwriting Maya Literature: Ts'íib as Recorded Knowledge*. Tucson: University of Arizona Press.

2

DULE MOLAS

The Counterpoint-Counterplot Practice of the
Traversable Cloth in (Non)Digital Realms

SUE P. HAGLUND

*Think like a Dule and abstract it down to the gwage, heart, corazón—essence.
What would it be if it were a mola with only what is necessary to tell the story
and image?*

—OLOEDIDILI MONIQUE MOJICA (DULE
RAPPAHANNOCK), PERS. COMM., 2009

"¡Mira y observa!" (Look and observe!) my grandfather once said to me as a
young child as I watched him weave the fronds of the palm trees to make
a roof of a Dule house for my dolls. *¡Mira y observa!* This call to "look and
observe" has remained with me ever since as an invitation to awareness of the
world around. Flash forward to my adulthood, this call to "look and observe"
must have been present within my subconscious mind on a rainy spring day
several years ago, when I entered a Starbucks coffeehouse on Alakea Street in
downtown Honolulu and encountered an image of a large advertisement for
a coffee product grown in Panama.[1] I looked at and observed this large motif
hanging on the wall, instinctively recognizing the design's origin. The motif
was an abstract floral design, surrounded by vertical columns in the space of a
squared outline border, which, in turn, is encircled by stitched fragmented lines
painted to simulate the look of thread stitches. This painted image was a replica
of a *mola* or blouse, a brightly colored, rectangular shaped reverse-appliqué
textile. The mola's origin is specific only to the Dule, an Indigenous people of
Gunayala residing on the Atlantic coast of Panama, as well as in Colombia.[2]
It is one of the most notable aesthetic textile pieces made by the Indigenous

Dule. There I stood in the middle of a coffeehouse, looking at this folk artform that Starbucks chose to *represent* its product through the cultural and political aesthetics of a culture quite unlike its own and of a people living thousands of miles away from downtown Honolulu.

Starbucks's relationship to the mola is based on its appropriation of Dule traditional dress in order to service its global economic interests. Yet as Starbucks harnesses the Dule art form for its own purposes, paradoxically, the company's practice of cultural appropriation physically and digitally reveals the Dule to the world. Economic appropriation unexpectedly also operates as Dule's political herald. While appropriation is not an uncommon occurrence in most colonized spaces, on this day it was so clear to me how closely Starbucks' appropriation of a Dule cultural aesthetic mirrors the relationship between the Dule and Panama. Like the image of the Starbucks's coffee product, the Dule textile narrative is apportioned for commercialization in Panama too. Here, the Dule and their cultural and aesthetic materials have been deeply woven into Panama's national story—both in printed and virtual forms. So much so that they have become an authenticating mechanism in a foreign national narrative, while the Dule themselves only interact tangentially, or as they please, with this colonial entity. Dule materials are showcased as Panamanian and never fully acknowledged as Dule.

Both Starbucks and Panama mold, develop, and mediate their commercialized narratives in (non)digital spaces by poaching Dule culture and their aesthetic products. They thus create a strained, binary relationship that plays a role in constructing national histories and defining "what is Panamanian," "who is Panamanian," and how is a "Panamanian" defined through appropriation (as well as possession) of indigeneity. These dynamics deny Dule a voice and, conversely, are processes that Dule push back, resist, and unravel. In this manner, Dule secure distinct political and cultural spaces across Panama and worldwide in physical and digital realms.

Like the layers of a mola, this chapter is composed of multiple stratums of text that tell the unique story of the Dule people and their/our Indigenous existence within newly propagated non-Indigenous spaces such as those represented in global digital realms. In this chapter, I will discuss molas as a theoretical practice and that practice's origin. Then I will examine the movement of molas from the physical space to the digital space. I will thus demonstrate how the textualities and realms of the virtual reproduction of mola images serve as conduits for an expanded digital discourse—a Dule digital literature that narrates the continued existence of the Dule nation.

PRACTICE AS THEORY

Theoretically, this chapter draws on a number of concepts that define and situate the positionality of the Dule people, their cultural practices, artifacts, and everyday movements in relevant contexts. These include the terms "poli-aesthetic" and "counterpoint-counterplot." First, it uses "poli-aesthetic" to define the political and aesthetic practices in Dule society that are layered, fused, and articulated as a single, collective unit. This term describes Dule social, political, cultural, and artistic in/visibilities, both in contemporary Panama and in cyberspace. Following Jacques Rancière's (2006, 9–45) model of a "politics of aesthetics," it examines how the Dule seamlessly, concurrently occupy and navigate seemingly non-Indigenous spaces and places, while still retaining an artful and political existence that supports Dule indigeneity.[3] Such politics determine areas that are perceived and expressed by those who are capable of observing and speaking "around the properties of spaces and the possibilities of time" (13). That is to say, concerning aesthetics, there is an occurrence in the partitioning and distributing of perception. Yet the political here is conditioned by the aesthetic possibility of shared sensory experience within inclusionary and exclusionary communities (12–13).[4]

In Dule society, aesthetics and politics alike are conditioned not by each other but rather by how they operate together as a single equivalent unit counterpoint within a natural ontological milieu, blended in all spaces. In so operating, they also enact a counterplot. In other words, aesthetics and politics combine to form one undivided entity. Dule governance structure and community-at-large, for example, are composed of political and aesthetic practices that are layered, combined, and expressed as a single unit. To this end, poli-aesthetic movements in these sociocultural and sociopolitical practices offer one set of equivalent components wherein aesthetics and politics intertwine. The usage of the term "poli-aesthetics," therefore, not only describes how the Dule engage with modernity but also how others engage with the Dule—even unconsciously.

Second, the term "counterpoint-counterplot" explains and reveals how the Dule, through poli-aesthetic movements, engage with and disengage from the Panamanian structural narrative by removing and replacing one plot for another. At the same time, the Dule is creating a subversive façade of being in compliance with the dominant regime. Edward Said's (1994, 51) concept of the "contrapuntal" and June Nash's (2001, 20–26) notion of "counterplot" are useful in revealing how the Dule, through poli-aesthetic movements, operate and live in a non-Indigenous space like Panama. Contrapuntal, according to Said (1994, 51), applies to the studying of histories and processes that are synchronized and intertwined, yet disjointed and apart. The corresponding histories and patterns may appear to be harmonious, yet they reveal conflicting developments and interpretations. A contrapuntal method unveils the networking links and articulations of Dule indigeneity with and against Panamanian narratives that express a national imaginary identity.[5] By de-centering the established Panamanian national narrative through this counterpoint practice, Dule histories are re-centered within it, making them visible.

Coexisting with the counterpoint practice, a counterplot act also appears and reveals Dule experiences that have been otherwise obscured within modern Panama. I use counterplot to distinguish and demonstrate how Dule poliaesthetic ontologies exist, reveal, and even replace prevalent histories that try to ignore or eradicate their experiences within and beyond the Panamanian region. By the same token, counterplot materializes as a practice of subversive acts that affords Dule a space for cultural manifestations and political actualizations with and against Panama's national government and identity.

Counterplot thus equals nonconformism, and the occurrence that takes place in these new positions for dissension, as described by Nash (2001, 20), represents nonconformity.[6] Indigenous cultural and political movements emerge from marginalized locations, therefore as counterplot to the previously dominant histories that have shadowed and, in many cases, even attempted to erase Indigenous languages, epistemologies, and histories through systematic colonialist policies.

In the physical realm, as well as the digital, Panama's official story (since 1903) has relied on an appropriation of Dule-specific experiences, such as molas, in order to define and create its national narrative. In addition, the molas become a site for commercial exploitation by online retailers. These virtual and corporeal forms of cultural appropriation and exploitation have continued to fail on many levels. Given the histories of the Dule in Panama (which existed as part of Gran Colombia until 1903) and their presence in cyberspace, there are visible manifestations of Dule as an Indigenous people that counterplot Panamanian narratives about them and the online commercial exploitation of molas. For example, through a counterplot practice, whenever a Dule or non-Dule person engages in Dule cosmopolitics, via the site of a mola, their engagement with such Dule experience(s) disassembles Panama's national narrative and dismantles the commercialized exploitation. In fact, a viewer's interaction with a mola, in the physical and digital realms, forces one to view a story through Dule experiences. The practice of counterplot takes apart both Panamanian narratives and the cyber marketing exploitation of molas, and it strains them in such a way that reveals and opens up sites for Dule poli-aesthetic ontologies in physical and digital realms.

ORIGIN OF MOLA

According to Dule oral history:

> Gikadiryai, great grandmother, also taught in Yoodiwala. . . . Before Gikadiryai, grandmothers and grandfathers were already dressed. They were using aramola, the dabumola and skins of animals. The kind of mola our women use today was not yet born. With Gikadiryai, they begin to use [different types of fabric molas] the diskelamola, masimola, abgimola, ubsanmola. The fabrics were subjected to various shades of dyes. Gikadiryai used seeds of avocado, the abgi, the gobirgwa, the roots of mangroves . . . to dye fabrics, giving color to their clothes and hammocks. The threads were extracted from the banana stem and the oa was used for weaving and sewing dresses. Gikadiryai taught Ogir, Inar, Aidikili. They prepared and made long dresses. The grandmothers were distributed into groups and the one who knew more directed each group. Gikadiryai directed all groups. (Wagua 2007b, 27)[7]

Dule poet and scholar Aiban Wagua (2007b, 27) recounted and translated the origin story of mola, which tells us of Gikadiryai's teachings. She teaches Dule women how to use plants, tree bark, and seeds in order to make, to tailor, and to color natural tree bark for clothes and hammocks. The narrative of mola's origination explains, from a Dule perspective, the production of their aesthetics and cultural practices—existing long before contact with outsiders such as the Spanish, English, Scots, and Americans.

The Dule are the artistic creators of molas. The quilted, reverse appliqué includes hand-stitched needlework designs from abstract geometric patterns to motifs of flora and fauna. After each cloth is completed, a mola-maker sews one mola onto the front and one onto the back of a blouse. From a young age, every Dule woman learns to embroider and sew, and she designs her own mola by watching "other women in the household" (Salvador 2003, 55). Dule mola-maker

Cristina de Martínez (pers. comm., March 7, 2009) explains, "from 7 to 8 years old you learn to sew, Grandma makes one to sew and how to tailor it. . . . [Also] you see Granny sewing and you sit also sewing. The lady who raised me taught me to sew things for myself. I used to sew, she used to cut and tailor it."[8] When a young Dule woman reaches marriageable age, she should have already accumulated a large quantity of her finest blouses (Shaffer 1982, 5). Before making a mola, each maker carefully selects a pattern, which may differ from that of other mola-makers, focusing closely on utilizing the space provided from the cloth material. As Clyde E. Keeler (1969, 85) observes with regard to the proportion and space used in the design, "mola art at its best cannot tolerate spaces, and all colors employed must be distributed. Bodily proportions may be exaggerated to fit a particular space." The selection of motif designs and the decision on how to space and place them onto fabric is governed by the norms of an artistic movement, not solely by individual choice. In Dule communities, there is art not only in the making of these pieces but also in how one wears the molas.

MOLAS AND SPACES

Molas perform spatial practices in physical and virtual spheres through conditions of everyday operational acts. As Michel de Certeau observes, space is "composed of intersections of mobile elements. It is in a sense actuated by the ensemble of movements deployed within it" (1984, 117). Stories form through the intertwining of movements in, out, and around various spheres. Where there was once nothing, these elemental motions develop a culture. The word "mola" translates to "cloth" in Dulegaya, Dule language. Mola's stories determine the cloth's "place" and "space," by the very act of it "being-there" and also through "operations" where "movement always seems to condition the production of a space and to associate it with history" (118).

Prior to commencing the creative process, a Dule mola-maker chooses a "placed" inanimate or animate object from one's surroundings—like a frog or the geometric motif of a patterned basket—and draws an outline of the item with a pencil onto the fabric. In doing so, the Dule artist takes the object (mobile and immobile) from its original location and transfers it onto fabric. By her stitching actions, she completes the creation of a new "space" for the original object. This space becomes a "visual dwelling" in which the embroidered design represents how Dule interpret and relate to their environment. The making of a mola perpetuates a process where "stories thus carry out a labor that constantly transforms places into spaces or spaces into places" (Certeau 1984, 118). While patterns that have been passed down from generation to generation can appear similar to one another, their mutual distinctiveness is clearer when comparing examples from the past and present.

The mola-maker's imagination ultimately becomes a kind of "space" as well, the dwelling in which the aesthetic sense and creativity of the artist comes to life. Through the eye and hands of a seamstress, the tactile motif she creates for her mola reflects a singular vision, of the world and her reality, within an identity as Dule. Her visual craft becomes a tangible, established place, where she re-visions, re-defines, and then re-establishes a confined, bordered reality—on textile. The spatial story occurs through the re-vision of artistic work. For example, simple abstract images of an animal, a plant, or even a bow tie (see fig. 2.1), or a more complex design documenting important events, such as a Dule girl's puberty ceremony, are reinterpreted in every generation.

In Dule molas, the design of animal or plant motifs is a process born from the artist's own imagination and creative language. The visual image is an ontological movement from nature. The mola-maker works as a creator of the visual design. In fact, the image itself also labors and acts as creator of the mola-maker, such that the visual image *instructs* her to create a presence on textile. Mari Lyn Salvador explains the mola-maker's creative process:

FIGURE 2.1. A work-in-progress mola with a bow tie repetition motif, made by the author's great-aunt. Photo by the author.

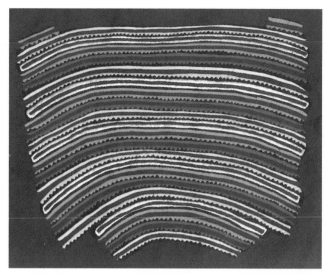

FIGURE 2.2. A *sue mor* (rainbow mola) from the Haglund family collection, circa 2005. Photo by the author.

Some *sergan* ["old" or "from the past" in Dule dialect] designs are simple geometric patterns, while others are inspired by patterns on baskets, beaded leg bands, and body painting, or from abstract designs based on images in nature or common household objects such as gourds, leaves, snakes, or wooden hangers used in the home. Some are easy to recognize, but others are so abstract that they require explanation. To create this type of abstract design, women scrutinize an object, often turning it to view it from all angles, and reduce it to what they consider the basic components of its form, then repeating the design over and over. (2003, 61)

These abstract, geometric images, as artistic expression and spiritual engagement, demonstrate the strong influence that their natural surroundings have on their designers. The mola patterns themselves become a medium for telling a story—the story of the artist. Figure 2.2, for instance, represents a *sue mor* or rainbow mola design.[9] As a mola captures a piece of history and a moment in time, passing them down from one generation to another, it engages an evolutionary movement that is reciprocal between both the artist and the image itself.

Molas and other Dule cultural products, in serving as poli-aesthetic texts that reveal social, cultural, political, and economic movements, also show the intrinsic relationship among the Dule, land, and nature. Dule mola patterns originating from early body-painting designs represented nature. As one seventeenth-century account states with regard to the act of art emerging onto the physical body:

> Both these and the Copper-colour'd Indians use painting their Bodies, even of the Sucking Children sometimes. They make Figures of Birds, Beasts, Men, Trees, or the like, up and down in every part of the Body, more especially the Face: But the Figures are not extraordinary like what they represent, and are of differing Dimensions, as their fancies lead them. The Women are the Painters, and take a great delight in it. The Colours they like and use most are Red, Yellow, and Blue, very bright and lovely. . . . The Men, when they go to War, paint the Faces all over with Red; and the Shouldiers, Breast and the rest of the Bodies, here with Black and there with Yellow, or any other Colour at pleasure, in large Spots; all which they wash off at Night in the River before they go to sleep. (Wafer 1699, 138–40)

The account is significant in its observation of Dule artwork moving from one realm to another. This transference of body-painting designs, such as the geometric images and flora and fauna motifs, onto cloth represents movement—a movement of designs from temporary canvases such as the human body onto more permanent ones such as the mola. These movements occur from within the artist's environment, which moves through her imagination and recycles (in)to her reality as an artwork form, on both the body and the fabric.

As the flora and fauna motifs are stitched onto its fabric, molas progress through another kind of "movement," linking art and environment together in one locale. This simple, physical technique creates a new reality of consciousness or spatial movement of knowledge. In other words, the knowledge of the five senses, the environment, history, language, tradition, and experience. For example, Dule artwork's movement from body to cloth represents not only a literal one but an epistemological movement, creating a link between two physical layers. Most importantly, however, it is not just the obvious creation of different physical spheres but also the transference process that takes place from Dule body to cloth. For most Indigenous peoples, including the Dule, spatial and place-based relationships do not explicitly demarcate the *here* and *there* worlds. Instead, a correlation of layers emerges within a variety of worlds; for instance, the physical and spiritual or the heavens and earth. The layers of the space and place, in both physical and spiritual realms, are not separated but rather synchronous spheres.

Lakota author and scholar Vine Deloria Jr. (2006, 202) explains the relationship between space and place as "one of relationships, and since the entire cosmos cannot be contained in our daily lives, we learn that sacred places represent the power by showing us that we can become a part of a preexisting set of relationships." The relationship between space and place reveals that consciousness is a flexible sphere—a spiritual realm that is not compartmentalized but rather becomes reality even when our physical body occupies the physical world in all locations ranging from a sweat lodge to a sacred mountain or land (Deloria 2006, 202). This is similar to Certeau's (1984, 117) assertion that "space is a practiced place."

The visual language of a mola represents how a Dule sees and relates to their natural surroundings. Some of the common mola designs include lobsters, turtles, parrots, leaves, canoes, and events of daily life. According to Dule educator Roberto Martínez Owen (pers. comm., March 7, 2009): "Well, in the drawings, we will always find animals. Animals because the Guna always want to preserve and to protect nature. They always want to take care of animals like dogs, cats, and parrots. Take care of all these animals. That is why we always find drawings on the mola. We always find drawings of flowers, we always find mountains, namely, we always find nature."[10] Aside from images of nature, other popular designs include, as mentioned earlier, geometric and abstract patterns. The diversity in motifs "illustrate[s] things that interest them [women, as mola-makers], and almost anything a woman sees or hears about may become the inspiration for a pictorial mola" (Salvador 1997, 191). Additionally, "women create designs from objects they see or events they participate in, such as the girls' puberty ceremony . . . they listen to narratives in the gathering house and illustrate the primary characters and activities in their molas" (191). As these mola-creators tell their stories, the pictorial designs become visual narrations of Dule ontology, identity, and culture.

THE DIGITAL MOVEMENT OF MOLAS

Molas are mutable stories that change and move. The digital movement of molas via the works of Dule artists, such as Oloedidili Monique Mojica and Achu Oswaldo De León Kantule, are two prime examples discussed in this section. These artists find their aesthetic inspiration via a mola where their artistry (on stage and on canvas) suggest multiple stories in multiple spaces that create a technological interplay between an online viewer and digital location (Deleuze 1989).[11] In the case of a mola in the digital terrain, the computer serves as an instrument that "mediate[s] the relation between" both the image and the physical mola, resulting in a virtual snapshot that reproduces itself as a cybertext to the observer (Certeau 1984, 141). This (cyber)operational interaction seemingly "organizes social space: it separates the text and the body, but it also links them, by permitting the acts that will make the textual 'fiction' of the model reproduced and realized by the body" (Certeau 1984, 141). Hence, it is evident, via the (cyber)operational relationship, that the images of Dule molas textually reproduce and manifest on any kind of fabric, visual painting, and stage set design.

For Dule-Rappahannock theater artist and playwright Oloedidili Monique Mojica,[12] theatrical performances serve as her molas. She explains, "These are my molas. I can't sew to save my life, I mean I can put a button back on, but this work [speaking of her collection of plays *Chocolate Woman Dreams the Milky Way*], these are my molas. These are all the layers that I'm trying to sew together and figure out how they fit to present this other perception that comes from within" (Oloedidili Monique Mojica, pers. comm., March 2, 2009). In the physical realm, Mojica is, therefore, a Dule seamstress working in an alternative medium and context, one who sews her plays—her mola—on stage: an embodiment of other Dule women wearing mola as they connect to the stories of their ancestors, in the sergan molas.

In the digital realm, Mojica extends the presence of her mola—her collections of plays like *Chocolate Woman Dreams the Milky Way* (Mojica, n.d.)—by establishing and creating a modern, technical form of material: a website[13] and social media (Facebook) presence of Chocolate Woman Collective.[14] For example, the visible website presence of Chocolate Woman Collective (Mojica, n.d.) provides space for Mojica, as an Indigenous playwright and artist, to narrate a type of mola via the narration of the play, the mola-inspired stage design, and the characters' costume design. Further, Chocolate Woman Collective website is a space where mola-inspired stories navigate effortlessly across physical and digital realms, while never losing their meaning. In Mojica's emphasis: "These stories need to be told, but who were we before the rupture? And if those entities, that energy, that spirit still exist in those dimensions, where they came from. They haven't gone anywhere. They haven't changed. We're the ones who've changed. And that means we can still find ways to connect ourselves to them. . . . I can connect myself to Buna Siagua [Chocolate Woman], . . . I can connect myself to Muu Bili [Grandmother Ocean] . . . connect myself to

Nis Bundor [Star Daughters], to Napguana [Mother Earth], Ibedon [a kalu or sacred land that overlooks Yandup-Nargana]"[15] (pers. comm., March 2, 2009). Mojica's connection to Buna Siagua, Muu Bili, Nis Bundor, Napguana, and Ibedon is a space of consciousness—a space where there is "constant movement" in the molas.

Similar to Mojica's theatrical artistry, Achu Oswaldo De León Kantule, a Dule painter and installation artist, finds inspiration for his artwork via molas. He sees the mola as representing a "moving place" on the bodies of Dule women (Achu Oswaldo De León Kantule, pers. comm., June 2, 2011). In this way, Dule women become "walking books" carrying their stories of culture and lifeworlds with them everywhere they go (Achu Oswaldo De León Kantule, pers. comm., June 2, 2011). Similarly, Achu's visual paintings and installation projects traverse and meld from the physical realm to the digital. On the physical canvas, the mola is an inspiration because the openness and evolution of the visual designs tend to craft and tell stories that are passed down from one generation to the next. Inspired by molas as "walking books," in the Montreal First Peoples' Festival 2005 visual art exhibition, *Artists' Books: Written Images of the First Nations* (organized by Terres en Vues/Land InSights), Achu created an "installation of a mola-book [that] pays homage to this ability to transmit a symbolic language" (Montreal's First Peoples' Festival, 2005).[16] The physical embodiment of this installation project involved the construction of a wooden book assembled with mola abstract and geometric designs.

Beyond the physical artwork, Achu makes use of millennial technology to promote and display his paintings, which reflect Dule culture, historical memory, and cosmology. A digital photo collection of his artwork is found on his personal website with an integrated approach using social media such as Facebook, Twitter, and Instagram (Achu Oswaldo De León Kantule, 2015).[17] The digital photographs showcase his paintings that reflect duality, repetition, and symmetrical designs. Often times, Achu includes prominent figures from Dule society and narratives in his paintings. These include: canoes, abstract figures of Dule women wearing molas, water, whirlpools, tornadoes, and *nuchus* [hand-carved wood figures used for ceremonial practices] (Achu Oswaldo De León Kantule, 2015). Achu's usage of technology for his paintings represents the (cyber)spatial layering of molas in a different context. His artwork's online presence communicates an aesthetic appeal of the mola as a traversable entity. Specifically, the (cyber)spatial operations of his paintings reflect the molas flexibility to function and occupy Indigenous and non-Indigenous spaces simultaneously (Certeau

1984, 115–53). The molas exist as practices of counterpoint-counterplot occurring in a variety of spaces where Achu's mola-inspired paintings become "packed into a text"—manufactured, reproduced, and disseminated to the public (local and international) for consumption (Certeau 1984, 140). The molas, as a result, become a virtual text.

Both Achu (pers. comm., June 2, 2011) and Mojica (pers. comm., March 2, 2009) describe Dule women as moving storybooks. Mojica (pers. comm., March 2, 2009) further explains that a mola reflects the practice and belief of Dule ontology and belief systems, especially its duality and multiple layers existing within Dule worlds. She describes her meeting with an *argar*, a specialist who interprets a *sagla*'s symbolic language on the teachings and ways of Babigala, during her travels to Gunayala in 2008 with Achu:

> I was here [in Panama] in September. Achu and I spent an entire afternoon with the *argar* Ricardo Arias Sipu from Agligandi, where you're from [referring to me]. He spoke to us in the same terms about multidimensionality, about the duality of Baba and Nana. Everything is Baba and Nana, everything is in twos or multiples of twos. It begins to get very mathematical; it starts to go into Dule physics, because it amplifies in terms of everything. Everything has eight levels. If you're looking at anything within the Dule culture, you're looking at eight levels; all at the same time. That's why, [with] the molas, you are looking from the top, from the bottom, [and] from the inside. There are just always eight levels because they're four times the sacred number two. (Oloedidili Monique Mojica, pers. comm., March 2, 2009)

In Dule ontology, all things exist in repetition, as multiple layers and symbolic language. This is notable in the way designs and motifs of molas appear in pairs, showing a repetition of patterns, layers of materials, and abstract symbols. Mojica, in the context of explaining how to interpret a mola, talks about the different activities "in constant movement" occurring simultaneously in her uncle's house: "kids all over, my tío Francisco's television blaring baseball, animals out on this level, and all my female cousins laughing really loud" (Oloedidili Monique Mojica, pers. comm., March 2, 2009). She recalls that her colleague, Erika Iserhoff (a James Bay Cree textile and costume designer), interpreted these things in the following way, after they had left her uncle's house together: "Erika said, 'well you know when you look at a mola, it is the same as being in your family's living room. There is all that cacophony, all those different layers and all that movement and all those different colors that seem they shouldn't go together, but they do'" (Oloedidili Monique Mojica, pers. comm., March 2, 2009). Thus, we find a similar cacophony in digital spaces.

The counterpoint-counterplot framework of mola stories displaying a poliaesthetic movement is embodied in its cacophonous (but ultimately harmonious) textile. At the same time, it also represents identity and unity similar to that lived by the Dule before and after the 1925 Dule Revolution. That year, a group of Dule revolted against the Panamanian government's attempts to assimilate them into Western culture—thus resulting and giving rise to the Dule Revolution (Tice 1995, 40). The primary catalyst of the insurgency was the unlawful and inhumane treatment Dule experienced under the colonialist Panamanian police. Tice (1995, 61) explains, "Kuna women in a number of Kuna communities had been forced to take off their *molas*, to wear western clothes, to remove their nose rings and *wini*. . . ." In one testimony, Elisa Blanco describes her mother's incarceration by colonial police during the Panamanian occupation in Gunayala to *La Prensa*, one of Panama's local newspapers. According to Arcadio Bonilla (2006): "Elisa Blanco, an 89-year-old woman, still remembers clearly some of the events they experienced during the revolution, because her mother, Hilda Campos, was one of the [Dule] people arrested by the colonial police. After finding out about the incident, Blanco tells the story of when she was nine years old [and] she brought her mother a corn drink. 'When I saw her, I began to cry. She confirmed to me that she was detained, along with other women, because they refused to take off the winis [bracelets] and mola.'"[18] This brief testimony is an example of how the (story)teller conveys their words into a materialized political medium, much as Dule women's acts of resistance to the prohibitions against wearing the mola and winis. Many Dule women, like Elisa Blanco's mother Hilda Campos, continue to proudly wear these cultural identity markers, which serve as sites of aesthetic production and political resistance.

TEXTUALITIES AND REALMS

We, the Dule, did not shun modernity—and we have made sure that modernity has not shunned us. Dule material culture, like the mola, is a ubiquitous way of being and knowing that dwells in the multilayered planes. A mola dwells in cyberspace through virtual storytelling on Facebook, technological photo archiving of paintings for online art galleries, and (cyber)writing a genre of digital literature that reflect Dule cultural-historical memory. In material culture and cyberculture, the mola physically links and digitally networks in locations, which reflect the abstraction as well as the total sum of Dule continued existence.

We find an example of Dule continued existence in the material world, as previously mentioned, in colonialist policies that restrict Dule women from wearing their mola. The act of prohibiting women from wearing their traditional dress "was considered by many Kuna as a way of stripping them of their identity," an "important symbol of the Kuna people's right to self-determination" (Tice 1995, 62). Their culturally specific ways of wearing the mola have and continue to distinguish Dule from the larger Panamanian population and reaffirm their resistance to colonial assimilation. The conservation of the mola is similar to the preservation of Mayan literatures and languages. These entities, Dule mola and Mayan languages and literatures, serve as expressions of "cultural agency" that highlight the means by which "subjects, often peripheral or subaltern, empower themselves through cultural practices" (Arias 2006, 167). The practice of cultural agency in "Maya literature began to appear for the first time written in Maya languages. . . . These Maya texts include a range of genres. One might think initially of testimonios, such as those of Rigoberta Menchú and Victor Montejo, which were a first attempt to frame a rhetoric of being and to name agency for Mayas, to state the right to be themselves" (Arias 2006, 171). The production of this literature mobilized the cultural revitalization of Maya people and reinforced their resistance to suppression and oppression. As political acts, they represent a poli-aesthetic practice of existence. Various groups and organizations began to look to the symbols of the collective past, such as the Mayan glyph writing system, and reintroduced them to the community (171). Maya literature demonstrates "a discursive performativity that explores the contours of a collective identity, representing the construction of a subjective and moral 'imagined community'" (171). In a similar fashion to Maya literature, the mola and wini serve as Dule cultural identity markers, as well as collective symbols of the Dule historical past and enduring present.

For the Dule, oppression under and occupation by police and government forces in Gunayala serve as catalysts of visual language that resists Panama's domination thereof, both prior to and after the 1925 Dule Revolution.[19] Everything in Gunayala and in Dule society becomes sites of poli-aesthetic counterpoint-counterplot acts. The poli-aesthetic movements of molas and winis construct a space for the Dule and demonstrate a continuity of existence.

The testimonies of the Dule people and the political manifestations of pictorial systems in their communities endured during the occupation in Gunayala by Panamanian colonial police. With respect to the 1925 Dule Revolution, Dule historian Iguanape Purbagana stresses the importance of this war:

> I will tell you the importance of the Dule Revolution. It was an important part in the lives of the Guna. Why did the Guna allow the North American Marsh to be involved? They just realized that (1) they have always been allied with the English, and (2) the Guna realized that they could not fight alone. Because they learned in their own history . . . to defend their own, defend their life, their law, their history, their congress, their mola, their way of life as a Guna they had to unite with someone who has a force that can support them, that's all. It is not like Marsh stayed for the revolution. It is like any other revolution. If you take a look at the American Revolution of Independence, many called for the support of the French. Because no one is alone in a war, in any war no one succeeds alone. That's simply what the Gunas did. (Iguanape Purbagana, pers. comm., March 6, 2009)[20]

There was a lot at stake for their culture, way of life, and practice. The very essence of being Dule and the continuity of Dule existence were determined by their traditional dress: the molas and winis. In order to honor their culture, the Dule made the decision to take up arms against the Panamanian government. Thereafter, Dule traditional dress becomes symbolic of cultural existence and agency, a site that defines who the Dule are as a people and how they perceive their history, way of life, and traditional practices. At the same time, the Dule dismantle the Panamanian national narrative. Furthermore, a mola is a place where Dule women, like my great-great-grandmother Muukuaiet, nonviolently express themselves by wearing their Dule story through these aesthetic blouses, and by culturally identifying and politically defining themselves through experience, representation, interpretation, and a philosophy that is strikingly different from the non-Dule's understanding and knowledge thereof. As Anne Waters (2004, 159) explains, "Over 500 years of cultural seeing of the resistance of American Indians to colonization, assimilation, and genocide have informed our hearing of a different drum." Waters refers to the senses of seeing and hearing as embodying the production of a collective experience of one's surroundings and the self. The markings of self-perception and existence (with)in a certain location draw out and disclose an interpretative experience of one's culture, way of life, and communication.[21] The development of multiple perspectives and understandings of it, however, is always vulnerable to the dangers of a dominant group's official story. These dangers create an absence of and/or a gap within the stories of a dominated group. Sagladummad Inakeliginya affirms the great difference between the Dule and many non-Dule interpretations of molas: "We must always bear in mind a great truth: we are different from those wagas, and we do not look alike. Our culture, compared with theirs, is different. They do not think like us, do not feel like us, do not plan like us. The wagas plan to finish us and they say that they love us" (Wagua 2007a, 18).[22]

For Dule, the mola reinforces unbroken Indigenous ties via traditional dress, political-cultural identity, and social connections among Dule women and men. Outside of the Dule realm, the mola continues to be recast from its true Indigenous Dule affiliation to that pertaining to the greater Panamanian national narrative. The mola is redistributed and repartitioned in physical and digital spaces from a Dule mola blouse to a virtual collection of stage design, including the cultural appropriated motif chosen by Starbucks for one of its Honolulu locations. These expressions collectively recognize and register Dule histories, intentionally or not (in regards to sense experience and perception of the visible and invisible, sayable and unsayable, and audible and inaudible), within the realm of Panama's modern territorial existence as well as beyond its territorialized identity (Rancière 2006, 12–14).[23] Regardless of the original intention and role that the mola may have in Dule society, it has appealed to and informed cultural-political movements in physical and technological terrains.

The mola is political. It exerts political intentions through visual and virtual modes of being via cyberspace and material culture. Also, the mola is simultaneously modern and traditional. It crosses all terrains. While the mola physically and virtually crosses various terrains, it creates, develops, modifies, and occupies more spaces and places along the way. Iguanape Purbagana describes it thusly:

In 1925 the mola was not appreciated. It was tumultuous that it was not wanted by the so-called civilized state and that is why they separated us because they wanted to ban the traditional mola. Today, but today mola is famous at the global level. Look how man's thought has changed. Today the mola is commercialized. Years before it was an object not appreciated because it wasn't commercialized. It wasn't money, now it is money. A changed world and that is why the Dule Revolution is just that: the defense of the mola, defense of culture, language, and everything of our own autonomy. (Iguanape Purbagana, pers. comm., March 6, 2009)[24]

NOTES

1. The product showcased in the Starbucks coffeehouse is the dark-medium roast coffee called "Panama La Florentina." To view the image of the advertisement canvas, see Garrett's blog post (2012).

2. I use the term Dule to describe this specific Indigenous people of Panama, a word that they use to identify themselves as a people. However, Guna (another term also accepted by the Dule) is a word more commonly used by others, including academic scholars, to identify this group. Other words that are often used to identify the Dule include San Blas Indians, San Blaseños, Kuna, Cuna, and Tule. Furthermore, the name "San Blas" (this is a Spanish term for Saint Blaise, a patron of the Catholic Church) is used (by others) to refer to the region Dule people inhabit, which today is called Gunayala (also with the spelling variation of Kuna Yala). I keep to the original diversity of references used by scholars in their own literary works, as to how each has addressed the Dule people and contexts—that is, Cuna, Kuna, San Blas Indians, or Tule, including also isle communities such as Ailigandi, and the Gunayala region as Kuna Yala or San Blas. However, in my own analysis, I use the word Dule to refer to the people, Agligandi (the proper Dulegaya spelling variation of Ailigandi), and Gunayala to refer to the region they inhabit in Panama.

3. Rancière suggests, that in the "politics of aesthetics" model, art: "as the systems of a priori forms determining what presents itself to sense experience . . . [offers] a delimitation of spaces and times, of the visible and the invisible, of speech and noise, that simultaneously determines the place and the stakes of politics as a form of experience" (2006, 13).

4. Following Rancière's (2006, 12–13) explanation on the "politics of aesthetics" model, inclusionary and exclusionary communities are defined by distribution of experiences by those who have access to a common experience and by those communities who are excluded from a shared experience.

5. This artful and political existence presents patterns and processes in polyphonous acts. In this sense, contrapuntal analysis points to numerous modes of arrangements and processes where Dule poli-aesthetic existence concurrently engages the dominant Panamanian structural narrative. At the same time, however, it disparately disengages from Panama's main story. This modern nation's narrative must also be experienced, viewed, engaged, and disengaged on the basis of Dule experiences that, even if they have been masked, are salient and sentient.

6. As Nash writes: "Global integration has disrupted old bases for collective action while creating new modes of organization. With the loss of stable production sites, the basis for collective action by an organized working class becomes fragmented, yet new sites for dissent emerge to contest the consolidation of power in global settings" (2001, 20).

7. Original: "Gikadiryai, la gran abuela, también enseñaba entonces en Yoodiwala. . . . Antes de Gikadiryai, ya se vestían las abuelas y los abuelos. Ellos y

ellas utilizaban el aramola, el dabumola y pieles de animals. Aún no había nacido el tipo de mola que utilizan nuestras mujeres de hoy. Con Gikadiryai empiezan a usar el diskelamola, masimola, abgimola, ubsanmola. Los tejidos fueron sometidos a las tinturas de diversas tonalidades. Gikadiryai utilizó las semillas de aguacate, el abgi, el gobirgwa, las raíces de los manglares . . . para teñir los tejidos; daba así los colores a sus ropas y hamacas. Los hilos se extrajeron del tallo del plátano y el oa se utilizó para tejer y coser los vestidos. Gikadiryai enseñó a Ogir, a Inar a Aidikili. Se elaboraron vestidos largos. Las abuelas se distribuían en grupos y cada grupo era dirigido por una que sabía más. Gikadiryai orientaba a todos los grupos" (Wagua 2007b, 27). The original quoted passage is translated by the author.

8. Original: "de 7 a 8 años uno aprende a coser, la abuela le pone a uno a coser y cómo confeccionarlo. . . . [Además] uno ve a la abuelita cosiendo y se sienta también a coser. La señora que me crió me enseñó a coser cosas para mí. Yo cosía, ella lo cortaba y lo confeccionaba." The original quoted passage is translated by the author. Cristina de Martínez (a Dule mola-maker from Agligandi, pers. comm.), interviewed by the author, Colón, Panama, March 7, 2009.

9. According to Nordenskiöld, in Dule storytelling, "The rain-bow is called a sue. One should not point at the rainbow, for if one does, one will get warts on the hand. When there are two rainbows, the brighter is looked upon as a man and the other one as a woman" (1938, 394). Nordenskiöld did not elaborate further, alas, on the reasoning for why the brightness of two rainbows should thus distinguish between genders. Achu Oswaldo De León Kantule (n.d.), an artist and grandson of Dule spiritual leader Nele Kantule, confirms that in Dule culture, the *sue* symbolizes fertility. For more information on Dule spirituality and symbolic images, see Achu Oswaldo De León Kantule's web page (n.d.), accessed October 6, 2017.

10. Original: "En los dibujos siempre vamos a encontrar animales. Animales porque el Guna siempre quiere conservar la naturaleza. Siempre quiere cuidar a los animales como los perros, los gatos y los loros. Todos esos animales ellos los quieren cuidar. Por eso siempre encontramos en la mola los dibujos. Siempre encontramos las flores, siempre encontramos las montañas, o sea siempre encontramos la naturaleza." The original quoted passage is translated by the author. Roberto Martínez Owen (retired physical education teacher and Dule from Agligandi, pers. comm.), interviewed by the author, Panama City, Panama, March 7, 2009.

11. This interplay is similar to the sensory-motor image experience of a viewer when s/he watches a film. In *Cinema 2*, for example, Deleuze states, "What a viewer perceived therefore was a sensory-motor image in which he [she] took a greater or lesser part by identification with the characters" (1989, 3). That is, the audience, as an observer, interacts with the film. Within this interaction then, a multidimensional relationship is created among viewer, camera, and director. In this dynamic, the audience, the director of the film, and the film itself operate as three entities that mutually require one another to serve as a conduit (Deleuze 1986, 202).

12. Oloedidili Monique Mojica (Dule Rappahannock artist and writer whose family is from Yandup-Nargana), interviewed by Sue P. Haglund, Panama City, Panama, March 2, 2009.

13. Mojica (website), accessed October 6, 2017.

14. Mojica, Facebook, accessed October 6, 2017.

15. Oloedidili Monique Mojica (Dule Rappahannock artist and writer whose family is from Yandup-Nargana, pers. comm.), interviewed by the author, Panama City, Panama, March 2, 2009.

16. For more information of Achu's *Mola-Book installation project*, see Montreal's First Peoples' Festival: Visual Art (website), accessed September 6, 2011.

17. To view more of Achu Oswaldo De León Kantule's artwork, see his online gallery website, accessed November 19, 2017.

18. Original: "Elisa Blanco, una mujer de 89 años, aún recuerda con claridad parte de los sucesos que se vivieron durante la revolución, porque su madre, Hilda Campos, fue una de las tantas personas arrestadas por la policía colonial. Al enterarse del incidente, Blanco, quien entonces contaba con nueve años de edad, le llevó chichi de maíz. 'Cuando la vi, comencé a llorar. Ella, me confirmó que estaba detenida, junto a otras mujeres, porque se negaban a quitarse los *uinis* y la mola'" (Bonilla 2006). The original quoted passage is translated by the author.

19. This is reiterated in Roberto Martínez's (pers. comm., March 7, 2009) account: "The war, I remember it. In 1926 all the people fled to the mountain over there, tierra firme. I was about seven years old. That old man, his name was Colman. That old man, when I saw him, he was already old then. People carried him when he went about. San Blas, when it was under Panamanian control, when the police lived over there in Tupile, Narganá, Corazón de Jesus, Playón Chico. People from Playón Chico come and say [to Simral Colman,] 'I cannot go to the mountain. The police catch you. The police want to stop everything during that time.'"
    Original: "La guerra yo me recordaba de esa. En 1926 toda la gente se fue para el monte por allá, tierra firme. Yo como a siete años, ese viejo él se llama Colman, este viejo cuando yo lo vi, ya está viejito ya, gente cargaba a este cuando él se va. San Blas cuando tiempo panameño cuando vive por alla policía que se llama Tupile, Narganá, Corazón de Jesus, Playón Chico. Gente de Playón Chico viene y dice [al Simral Colman], 'yo no puedo ir al monte policía te agarra. La policía quiere parrar todo ese tiempo.'" The original quoted passage is translated by the author. Roberto Martínez (brother of Baby San Blas, pers. comm.), interviewed by the author, Colón, Rep. of Panama, March 7, 2009.

20. Original: "Yo le digo la importancia de la revolución Dule. Hubo un papel importante en la vida de los gunas. ¿Por qué los gunas hizo participar al norteamericano Marsh? Simplemente ellos se dieron cuenta que (1) siempre ha sido aliado con los íngleses, y (2) los gunas se dieron cuenta en que ellos no podían pelear solos. Porque aprendieron en su propia historia . . . para poder defender lo suyo, defender su vida, su derecho, su historia, su congreso, su mola, su forma de vivir tal como guna ellos

tenían que unirse con alguien que tenga una fuerza que la pueda apoyareso es todo. No es como Marsh quiso quedar por la revolución, sino es como cualquier otras revoluciones. Si tu ves la revolución Americana de Independencia muchos pidieron el apoyo de los franceses. Porque nadie ha salido solo en la guerra. En ninguna guerra que una triunfa solo. Eso lo que hizo los gunas simplemente." The original quoted passage is translated by the author. Iguanape Purbagana, as known Miguel de León (Dule historian, pers. comm.), interviewed by the author, Panama City, Rep. of Panama, March 6, 2009.

21. Waters explains: "In this way, what I see when I look in a mirror, or hear myself speak, is not only what is in the playful mirror or voice, but it may be radically different from what you see or hear. I, and not you, am in the place of experiencing self-reflection on my identity in the present, the very moment that I live the experience. This is one way we can be tricked in the game of identity—for what we appear to be to ourselves may not be what we appear to be to others" (2004, 161). The "I" and self-experience, as she mentions, articulate and put together a space for self-reflection and self-identification. In terms of literary production, the readings of texts like molas or *quipus* create a space for multiple interpretations and understandings of Indigenous identity and experience, even though these texts are normally not classified as literature or cataloged in a Western literary genre. Mesoamerican glyphs serve comparable roles to those of the Andean quipus and Dule molas and "could be read or interpreted by many people other than their creator" (Boone 1994, 22). The interpretations and readings of texts generate similar yet different relationships therewith. For example, the experience is different for a non-Indigenous than an Indigenous person when reading an Indigenous text. A space for discussion of multiple stories and multiple interpretations emerges from the production of reading a text.

22. Original: "Siempre tenemos que tener presente una gran verdad: somos distintos de los wagas, y no nos parecemos. Nuestra cultura, comparada con la de ellos, es distinta. Ellos no piensan como nosotros, no sienten como nosotros, no planean como nostros. Los wagas planean para acabarnos y dicen que nos quieren mucho" (Wagua 2007a, 18). The original quoted passage is translated by the author.

23. In addition, the mola serves as a reflection of unity and equal distribution of the sensible within Dule political terrain, as well as that developed in Panamá's national political terrain. The distribution of the sensible from Dule society thus is redistributed in Panamanian society. For more details on the distribution of the sensible see Rancière 2006, 12–14.

24. Original: "En 1925 la mola no era apreciada. Era un tumultuario querido de lo llamado civilización estatal y por eso nos separen porque quisieron acabar con esa tradición de mola. Hoy, pero hoy la mola es famosa a nivel mundial. O sea, mira como cambia la mentalidad del hombre. Hoy se comercializa la mola. Hace muchos años que era una cosa no apreciada porque no se comercializaba. No era dinero, por eso dinero. El cambio del mundo y por eso la revolución Dule es esta: defensa de la mola, defensa de su cultura, idioma, y todo de su propia autonomía."

The original quoted passage is translated by the author. Iguanape Purbagana, as known Miguel de León (Dule historian, pers. comm.), interviewed by the author, Panama City, Rep. of Panama, March 6, 2009.

REFERENCES

Arias, Arturo. 2006. "Conspiracy on the Sidelines: How the Maya Won the War." In *Cultural Agency in the Americas*, edited by Doris Sommer, 167–77. Durham and London: Duke University Press.

Bonilla, Arcadio. 2006. "El año en que los kunas se alzaron." *La Prensa* (Panama City, Panama), February 26.

Boone, Elizabeth Hill. 1994. "Introduction: Writing and Recording Knowledge." In *Writing Without Words*, edited by Elizabeth Hill Boone and Walter D. Mignolo, 3–26. Durham and London: Duke University Press.

Certeau, Michel de. 1984. *The Practice of Everyday Life*. Translated by Steven Rendall. Berkeley: University of California Press.

De León Kantule, Achu Oswaldo. n.d. "Gallery 1-Chants for Life and Fertility," Oswaldo De León Kantule-"Achu"-Dalagi Sobet-Artista Visual-Visual Artist (website). Accessed October 6, 2017. http://deleonkantule.tripod.com/antigua/old/obras.htm.

De León Kantule, Achu Oswaldo. n.d. Oswaldo De León Kantule (website). Accessed November 19, 2017. http://deleonkantule.wixsite.com/achu.

Deleuze, Gilles. 1986. *Cinema 1: The Movement-Image*. Translated by Hugh Tomlinson and Barbara Habberjam. Minneapolis: University of Minnesota Press.

Deleuze, Gilles. 1989. *Cinema 2: The Time-Image*. Translated by Hugh Tomlinson and Robert Galeta. Minneapolis: University of Minnesota Press.

Deloria, Vine, Jr. 2006. *The World We Used to Live In*. Golden, Colo.: Fulcrum Publishing.

Garrett, Jerry. 2012. "World's Best Coffee? Snobs Cast Their Votes for Kean's." *Garrett On The Road* (blog). June 5, 2012. https://jerrygarrett.wordpress.com/2012/06/05/worlds-best-coffee-snobs-cast-their-votes-for-keans.

Keeler, Clyde E. 1969. *Cuna Indian Art*. New York: Exposition Press.

Mojica, Oloedidili Monique. n.d. Buna, Siagua, Sordamar: Chocolate Woman Collective (website). Accessed October 6, 2017. http://www.chocolatewomancollective.com.

Mojica, Oloedidili Monique. n.d. "Buna, Siagua, Sordamar: Chocolate Woman Collective." Facebook. Accessed October 6, 2017. https://www.facebook.com/chocolatewomancollective.

Montreal's First Peoples' Festival: Visual Art (website). n.d. Accessed September 6, 2011. http://www.nativelynx.qc.ca/05/en/arts.htm.

Nash, June C. 2001. *Mayan Visions: The Quest for Autonomy in an Age of Globalization*. New York: Routledge.

Nordenskiöld, Erland, with Rubén Pérez Kantule. 1938. *An Historical and Ethnological Survey of the Cuna Indians*. Edited by S. Henry Wassén. Göteborg: Etnografiska Museum.

Rancière, Jacques. 2006. *The Politics of Aesthetics*. Translated by Gabriel Rockhill. London: Continuum.

Said, Edward W. 1994. *Culture and Imperialism*. New York: Vintage Books.

Salvador, Mari Lyn. 1997. "Contemporary Kuna Women's Arts." In *The Art of Being Kuna*, edited by Mari Lyn Salvador, 151–211. Los Angeles: UCLA Fowler Museum of Cultural History.

Salvador, Mari Lyn. 2003. "Kuna Women's Arts: Molas, Meaning, and Markets." In *Crafting Gender: Women and Folk Art in Latin America and the Carribbean*, edited by Eli Bartha, 47–72. Durham: Duke University Press.

Shaffer, Frederick W. 1982. *Mola Designs*. New York: Dover Publications.

Tice, Karin E. 1995. *Kuna Crafts, Gender and the Global Economy*. Austin: University of Texas Press.

Wafer, Lionel. 1699. *A New Voyage and Description of the Isthmus of America*. London: Printed for James Knapton.

Wagua, Aiban. 2007a. *Así lo vi y así me lo contaron: Datos de la Revolución Kuna Versión del Sailadummad Inakeliginya y de kunas que vivieron la revolución de 1925*. 2nd ed. Panama: Nan Garburba Oduloged Igar.

Wagua, Aiban. 2007b. *Relatos de mi gran historia*. Panama: Nan Garburba Oduloged Igar.

Waters, Anne. 2004. "Ontology of Identity and Interstitial Being." In *American Indian Thought*, edited by Anne Waters, 153–70. Malden: Blackwell Publishing Ltd.

3

USING TECHNOLOGY TO REVITALIZE ENDANGERED LANGUAGES

Mixe and Chatino Case Studies

EMILIANA CRUZ AND TAJËËW ROBLES

In 2003, the Mexican federal government enacted the General Law on Linguistic Rights of Indigenous People. This act officially recognized eleven Indigenous language families and the 364 individual languages that comprise them, which marked a significant step in the advancement of language rights in Mexico.[1] Still, many scholars and Indigenous community members express great concern for the future of Indigenous languages (Cruz and Woodbury 2014; England 2013; Hill 2002; Robins and Uhlenbeck 1991; Hale 1992; Nettle and Romaine 2007; Crystal 2000; Austin and Sallabank 2011). These stakeholders continue to advocate for endangered Indigenous languages by promoting the aforementioned law, identifying the number of Indigenous languages spoken, collaborating with Indigenous communities to revitalize their local languages, and joining forces to document Indigenous languages. In theory, the law defends the right of Indigenous Mexicans to use their language in private and public spaces, such as at home, in education, and in legal, cultural, religious, and political settings. However, the law has been poorly enforced and often altogether ignored. There is little space for Indigenous languages in mass media. Most local television and radio broadcasts are solely in Spanish and funding for community radio stations is negligible.

While traditional media lacks robust Indigenous language programming, there was hope that new and rapidly evolving communication technologies

(Facebook and Skype, for instance) might fill the void. Whether or not digital activism for Indigenous language rights will be the best pathway to preserve these languages, these technologies can provide new and expanded venues for revitalization efforts. New communication technologies can draw societies closer together, but their use is a double-edged sword for Indigenous language activists. Some Indigenous activists and allies use technology to revitalize their native languages and communities. However, these same communication platforms are dominated by majority languages—such as Spanish in the case of Mexico—that threaten the very survival of Indigenous languages. In fact, new communication technologies, such as cell phones and computers, present obstacles to language preservation in that they are designed for use in majority languages. Nonetheless, many young people have started to consciously subvert these standards, developing novel ways to use their native languages instead. Digital technologies (megaphones, telephones, telecommunication, the Internet) can be powerful tools for language maintenance.

The present chapter discusses the role of modern technologies in the revitalization and language loss of two languages spoken in Oaxaca, Mexico: the variety of Chatino spoken in San Juan Quiahije (hereafter, Quiahije) and the variety of Mixe spoken in Santa Maria Tlahuitoltepec (hereafter, Tlahuitoltepec) (map 3.1). This research draws from the experiences of each author. We were interested in comparing these two communities because they have different language revitalization experiences. At the same time, both places struggle to keep their language alive for younger generations. We hope that the comparison will allow Chatinos from Quiahije and Mixes from Tlahuitoltepec to learn from each other. We are both language activists who have trained young people for the last fifteen years to promote the use of their languages, using a variety of new media, including Facebook and YouTube.

For the last decade, a series of new technologies have been introduced into Indigenous communities in Oaxaca. Communication technologies have moved from radio stations to telephones, including landlines and cellular phones; megaspeakers; and, more recently, social media, especially Facebook, Twitter, and WhatsApp. Social media is used mainly by young people and migrants who reside in the United States or other cities in México. The use of writing in technology is connected to social class, generations, and formal education. Those who have high-quality phones and can read and write use social media, WhatsApp, and the Internet in general. Even though the use of technology is somewhat new, there are still some elders who participate in and who highly

MAP 3.1. Map of the two towns where the Chatino and Mixe languages are spoken. Copyright Google Earth.

value technology. For example, one morning about ten years ago, Emiliana Cruz was standing in the town center of Quiahije, when her uncle, Gonzalo, who was seventy-five years old, stopped to greet her. While they were chatting, his cell phone rang. He took the phone out of his shirt pocket. The cell phone was wrapped up in a plastic bag. With careful grace, he took the phone out of the plastic bag. Then he started to have a phone conversation in Chatino, using gestures as though he were face-to-face with the other person. Once he was done talking, he put the phone into the plastic bag and then back into his shirt pocket. This story might sound strange to those who are used to seeing elders using technology, but this was not common ten years ago. Elders are now more accustomed to using cell phones.

The use of technology is similar in Tlahuitoltepec. The local radio station Jën Poj in Mixe is popular among all ages (Quiahije does not have a radio station). People with a formal school background use technology that requires writing, such as texting, social media, and Twitter. The elders use cell phones, but only for oral communication. In a social space, like the market, elders will go outside to use the phone, as it would be disrespectful to answer the phone in front of everyone in the space.

Technology offers Indigenous communities many benefits (King and Berners-Lee, 2005). The ease of communication across distances helps people from smaller communities remain in contact with those who have migrated to other places, such as urban areas within the home country or abroad. Video conference platforms such as Skype and Facebook also facilitate communication between linguists and speakers, which helps ensure the study and preservation of endangered languages. We have found that speakers of Chatino tend to write in Spanish when they send a text, but those who do not write often use WhatsApp using their voice. People in Quiahije are active on Facebook, though there is more preference for video and audio versus writing. As access to the Internet grows daily, so too does the potential for technology to revitalize Indigenous languages.

Despite these new interactions with technology, Indigenous languages are rapidly disappearing. According to a survey conducted by the Linguistic Society of America, 19 percent of the world's living languages are no longer being learned by children. Scholars indicate that there are many factors that affect the vitality of Indigenous languages, and that these factors vary greatly between countries (Rogers and Campbell 2011; Swadesh 1948; Brenzinger 2007; Grenoble and Whaley 1998; and Nettle and Romaine 2007). In Mexico, language use and transmission are impacted by economic disadvantages, local and national politics, language ideologies among the speakers, demography, geography, history, religion, urban migration, and education, among other issues (Simons and Lewis 2013; Rogers and Campbell 2011). An important factor to consider with regard to Mexico is the imposition of Spanish onto the country's Indigenous peoples since the colonial period, in tandem with the intensified suppression and sabotage of native language use after the country's independence.

CHATINO LANGUAGES

Chatino languages are spoken in the southern part of Oaxaca state. Chatino languages are members of the Otomanguean language stock and form a genetic subgroup within Zapotecan (Kaufman 2006; Campbell 2013). There are three Chatino languages: Zenzontepec, Tataltepec, and Eastern Chatino (Campbell 2013). Eastern Chatino is spoken across twenty-one communities (Cruz 2011). Within these twenty-one villages, fifteen varieties of Chatino are spoken (Cruz and Woodbury 2014). Eastern Chatino comprises a set of fifteen varieties that share a number of phonological, morphological, and lexical innovations

(Campbell 2013). These varieties are to some degree mutually intelligible (Cruz and Woodbury 2014), however each of the fifteen Eastern Chatino varieties is distinct enough to constitute a dialect.

The Mexican Census Bureau, Instituto de Estadística y Geografía (INEGI), counted 51,612 Chatino speakers, with 4,233 people living in Quiahije, in 2015 (INEGI 2015). More than half are bilingual in Chatino and Spanish, largely because of the number of inhabitants who are under thirty years old. It is likely that bilingualism will transition to monolingualism in Spanish due to the relatively low status of Chatino. Moreover, Chatinos have not been afforded opportunities to study their language. Since 2003, the Mexican Constitution has acknowledged that Chatino and other Indigenous languages spoken in Mexico are part of the country's linguistic diversity, but this recognition has not resulted in Chatino language instruction in schools. Public education remains monolingual in Spanish, even in supposedly bilingual schools. Additionally, two decades of migration to the United States have resulted in many linguistic changes to Quiahije. Community members face an increased need to learn Spanish and English but a diminishing need to speak Chatino.

THE MIXE LANGUAGE

The cases of Chatino and Mixe are very different, in part because of geography. Mixe is closer to the city of Oaxaca, and thus many more people have access to education. The Mexican Census Bureau counted 8,473 Mixe speakers out of 9,663 people living in Tlahuitoltepec in 2010 (INEGI n.d.). Among Indigenous communities, Mixe, and Tlahuitoltepec in particular, is known for its strong educational programming. Many young people, inspired by the work in this community, wish to expand the model of Tlahuitoltepec to their own communities.

The Mixe language belongs to the Mixe-Zoque language family. Tlahuitoltepec is located in the northern highlands of the state of Oaxaca. According to the classification proposed by Wichmann, Mixe is divided into four variants: (1) northern highlands: Totontepec, Moctum; (2) southern highlands: Ayutla, Tamazulapan, Tlahuitoltepec, Tepuxtepec, Tepantlali, and Mixistlán; (3) middle zone: Jaltepec, Puxmetacán, Matamoros, Cotzocón, Juquila, and Cacalotepec; and (4) low zone: Camotlán, Coatlán, Mazatlán, and Guichicovi (Wichmann, 1995).

According to the 2015 Mexican census, Mixe is among the largest Indigenous languages in Mexico with a total of 117,935 speakers. While this data suggests that there is a large number of Mixe speakers, in reality many young people do not speak the Mixe language. This is true especially for those who are under fifteen years of age, those who live in larger communities or in municipal headwaters, and those Mixes with more means of communication and exchange with Oaxaca City.

For the last twenty years, compared to other languages in Oaxaca, Mixe has been well documented. This is due in large part to the fact that there are at least ten linguists who are native speakers dedicated to the study of the language. In addition, in the last thirty-five years, many Mixe speakers with no formal linguistic training have also documented and studied their language. In Tlahuitoltepec, community members have pioneered local education projects, which have helped the community thrive as a leading example of Mixe literacy. This success has translated into high numbers of young people attending high school and graduating from college. According to the education board of this municipality (Regiduría Municipal de Educación y Cultura de Tlahuitoltepec Mixe Oaxaca [REME]), in 2015 about 30 percent of the total population of Tlahuitoltepec had attended high school (REME, 2015).

PRACTICAL ORTHOGRAPHY

In the twenty-first century, many Indigenous languages do not have a standardized orthography and so must maintain their languages orally. There are many circumstances that lead Indigenous speakers to not write in their languages (Hinton 2014). In Mexico, a challenge to the writing of Indigenous languages is simply that more people are literate in Spanish. In addition, Indigenous languages do not hold the same social status as majority languages, and so their use is suppressed.

The two communities presented in this chapter have different experiences with writing. There is no practical orthography for writing Chatino in Quiahije, nor in other Chatino communities, though there have been recent attempts to develop one. In Tlahuitoltepec and many other Mixe communities, a practical orthography and written language have been used since the 1980s. Notably, however, writing systems alone do not guarantee the survival of an Indigenous language. Many other factors must come together to preserve Indigenous languages, especially the use of these languages in educational settings.

CHATINO

There are many different reasons a language can be complex. In the case of Chatino languages, complexity is the result of a large set of tones. Between 1970 and 1980, the Summer Institute of Linguistics researched Chatino communities and translated the Bible into the Tataltepec de Valdés language. They also made pedagogical materials and a dictionary for the San Miguel Panixtlahuaca variety. A group of teachers, only some of whom spoke Chatino, gathered in 1990 to create a practical orthography for the Chatino languages. These teachers created a writing system, but it has not been integrated into classrooms. There is no formal training for teachers to introduce the Indigenous language into classrooms. Also, teachers have been trained and educated in Spanish, making it their default language, and the classroom materials provided by the state are solely in Spanish. To add to these challenges, as we mentioned above, there are three Chatino languages, and Eastern Chatino alone has fifteen varieties, most of them mutually unintelligible. Finally, decisions about the geographic placement of teachers is not based on linguistic area of competence but instead on teacher preference and seniority.

Starting in 2003, Emiliana Cruz began working with a group of linguists from the University of Texas and spent a decade researching in each of the Chatino villages. They worked on creating a writing system for the communities where they did their research (tables 3.1 and 3.2).

TABLE 3.1 Consonants[2] in Chatino

	BILABIALS	APICO-DENTALS	LAMINO-ALVEOLARS	PALATALS	VELARS	LABIO-VELARS	LARYN-GEALS
stop	p b	t d	tʸ [t̪] dʸ [d̪]		k g		q,7,' [ʔ]
affricates		ts	ch [tʃ]				
fricatives		s	x [ʃ]				j [h]
nasals	m	n	nʸ [ɲ̪]				
tap		r [ɾ]					
laterals		l	lʸ [l̪]				
glide				y [j]		W	

TABLE 3.2 Vowels in Chatino

	FRONT	CENTRAL	BACK	FRONT	CENTRAL	BACK
high	i [i]		u [u]	in [ĩ]		
mid	e [e]		o [o]	en [ẽ]		on [õ]
low		a [a]			an [ã]	

With this, they contributed a study of the language's tones, which was incorporated into the writing system (Cruz and Woodbury 2014) (table 3.3).

TABLE 3.3 Tones in Chatino

LEVEL TONES:	PHONETIC	TONE REPRESENTATION	GLOSS
kna^E	high	E	'snake'
kak	super high	K	'cow'
kna^C	mid	C	'theft'
kna^A	low	A	'sandal'
RISING TONES:			
kon^H	mid super high	H	'I will eat'
sqen^I	mid high	I	'scorpion'
kon^G	low high	G	'tuber'
skwan^L	low super high	L	'I threw'
si^F	low mid	F	'butterfly'
DESCENDING TONES:			
tla^B	high low	B	'night'
kla^J	mid low	J	'twenty'

MIXE

Unlike the Chatino experience, Mixe speakers have been working on a writing system since the 1980s.[3] On the initiative of the Mixe Basic Education Instrumentation Team, and supported by the Committee for Defense and Development of Natural, Human and Cultural Resources of the Mixe Region, local stakeholders have started to hold weekly meetings committed to the preservation of the Mixe language. Between 1984 and 1986, Mixes from different communities met for the first time to discuss their linguistic diversity and the development of a writing system. At that time, different stakeholders promoting the writing of Mixe used varying graphic systems. Following the development of an agreed upon graphic system, 1994 marked the beginning of a second phase of the initiative, which aimed to disseminate the graphic system and teach literacy in the Mixe language to community members. This project also provided space for people dedicated to the study of the language, as well as for children, young people, and adults who were interested in the language, to come together and learn. Despite their progress, the writing system remains an ongoing topic of conversation among the Mixe people (Díaz Robles and Vásquez, 2011).[4] What follows in tables 3.4 and 3.5 is the practical alphabet used in Tlahuitoltepec.[5]

TABLE 3.4 Awätspë Vowels

AWÄTSPË	MIXE	GLOSS	MIXE	GLOSS
a	kajaa	alot	kapy	Bamboo
ä	ääy	leaf	jäj 'luz'	Light
e	pejk	feather	tsep	conflict/difficult
ë	yëjk	black	tëjk	House
i	kipy	tree/wood	mi'iky	Tamal
ï	witsuk	thunder	jïyujk	Animal
o	koots	night	mo'nts	Mud
u	ju'uy	charcol	utsj	Plant

TABLE 3.5 Atujkpë Consonants

CONSONANTS	MIXE	GLOSS	CONSONANTS	MIXE	GLOSS
p	poj viento	wind	x	xëëw	sun/name/day
t	tuu' lluvia	rain	w	wejkxy	tortilla grill
ts	tsääj piedra	rock	y	yoots	cloud
k	ka' no	not	'	n'uk	my dog
j	jëën lumber	fire	l	lëjtsy	Calf
m	mejy laguna/ mar	lagoon/sea	s	sää	What
n	nëëj agua	water	r	kapreen	type of orchid

PRESERVATION AND REVITALIZATION
OF CHATINO AND MIXE

Differences in Chatino and Mixe communities translate into differences in the effectiveness of their use of technology for language revitalization. There is less technology used in Quiahije, and it seems that the people in Tlahuitoltepec have more access to the Internet. For example, in Quiahije there is a cell phone tower, but it is extremely difficult to access the Internet, even on smart phones. Tlahuitoltepec has better phone and Internet service due to its proximity to Oaxaca City. Also, being closer, young people have more contact with the urban center. In Quiahije, most people speak Chatino, while in Tlahuitoltepec most do not regularly speak Mixe and fewer children acquire their Indigenous language. However, Tlahuitoltepec has a tradition of linguistic activism that has created a stronger sense of Mixe identity (fig. 3.1). Chatinos are about ten hours from Oaxaca City. They only recently started to write their language, and literacy levels are not as high as in Tlahuitoltepec. Further, the Chatino language is not as central to the identity of people in Quiahije as the Mixe language is to the identity of the people in Tlahuitoltepec.

FIGURE 3.1. Natalia Cruz Cruz, from the Santa María Ixpantepec community, teaching a group of women to write in Chatino. Photo by Gibrán Morales Carranza.

The different degrees of pride that members of both communities have toward their languages is exemplified in their respective linguistic landscapes. In Tlahuitoltepec, there are many signs in Mixe, such as in local stores, government offices, schools, and many other places, including street signs. In Quiahije, there are not any Chatino signs in schools. The Land Commissioner's office has a single sign, and only a few Chatino street signs can be seen around the community. In both communities, however, public announcements are made in the local language.

The people in Quiahije pay less attention to written Chatino. Many Quiahije citizens still believe that Chatino is only a spoken language, while Spanish is the language that can be written. As such, literacy among Chatino speakers is almost null. In contrast, the written aspects of Mixe are more important to speakers in Tlahuitoltepec, yet many children are not acquiring the language. Interestingly, speakers of both communities share a linguistic ideology that does not always recognize that their native languages are endangered. When members of both communities reflect on the future of their languages, sometimes they maintain that their own language is not at risk, even as they recognize that neighboring local languages are disappearing. Even with the obvious and well-documented importance of speaking Indigenous languages in Mexico, the Spanish language has served as a unifying force among Mexicans for centuries. Mexico has many Indigenous languages and cultures and adheres to many linguistic ideologies. In Mexico, the need for Indigenous people to learn Spanish falls into a pattern, with Spanish being connected to success and economic opportunity. To learn Spanish is a winning formula that Indigenous people follow to reproduce success stories of "Mexico the Great." Chatinos and Mixes are caught up in this ideology. As we see in the following narratives, such language ideologies play an important role in revitalization efforts in Quiahije and Tlahuitoltepec.

QUIAHIJE

Emiliana Cruz had a conversation with the local government officials in Quiahije about language loss in the Chatino region after visiting other Chatino communities.[6] The local authorities were interested in the linguistic situation of other villages where Emiliana had traveled: "So, how is the language in San Marcos Zacatepec?" She responded, "Only elders speak the language." They continued: "What about Santiago Yaitepec?" She responded that people there

FIGURE 3.2. Presenting the children's book *Ja Nanociencia jïts ja nanotecnología* in San José Chinantequilla (2014). Photo by Yásnaya Aguilar.

still use Chatino. They continued asking, "What about Quiahije? Since you are familiar with other communities, in your opinion, what community has better language vitality." She responded that many communities speak Chatino. In Quiahije, one can hear more children speaking Chatino in the streets. She described language loss in other communities in Oaxaca and across Mexico. They were happy to hear about language vitality in Quiahije. Yet when she returned the following year, the teachers at the local middle school had prohibited Chatino in the classroom. The parents and the local authorities supported this initiative as well, regarding Spanish as the only language necessary for success in school and for finding work.[7]

People in Quiahije do not typically believe that Chatino is endangered, and there are no local-level initiatives to preserve it or to counteract prohibitions against its use in schools. As a result, there are only a few projects run by outside institutions, academics, and speakers who do see the need to protect the language. Notable projects include the Center for the Study and Development of Indigenous Languages (CEDELIO), which published several children's books in Chatino (fig. 3.2).[8] In addition, the Chatino Language Documentation

Project created a blog to provide material about different Chatino languages, including pedagogical and academic publications, film production, and a Facebook page that promotes the use of Chatino and Chatino writings.[9] Director Yolanda Cruz has made documentaries of Eastern Chatino. There is a personal Twitter account in Chatino (Lillehaugen 2016); and Sha Kuii, an organization created by young people from Quiahije, uses Facebook to promote sports and social activities around the San Juan region. While the latter do not write in Chatino, their mission is to speak Chatino at their public events.

TLAHUITOLTEPEC

As opposed to Quiahije, in Tlahuitoltepec people are highly aware of the importance of the Mixe language. The local authorities promote the use of Mixe language in all spaces, schools, churches, and local assemblies. The local assembly space exclusively uses the Mixe language. However, in some cases the administrative and governmental technical language used in assemblies is Spanish. People bemoan language loss in Tlahuitoltepec and discuss it in public. In 2012, I was at a local Catholic church when the original bells were being replaced. The old bells had a very particular sound that everyone in the community was familiar with. The sound was part of the landscape of Tlahuitoltepec. When the new bells were installed, I heard a few grandmothers saying they sounded different, more tenuous, just like Mixe language. From their perspective, Mixe is weakening, just like the sound of the bells.

There have been considerable efforts to counteract this decline. A community radio station called Jën Poj has actively broadcast for the last sixteen years in Tlahuitoltepec. Transmitting live from 107.9 FM and through the Internet, Jën Poj has been able to reach a wide audience.[10] The program is mainly in Spanish but features some content in Mixe. Proyecto *Nayuujk* is a similar project that lasted about two years and functioned as a space for young writers to share their work.[11] Mixe scholars from different communities founded the Colegio Mixe (Colmix) in 2012 with the intention of disseminating knowledge and collaborating with each other. Colmix operates a Facebook page dedicated to Mixe and other Indigenous groups. Because many of its 2,210 followers do not speak Mixe, the Colmix Facebook page posts in Spanish. Other Facebook pages also promote the Mixe language, such as the Tlahuitoltepec page, which focuses on interests of the followers. Here, posts range from personal updates to announcements regarding cultural events in the community. People who do not necessarily have a community or local government connection have created other independent and privately run Facebook pages and websites. These independent pages aim to spread the importance of the Mixe language and culture to the community and outsiders. While these initiatives aim to preserve Mixe, they mostly use Spanish to reach broader audiences. A website run by Luis Balbuena Gómez, from Tlahuitoltepec, uses Mixe to disseminate cultural information and resources to learn Mixe. Luis is a Tlahuitoltepec citizen who is interested in promoting Tlahuitoltepec culture. Teachers in Tlahuitoltepec get students involved in different projects related to Mixe and post the materials they produce on Facebook and YouTube. One company, called Yinet, is an Internet service provider in Tlahuitoltepec. It offers WiFi services to the community as well as an Internet radio station and a Mixe encyclopedia built in the wiki platform. However, this resource is mostly in Spanish.

In recent years, institutions and organizations have developed initiatives to revitalize Mixe in Tlahuitoltepec. These efforts are focused on strengthening writing and reading skills in the language rather than addressing the growing decline of young speakers. Of note are the Mixe classes taught in schools, even though these schools do not belong to the bilingual education system. Local schools also celebrate February 21, the International Day of the Mother Tongue, in which students engage in activities that highlight the importance of preserving Mixe. One initiative has ensured the use of street signs written in Mixe around Tlahuitoltepec.

CONCLUSION

The creation of a writing system and the use of new technologies will not guarantee the survival of Chatino and Mixe languages. In both Quiahije and Tlahuitoltepec, there are only a few blogs, Twitter accounts, Facebook pages, and radio programs that show potential for language revitalization. That said, as a platform for activism, technology may help in revitalization efforts. Technology is one tool, among many, that must be used in tandem with proven revitalization mechanisms, such as entertainment for different ages, news, games for children, and more. New generations are very active on social media, watch online media, and like to be connected to the world via the Internet. Though technology helps increase the visibility of Indigenous identities, Twitter and Facebook posts alone do little to revitalize Indigenous languages. As mentioned above, most of the digital projects are in Spanish and have not been implemented locally. For example, the websites that focus on Indigenous languages are only known outside of the Indigenous communities.

Technology presents many challenges for revitalizing Indigenous languages. In addition to problems of access faced by many communities, the fact that nearly all websites are in Spanish only reinforces the pattern in which children become more familiar with Spanish than their own Indigenous language. Children will still use technology regardless of whether there is content in their native languages. As such, we must have a careful plan when we think about using technology for revitalizing Indigenous languages. Any plan to support Indigenous Mexican languages through the Internet must take all of these factors into account. There are many digital platforms with scattered use, but no single place where speakers of Mixe and Chatino can find information about their languages. There needs to be a broader variety of platforms dedicated to using these endangered languages, as opposed to platforms that operate in Spanish. Technology can help spread word of Indigenous activism and build community, but it will not guarantee the survival of endangered languages for future generations. In fact, it may pose additional challenges to revitalization efforts.

Indigenous movements in defense of lives and resources are gaining strength. It is possible that, through these struggles, language can be fought for as well. The ideology of resistance influenced our own use of native languages. If we can make the case for the importance of Indigenous languages, their loss would be decelerated. Especially vital is the use of Indigenous languages in legal, health, and educational settings, as well as in the communities, such as for local assemblies, celebrations, and locally important loudspeaker announcements. We must also unite and share digital technology resources, such as the Digital Activism in Indigenous Languages of Latin America initiative (DAILLA). DAILLA supports initiatives using digital media and the Internet to revitalize and promote native languages online. In the state of Oaxaca, we should have resources dedicated to Indigenous language programming on community and local radio stations. Unfortunately, we have little support for such initiatives. Although we do not know if digital activism will be the ultimate key to preservation, we do believe that it is necessary for Indigenous people to promote the use of our native languages across as many platforms as possible.

NOTES

1. Moraila 2008.
2. The consonants and vowels in the [brackets] represent the phonetic representation of sounds.
3. Adapted from Colmix 2014.
4. Instituto De Investigaciones Estéticas De La UNAM 2011.
5. These examples were derived from Colmix 2015.
6. This interview took place in 2012 in Cieneguilla, San Juan Quiahije, between the authors and local authorities.
7. These are personal interviews that were held in Tlahuitoltepec and Quiahije.
8. http://www.cedelio.edu.mx/chatino.
9. "Lengua Chatino: Recursos" (website), last modified September 28, 2017.
10. "Jënpoj Radio" (website), last modified 2017.
11. http://www.tlahuitoltepec.com.

REFERENCES

Austin, Peter, and Julia Sallabank. 2011. *The Cambridge Handbook of Endangered Languages*. Cambridge: Cambridge University Press.

Brenzinger, Matthias. 2007. *Language Diversity Endangered*. Berlin: Mouton de Gruyter.

Campbell, Eric. 2013. "The Internal Diversification and Subgrouping of Chatino." *International Journal of American Linguistics* 79: 395–420.

"Chatino." n.d. Cedelio (website), last modified 2015, http://cedelio.ieepo.oaxaca.gob.mx/chatino.

Cruz, Emiliana. n.d. "Conflicting Ideologies of Indigeneity and Nationalism in the Translation of the Mexican National Anthem" (unpublished).

Cruz, Emiliana. 2011. *Phonology, Tone and the Functions of Tone in San Juan Quiahije Chatino*. PhD diss. University of Texas.

Cruz, Emiliana, and Anthony Woodbury. 2014. "Collaboration in the Context of Teaching, Scholarship, and Language Revitalization: Experience from the Chatino Language." *Language Documentation & Conservation* 8: 262–86.

Crystal, David. 2000. *Language Death*. Cambridge: Cambridge University Press.

Díaz Robles Tajëëw and Tonantzin and Julio C. Gallardo Vásquez. 2011. "Semana de Vida y Lengua Mixes 2011: Preservar un mundo originario." *Revista El Jolgorio*, no. 41, https://issuu.com/eljolgorio.

England, Nora C. 2013. "Logros y desafíos de la lingüística Maya." *Voces, Revista Semestral del Instituto de Lingüística e Interculturalidad* 8 (2): 71–94.

"Et Wënmää'Ny." n.d. Enciclopedia Mixe (website), last modified May 5, 2017, http://www.enciclopediamixe.com/index.php?title=P%C3%A1gina_principal.

Grenoble, Lenore A., and L. J. Whaley, eds. 1998. *Language Loss and Community Response*. Cambridge: Cambridge University Press.

Hale, Kenneth L. 1992. "Endangered Languages: On Endangered Languages and the Safeguarding of Diversity." *Language* 68 (1): 1–42.

Hill, Jane H. 2002. "'Expert rhetorics' in Advocacy for Endangered Languages: Who Is Listening, and What Do They Hear?" *Journal of Linguistic Anthropology* 12 (2): 150–56.

Hinton, Leanne. 2014. "Orthography Wars." In *Developing Orthographies for Unwritten Languages*, edited by Michael Cahill and Keren Rice, 139–68. Dallas: SIL International Publications.

Instituto Nacional de Estadística y Geografía (INEGI). n.d. "Diversidad." Accessed May 20, 2018. http://www.cuentame.inegi.org.mx/monografias/informacion/oax/poblacion/diversidad.aspx.

"Informe Final." n.d. Global Voices—Lenguas Indígenas (website), last modified April 28, 2017, https://rising.globalvoices.org/lenguas/investigacion/activismo-digital-de-lenguas-indigenas/informe.

Instituto De Investigaciones Estéticas De La UNAM. 2011. "Una Mirada Al Pasado Y Presente Del Arte En Oaxaca." *El Jolgorio Cultural* 41, https://issuu.com/eljolgorio/docs/el_jolgorio_cultural_41.

"Jënpoj Radio." n.d. Radio Jënpoj de Tlahuitoltepec (website), last modified 2017, http://jenpojradio.info.

Kaufman, Terrence. 2006. "Oto-Manguean languages." In *Encyclopedia of Languages & Linguistics*, edited by Keith Brown, 118–24. Oxford: Elsevier.

King, Lila, and Tim Berners-Lee. n.d. "Web Inventor: Online Life Will Produce More Creative Children." CNN: Technology (website), last modified October 10, 2005, http://www.cnn.com/2005/TECH/Internet/08/30/tim.berners.lee.

"Lengua Chatino: Recursos." n.d. The Chatino Language Documentation Project (website), last modified September 28, 2017, https://sites.google.com/site/lenguachatino/recursos-academicos.

"Lenguas indígenas en México y hablantes (de 3 años y más) al 2015." n.d. INALI (website), last modified 2015, http://cuentame.inegi.org.mx/hipertexto/todas_lenguas.htm.

Lillehaugen, Brook Danielle. 2016. "Why Write in a Language That (Almost) No One Can Read? Twitter and the Development of Written Literature." *Language Documentation & Conservation* 10: 356–93.

Moraila, Fabricio Gaxiola. CATALOGO de las Lenguas Indígenas Nacionales: Variantes Lingüísticas de México con Sus Autodenominaciones y Referencias Geoestadísticas. Mexico, D. F.: Instituto Nacional De Lengua Indigenas, Lunes 14 de enero de 2008. 2008. http://www.inali.gob.mx/pdf/CLIN_completo.pdf.

"Nayuujk Project." http://www.tlahuitoltepec.com/archives/1589. Last modified November 6, 2009.

Nettle, Daniel, and Suzanne Romaine. 2007. *Vanishing Voices: The Extinction of the World's Languages*. New York: Oxford University Press.

Regiduría Municipal de Educación y Cultura de Tlahuitoltepec Mixe Oaxaca. 2015. Annual Report. Unpublished.

Robins, Robert H., and Eugenious M. Uhlenbeck. 1991. *Endangered Languages*. Oxford: Berg.

Rogers, Chris, and Lyle Campbell. 2001. *Endangered Languages*. New York: Oxford University Press.

Romero Méndez, Rodrigo. 2013. *Historias Mixes de Ayutla. Así contaron los Abuelos.* Mexico City: Universidad Autónoma de México.

Simons, Gary, and Paul Lewis. 2013. "The World's Languages in Crisis: A 20-Year Update." In *Responses to Language Endangerment. In Honor of Mickey Noonan,* edited by Elena Mihas, Bernard Perley, Gabriel Rei-Doval, and Kathleen Wheatley, 3–19. Amsterdam: John Benjamins.

Swadesh, Morris. 1948. "Sociologic Notes on Obsolescent Languages." *International Journal of American Linguistics* 14 (4): 226–35.

"Tlahuitoltepec." n.d. http://www.tlahuitoltepec.com. Accessed October 18, 2018.

Valiñas, Leopoldo y Tonantzin Díaz Robles. *Las lenguas mixe-zoques. Sombra y Luz.* Unpublished manuscript.

Wichmann, Søren. 1995. *The Relationship Among the Mixe-Zoquean languages of Mexico.* Salt Lake City: University of Utah Press.

YouTube. n.d. youtube.com/results?search_query=Aprender+mixe. Accessed October 18, 2018.

PART II

CYBERSPATIAL
NATION BUILDING

4

YOUTUBING MAYA ROCK

B'itzma Sobrevivencia's Aural Memory of Survival

ALICIA IVONNE ESTRADA

In 2014, while participating at a music festival in Mexico City's Palacio de Bellas Artes, Maya Kaqchikel singer and songwriter Sara Curruchich Cúmez was invited by a group of Mexican musicians to record her song "Ch'uti'xtän (*Niña*/Girl)." A music video of the production was uploaded to YouTube and, as of October 2017, has more than 344,306 views. The video and Cúmez's music have been widely circulated on social media, expanding the musician's fan base as well as further presenting other forms of Maya musical expressions to a global audience.[1] While access to the Internet continues to be limited for Indigenous communities, young Maya musicians and their fans have produced as well as uploaded their music videos to YouTube since 2005 when it was launched.[2] These new mediums, both the hybrid musical productions and the use of social media technologies, serve not only as a mode of self-expression and representation but also as important tools for the revitalization of Indigenous cultures among youth.

At the same time, these musical and video productions function as vehicles for community-building and Maya sociocultural activism that form part of local/hemispheric Indigenous struggles and resistance movements. For more than two decades, these collective endeavors have rooted the music and videos produced by the Maya rock group B'itzma Sobrevivencia. As a way of addressing the limited broadcast of their music on mainstream media in Guatemala and abroad, both the group and their fans have used the Internet, particularly social media like Facebook and YouTube, to transmit their music to a wider national and transnational audience.[3] By strategically using these online outlets to circulate songs that emphasize Maya knowledges and culture, they contest racist representations that dominate mainstream Spanish and English media as well as the Internet.

As scholarship on digital technologies highlights, the accessibility of social media spaces, which require basic technology and skills, allows Indigenous musicians as well as their fans to frequently upload music tracks and videos (Hilder 2017; Montero-Diaz 2017; Snickars and Vonderau 2009). For instance, on YouTube there are more than twenty videos of B'itzma Sobrevivencia's music. The band has only uploaded a couple of those videos, but fans living in Guatemala and those constituting the diaspora have created many others. In fact, B'itzma Sobrevivencia's fans have produced the YouTube videos with the most views and likes. Because the band creates multilingual music that includes Maya Mam, Achi, Kaqchikel, K'iche,' and Q'anjob'al, as well as Spanish and, most recently, English, the songs and, by extension, the videos construct a sense of community that crosses various linguistic regions as well as borders. Additionally, the songs in Spanish, or in Maya languages with Spanish subtitles, incorporate and impart lessons on Maya culture to diverse global audiences. Their music videos, which are often self-produced, are equally invested in actively contributing to social justice efforts through the transmission of songs like "Chjontela Qajwil" (*Gracias a nuestro creador*/Gratitude to Our Creator) and "Un'oj numam" (*Consejos del abuelo*/Advice from the Elder), which emphasize Maya knowledge and spirituality. Moreover, the production of videos by their fans not only illustrates their active engagement with B'itzma's music but also with the band's efforts to affirm Maya land and cultural rights. This is evident in the images employed in songs like "Amatitlán" that denounce the contamination of this revered lake and use the YouTube platform to make a direct call for social action.

Building on scholarship that examines contemporary Indigenous music and the use of digital media (Chadwick 2006; Hilder, Stobart, and Tan 2017; Montero-Diaz 2017; Wilson and Stewart 2008), this chapter begins by arguing that the production and transmission of B'itzma Sobrevivencia's music videos on YouTube serve as strategic tools in countering racist dominant depictions of Mayas that continue to circulate in Guatemala and beyond. The contestation of these dominant representations takes places through the images incorporated in videos created by fans and the group as well as in the songs' lyrics, which offer positive and complex representations of Maya peoples, their languages and communities. This is particularly illustrated in their most popular song, "El grito/The Cry," which also has several videos created and uploaded by fans. Furthermore, the YouTube platform provides viewers with suggestions of videos and thus allows for songs that focus on issues like cultural rights and environmental struggles to be broadcasted to users that include Mayas and non-Mayas across the globe. In this way, the songs and the videos challenge the varied forms of erasure that take place in Guatemala and through other mainstream media spaces like monolingual Spanish-language networks, including Univision, Telemundo, and Televisa, which maintain a monopoly in the dissemination of information in and about Latin America. At the same time, the fans as well as B'itzma's direct dialogues with other Indigenous and non-Indigenous peoples through the comments section on YouTube create a web of communities, and communities on the web, that are inclusive of the diaspora. The chapter concludes by noting the ways that B'itzma Sobrevivencia's "survival aesthetics" provide the Maya diaspora in the United States an important medium to reaffirm their identity and place in the world (Wide Web).

B'ITZMA'S *GRITO*

B'itzma Sobrevivencia was formed in 1995, a year before the signing of the Guatemalan Peace Accords that officially ended a U.S.-backed civil war and genocide. At the end of the thirty-six year (1960–96) civil war, the United Nation's Truth Commission reported that more than 200,000 people were killed, there were more than 40,000 widows, and 1.5 million people were displaced and living in exile or as refugees. Additionally, the report states that military, police forces, or government officials committed 93 percent of these crimes. It further notes that 83 percent of those killed were Maya. For this reason, the U.S.-backed civil war in Guatemala was marked by genocide. Thus, B'itzma Sobrevivencia's name also reflects the *grito*, cry, of Maya genocide survivors.

In an interview on December 26, 2011, with the Los Angeles-based Maya radio program *Contacto Ancestral*, founding member Jorge Xulen Ortiz Sales explains that "B'itz" means song and harmony in Mam and "ma" refers to the word Mam, the language spoken by the two founding members, but also alludes to the "ma" in Maya.[4] B'itzma functions as a fusion, like their music, of the two words: B'itz and ma, suggesting a form of harmonious song for Mayas.

For Ortiz Sales, the use of Sobrevivencia as part of the group's name serves to emphasize and remember the historical struggles they face as Mayas as well as the ancestral survival strategies they continue to use (*Contacto Ancestral* 2011). Similar to Gerald Vizenor's narratives of survivance, B'itzma's "*sobreviven-cia* aesthetics" focuses on an active survival that goes beyond subsistence and includes a conscious refashioning of the musical styles they employ as well as create (1999, vii).

Considered one of the first Maya groups to bridge Indigenous musical forms with rock 'n' roll, B'itzma Sobrevivencia musicians have endured violent forms of racism in Guatemala and abroad. While reception in Indigenous communities has been positive since their first concerts, in non-Indigenous musical festivals the group initially faced violent racist reactions. For playing rock 'n' roll and singing in Maya languages they were sometimes ridiculed and booed off stage, with bottles filled with urine thrown at them both at Guatemalan and Mexican music festivals (*Contacto Ancestral* 2011). Steeped in colonialism, these overtly violent reactions to their musical productions as well as to their presence onstage expose vested interests in viewing Mayas outside of modernity and bounded in "tradition" (Teves 2015, 216). At the same time, the group's disruption of the universality often ascribed to music revealed, as Roshanak Kheshti (2015) affirms, that this cultural form is highly racialized and gendered. Yet as Ortiz Sales notes, B'itzma Sobrevivencia's long musical trajectory illustrates that the group continues to survive, like their ancestors, as well as contest these systemic forms of violence that seek to erase and eradicate them from asserting their place in these public and global spaces.

By 1997, the duo led by Jorge Xulen Ortiz Sales and Eduardo Ramírez had become a multilingual group of six.[5] Their second CD titled *Itz'x Q'anQ'ib'il*,[6] produced in 2003, includes "El grito"—the group's most popular song to date.[7] Consequently, there are several videos of the song on YouTube, but none produced by the group. The first video of this song was part of a collaborative project with a university student, Matt Gardner, from the United States, who traveled to Guatemala to interview the musicians. In 2008, Gardner published a compilation of three songs along with a short interview on YouTube, which at the time of writing this chapter had received more than 69,570 views. The video begins with the song "Tzan atqueya ow" (*Salud amigos*/Greetings Friends), followed by "El grito" and the interview. It includes footage of the six original band members playing "El grito" and using what audiences may identify as Western instruments. This image of the young Maya band members playing electric instruments as they jump to the sounds of rock is contrasted by the earthy color of the humble adobe home in the Guatemalan highlands where the band plays. The approximately six-minute video is longer and the production quality more complete than others uploaded by B'itzma fans.

A year later, in 2009, Gardner's video is republished, with a small modification, by Maya YouTube user Elias Itzep. This shorter (four minutes) version had 28,670 views at the time of this writing. There are also comments predominantly from members of the Maya diaspora in the United States.[8] And as of September 4, 2017, the song's most replayed video with more than 112,680 views was uploaded by "albeatman." Unlike the previous two, albeatman's video employs a variety of stock Guatemalan images, including natural scenery and popular cities that evoke a form of nostalgia for the nation. While the nostalgic landscapes do not reaffirm Maya culture, nor incorporate a photo of the Maya band members, they do attract viewers not familiar with B'itzma's music, thus aiding in the expansion of their listenership. The multiple layers of production and reproductions that take place around "El grito" on YouTube between the group's fan base and collaborators reveal the varied fusions and strategic appropriations by Maya cultural activists of this particular song. That is, Maya YouTube video producers and users, like the music created by B'itzma, participate in an artistic process that appropriates Western code systems for their own cultural expressions and purposes.

"El grito (Yo soy puro guatemalteco)" was written in the 1950s by José Ernesto Monzón Reina, whose musical career focused on writing and singing about the Guatemalan landscape. His popular songs, which include a compilation that consists of twenty-two melodies that pay tribute to the departments that form the Guatemalan nation-state, express a strong sense of national pride and belonging. To date "El grito (Yo soy puro guatemalteco)" is considered a type of popular national anthem for Guatemalans. Since its production, many Guatemalan musicians have "covered" the song. Often accompanied by marimba, Monzón Reina's version cries of national melancholy and pride. Similar to the official Guatemalan anthem, Monzón Reina's "El grito (Yo soy puro guatemalteco)" is taught at schools, and often children will dance traditional *sones* to the song on Independence Day celebrations. It is also a song that is widely circulated on the Internet, including many versions on YouTube.

Monzón Reina's lyrics, like the nation-state, reproduce racist and sexist ideologies and practices. In this national cry, the body of Maya women is the site of *Ladino*[9] desire and control:

cuando bailo con mi María	*when I dance with my Maria*
hasta un grito me sale así	*even a cry comes out like this*
que rechulas son las inditas	*how pretty are the little Indian girls*
cuando las veo bailar el son	*when I see them dancing the son*
con sus faldas levantaditas	*with their skirts lifted*
van taconeando con suave	*rumor they go about tapping*
	their heels with slight shyness[10]

The term *India* imposed by the Spanish during the process of colonialism continues to maintain racist connotations in Guatemala. It is often used by non-Indigenous Guatemalans to justify and assert racial hierarchies and power. In the song, the diminutive "Indita" also reinforces the dominant and paternalistic gaze of the *Ladino* man over the Maya woman's body. This is evident in the use of the pronoun "*mi* (my)," as belonging to the male Spanish-speaking voice, and the stereotypical name "María" often employed interchangeably in Guatemala when referring to Maya women. Her "lifted skirt" serves as another marker of the *Ladino* man's (sexual) desires and control over the racialized Maya woman's body.

Anne McClintock's foundational work on race, gender, and sexuality in the colonial context reminds us that these racialized and sexualized images of Indigenous women serve as metaphors that assert (European) men's "territorial rights of her body and by, extension, the fruits of her land" (1995, 26). Hence, in this popular Guatemalan national anthem, the Europeanized *Ladino* man asserts his power over the Maya woman's body and the (Indigenous) nation. The melancholic tones played on the marimba, Guatemala's national instrument, further reinforce these racial and gender hierarchies. The subtitle of the song, "(Yo soy puro guatemalteco)," emphasizes the colonial difference between the national *Ladino* subject ("Yo/I") and the Indigenous Other as the object of control and subjugation. In addition to the privileged and prominent place of Monzón Reina's "El grito (Yo soy puro guatemalteco)," the circulation of this song in grammar schools and on the Internet continues its racist and misogynist discourse across generations as well as regions.

Aware of the song's popularity and the reverence of this (un)official national anthem, B'itzma rewrote the chorus and music. The practices of appropriation, subversion, and repurpose as a strategy for survival have existed, as Aníbal Quijano notes, since the colonial period (1993). For instance, both Quijano and Walter Mignolo (1995) remind us of the strategic use of alphabetic literacy evident in Indigenous texts like the *Popol Wuj* and the writings of Felipe Guamán

Poma de Ayala. Therefore, B'itzma's fusion of Western musical styles, technologies, and traditional songs, like "El grito," serve to contest racist ideologies and hierarchies. In their version, the young Maya woman's body is a site of cultural empowerment:

Que rechulas son las patojas	*how really pretty are the young women*
Cuando las veo bailar el son,	*when I see them dance the son*
con sus cortes bien adornados	*with their woven skirts well-adorned*
van taconeando con un suave rubor.	*they go tapping their heels with slight shyness.*

It is in the heart of the song (chorus) that B'itzma changes how Mayas, and Maya women in particular, are viewed in the nation. Transforming the language in which Maya women are constructed within national cultural signifiers, they reaffirm an admiration for Maya textiles and the young women, "las patojas," that weave and wear them. The nostalgia evoked by the melancholic marimba rhythms in Monzón Reina's version is replaced by the fast and exhilarating beats of electric guitars, bass, and drums, thus suggesting an energetic and youthful ode to the nation. The sounds of marimba are introduced toward the end of the song as homage to the land and nation: "Te canto a ti / mi Guatemala, tierra querida / donde yo nací (I sing to you / my Guatemala, my beloved land / where I was born)." This last verse, like the first, is reproduced from Monzón Reina's version, but the marimba in B'itzma's is much faster and is later accompanied by the sounds of rock. In his work on Indigenous musicians' use of digital media, Thomas R. Hilder suggests that these artists, like the Maya members of B'itzma, create new narratives in their musical productions that articulate Indigenous histories and challenge "the national and imperial histories of settler societies" (2017, 5).

Hence, by appropriating Monzón Reina's lyrics, B'itzma uses the musical voice of the nation that privileges *Ladino* men to dismantle their racist and misogynist discourses. As the Maya voices of the young musicians reaffirm in energetic unison "*mi*/my Guatemala," they claim a sense of belonging and their birthrights to their ancestral land. In this way, the song constructs an active Maya subject that affirms her/his own place in the nation and, through the videos on YouTube, in the world (Wide Web). The band's strategic repurpose of this popular (national) song to subvert the social political structures that oppress Maya communities is also evident in the music videos produced by their fans on YouTube.

SOBREVIVENCIA ANCESTRAL

B'itzma's blending of songs in Maya languages with rock 'n' roll musical rhythms functions as an important cultural survival strategy and medium to reaffirm Indigenous worldviews. Much of the music produced and the videos uploaded to YouTube emphasize the revitalization of Maya identity, culture, and spirituality. At the same time, several songs in the group's discography focus on denouncing the ongoing legacies of colonialism that produce forced displacements as well as environmental degradation and global warming. The music videos uploaded to YouTube serve to create a local/global awareness and engagement around Maya cultural rights, spirituality, and the daily struggles faced as a result of ongoing neocolonial legacies. These songs, unlike "El grito," are written and composed by B'itzma. Often the songs are in Maya languages and then translated into Spanish. In some of the YouTube videos uploaded by fans and the musicians, subtitles are provided to give access to non-Maya language speakers.

While all B'itzma's music emphasizes a Maya identity and culture, specific melodies highlight Maya spirituality. Some of these songs on YouTube include "Un'oj numam" (*Consejos del abuelo*/Advice from the Elder), "Txe witz" (*Al pie del cerro*/At the Foot of the Hill), "Ruq'ojom Tat Mak" (*El son de Don Marcos*/The Son of Don Marcos), and "Chjontela Qajwil" (*Gracias a nuestro creador*/Gratitude to Our Creator). They often evoke a celebratory feeling as they impart ancestral lessons about harmony, life, offerings, nature, and ceremony. These songs frequently employ a narrative quality that reproduces storytelling practices. For Laguna Pueblo writer Leslie Marmon Silko, storytelling is a survival strategy that has "worked for the Pueblo people for thousands of years" (1981, xviii). She particularly stresses that telling and sharing stories is not simply relegated to writers that make up, or create, fictional stories but rather it is an act and practice that is shared by everybody in the community (1981, xix). Silko emphasizes that in the Laguna Pueblo communities "everyone [can] tell stories, and everyone [feels] responsible for remembering stories and retelling them" (1981, xix). In this way, both the music and lyrics that tell stories about Maya spiritual practices form part of these ancestral survival strategies. At the same time, like stories, the videos uploaded to YouTube conjure multiple sensorial memories for the Maya viewers through the embodied practices performed in the videos. Embodied practices have historically been fundamental for Indigenous communities as a way of transmitting communal memories, histories, and values from generation to generation in the midst of violent ongoing colonialism (Taylor 2003). Hence, the videos created and uploaded by Maya fans that incorporate images of Indigenous cultural practices, ceremonies, and important spiritual sites illustrate not only the ways B'itzma's music evokes these memories for them but also their participation in the transmission of these embodied histories.

B'itzma's second most viewed video on YouTube is "Ruq'ojom Tat Mak" (*El son de Don Marcos*/The *Son* of Don Marcos). There are three different linguistic versions of the song (Mam, Kaqchikel, and Spanish). Fans have uploaded at least eight videos and together they have garnered more than 200,000 views. At the heart of this song is a celebration of Maya culture. The festive tones vibrate in every aspect of the song including the music, lyrics, and videos taken by fans at B'itzma concerts. In "Ruq'ojom Tat Mak," the fusion of rock 'n' roll and traditional Maya music includes the incorporation of several ancestral instruments like the *tzicolaj* (*chirimía*), marimba, *ayotl*, and *tunkul* (drum).[11] It begins with the rhythms of marimba and the merging of those ancestral sounds with rock.

The chorus affirms Maya identity through celebratory references of everyday practices:

Se me antojaba tomar una bebida ancestral	*I craved an ancestral drink*
Se me antojaba comer un plato de kaq ik.	*I craved a plate of ka qik.*[12]
Que grande es la cultura	*How great is the culture*
que los abuelos dejaron.	*that our elders left us.*
Que vida tan hermosa	*What a beautiful life*
somos de Paxil.	*we are from Paxil.*

This emphasis on the greatness of customary cultural practices is further stressed in the song's title "Ruq'ojom Tat Mak." As with this song and others in their discography, B'itzma's inclusion of frequently used names in highland Maya communities, like Marcos, Natividad, Andrés, Alonso, and Juan, roots the music and the stories they tell in the daily experiences of everyday people. Additionally, the songs celebrate familiar community identities and roles like the *señora vendedora* (market woman), *abuelo* (grandfather/elder), *madre* (mother), *juventud* (youth), and *campesino* (farmworker). Hence, the music created by B'itzma aids in the transmission of a collective history that is rooted in the everyday person. At the same time, in the song "Ruq'ojom Tat Mak," the act of naming their territories in Maya languages further grounds the region within Maya history and knowledge. This is particularly evident in the last line where they affirm "*somos de Paxil*/we are from Paxil." Mentioning Paxil is also a reference to the *Popol*

Wuj, which names the place as the origin of maize. Evoking Paxil, instead of the imposed Spanish name (Guatemala), contests European colonialist powers that (re)named and claimed Indigenous territories as their own. Reclaiming in Mam the territory's ancestral name, Paxil, symbolically reaffirms Maya peoples' historical place and rights to the land.

Central to the revitalization of Maya culture is teaching younger generations ancestral knowledge and spiritual practices. Three of B'itzma's songs on YouTube, "Un'oj numam" (*Consejos del abuelo*/Advice from the Elder), "Txe witz" (*Al pie del cerro*/At the Foot of the Hill), and "Chjontela Qajwil" (*Gracias a nuestro creador*/Gratitude to Our Creator), specifically stress the pivotal role of Maya spirituality and knowledge in community construction. Uploaded to YouTube by two different highland Guatemalan groups, the most popular videos that circulate are for the song "Chjontela Qajwil." A television station from the Guatemalan highlands created the first video. The online video by OTVO Ostuncalco TV, a local station from Quetzaltenango, provides Spanish subtitles to the Maya-Mam song. In their version of the video, a young man carrying a *morral*[13] pensively climbs to the top of a local *cerro* (hill). Snapshots of the valley, trees, yellow carnations, and rocks that surround the area, and the small silhouettes of other members of the Maya community climbing, accompany the image of the young man. The video and song end with a blurry close-up of four Maya elders, two women and two men, preparing a ceremony. The out-of-focus image of the elders at the end of the video, as well as the use of Spanish subtitles, creates a closeness and distance for the Maya and non-Maya viewers. Though the Spanish subtitles give access to the lyrics for a non-Mam speaking audience, the spiritual meaning of the *cerro* and of the ceremony are reserved for members of the community and their memory of these places as well as practices.

The video created by Guatiendavirtual.com[14] forgoes the Spanish translation and engages non-Mam speaking viewers through a visual narration of the song. At the beginning and end of the video, four of B'itzma's musicians, wearing regional Maya clothing, appear walking through a steep street in a highland community. Most of the video is composed of footage taken at different Maya spiritual sites and ceremonies. These snapshots are often close-ups of yellow candles lit by elders, the ceremonial fire, *copal*, and flowers. It also includes footage of elders kneeling in ceremonies, holding hands around the fire surrounded by lakes and *cerros*. The images and the song evoke varied layers of sensory and embodied memories for Maya viewers. This is evident in the comments section where viewers note in Mam and Spanish the joy they feel as they listen to the song and watch the video. At the same time, both videos provide a different understanding of Maya knowledge and spirituality for a non-Indigenous cyber audience through the Spanish subtitles and the ceremonial images incorporated. In particular, the song reveals several central elements of Maya spirituality, like the role of duality and harmony and the respect of life, nature, and the creator. The lessons on the vital place of nature in Maya spirituality become an activist cry in songs like "Amatitlán" that overtly denounce environmental degradation in Guatemala. On the YouTube videos uploaded by B'itzma's fans, these local struggles are visually connected to global systems that contribute to the lake's destruction. For instance, Junajbe Ramírez's video merges stock images of (il)legal dumping by factories in different global landscapes, contaminated rivers and oceans, and agricultural fields and forest fires in the United States with B'itzma's song about the local destruction of Lake Amatitlán. Ramírez's audio-visual fusion proposes that the specific local struggles of Mayas in Guatemala are not isolated from the effects of globalization.

Uploaded in 2009 and with more than 40,160 views at the time of this writing, Kyxhpi's video for the song "Amatitlán" uses footage from different angles of Atitlán, another revered lake in Guatemala that has been contaminated by different (trans)national industries in the area. While Junajbe Ramírez visually engages YouTube viewers with environmental local/global struggles, Kyxhpi's video ends with a direct call to action that echoes the last verse in B'itzma's song: "Amatitlán, es la evidencia de / la falta de conciencia (Amatitlán, is evidence of / the lack of consciousness)." B'itzma's appeal for social consciousness is not simply an environmentalist cry in the defense of "Mother Nature." In their call to action, Maya knowledge and practices are posited as essential in creating local/global social changes.

The songs and videos illustrate the ways Mayas strategically use the YouTube platform to create awareness to a virtual global audience about the local/transnational struggles Maya communities face. At the same time, this virtual mediated exchange serves to educate non-Indigenous viewers about Maya culture, spirituality, and knowledge. In doing so, the space provides another medium for Maya activism in their strategic local/global networking with Indigenous and non-Indigenous peoples. For Kyra Landzelius, these types of computer-mediated communications function as "implicit and explicit tools of solidarity-building" as well as "digital contact zones" that include diasporic communities (2006, 18).

WEAVING VIRTUAL MAYA DIASPORIC COMMUNITIES

YouTube is considered the largest video-sharing site in the world. Since its launch in 2005, it has made video sharing accessible through the use of various formats that include "nearly every device with an Internet connection—from desktops to phones, tablets to TVs, game consoles, and even VR headsets" (https://youtube.googleblog.com). In his work on video activism, William Merrin notes that much of the material produced and uploaded to YouTube continues to be nonprofessional, despite the fact that it remains "the leading site and center of online video production and sharing" (2012, 98). This accessibility gives B'itzma musicians and fans a space where they can represent themselves as they create awareness around issues that impact Maya communities across territorial borders. The exchanges created in these sites, as Bronwyn Carlson explains, also produce another space for Indigenous people to interact "with one another, have conversations, debates and form relationships" (2013, 164). Hence, it is not a coincidence that several of the music videos produced by B'itzma fans were uploaded by members of the Maya diaspora in the United States. The videos contribute to the affirmation of Maya culture and serve to virtually (re)connect fans in the diaspora with their (home) land.

Though many of the songs by B'itzma are not specifically about forced migration, the legacy of displacement and its roots in the violence of colonialism are made visible in one of the songs on their first CD, *Twi'Witz: En la cima del Cerro/At the Top of the Hill* (1999), as well as in their most recent production, *Dualidad/Duality* (2016). These songs forgo the fast and electric sounds of rock 'n' roll and instead borrow elements from the *corrido* tradition.[15] The tragic stories of displacement, broken families, and exploitive labor conditions are musically reproduced by the melancholic rhythms of the songs. For example, in "Tat Lox (Don Alonso)" the profound sadness produced by forced displacement is stressed through the repetition of the line "Ma Tz'ex, Ma Tz'ex (Se fue, se fue / He left, he left)."

Jorge Xulen Ortiz explains that the song was written in the aftermath of the U.S.-backed Guatemalan genocide and the mass forced migration of thousands of Mayas to Mexican coffee plantations (*Contacto Ancestral* 2011). As with many migrant stories, Tat Lox/Don Alonso's begins at dawn. He leaves in the shadows, alone with nothing but "un viejo morral / su mecapal (an old *morral* / and his *mecapal*)"[16] as well as "tayuyos para el camino (*tayuyos* for the road)" and his immense "*tristeza* (sadness)." The continued violence of colonialism is symbolically present in the song's reference to the *mecapal*, a forehead strap used to carry heavy loads on the back. While both the *morral* and *mecapal* are prominent signifiers of Maya labor, the *mecapal* alludes to the historical weight of the poverty and exploitation that force Maya workers to bow their heads down. In the song, Tat Lox/Don Alonso also takes *tayuyos*, tamales filled with black beans, on his long journey because the *tayuyos* literary and metaphorically provide the ancestral nourishment essential for his survival.

Nearly two decades since their release of "Tat Lox (Don Alonso)" B'itzma composed the song titled "Al otro lado" (On the Other Side) as part of their latest compilation. Rooted in the personal experiences of several former band members' own migration to the United States as Florida citrus fieldworkers, the bilingual song (Spanish and Maya Mam) overtly denounces "lo inhumano (the inhumane)" and "la injusticia del sistema (the injustice of the [social and political] system [in the United States])" that "cada ves inventa más leyes con el fin de discriminar (each time [this unjust social and political system in the United States] creates more laws with the intent to discriminate)" against migrants.[17] As with the song about Tat Lox (Don Alonso), the exploitative labor conditions and isolation are stressed throughout "Al otro lado." The song begins with the melancholic sounds of marimba echoing the deep sadness experienced by Maya migrants and their families. Additionally, in this new song the forced migration of the "gente de maíz (the people of corn)" is no longer relegated to men, but now also "niños y mujeres (children and women)." This inclusion illustrates the ways B'itzma continues to use their music as a platform to expose structural inequalities that impact Mayas today. In doing so, the songs can function as important vehicles for community-building as they begin to make the circumstances of these historical forced migrations visible, thus creating an important space that provides Mayas a place for contact across borders as well as generations.

Furthermore, the comments below each video uploaded to YouTube reproduce a sense of community through the multiple dialogues that take place in the music, lyrics, and images, and the variety of issues, emotions, and memories they evoke. This is particularly important for the Maya diaspora since physical mobility from their place of residence is often limited because of their undocumented status. These online exchanges on B'itzma's music and the videos with and between the Maya diaspora make their presence visible, since their experiences and struggles are often erased from dominant media spaces in Guatemala and the United States (Estrada 2013).

Moreover, as Kyra Landzelius explains, "unlike immigrants of yesteryear, the displaced of today can 'stay connected' in ways that were inconceivable to their forebears" (2006, 20). As scholarship on YouTube suggests, the site not only enables its viewers and video producers a space from which to construct and reconstruct identity but also a place for people to interact with others across regions (Snickars and Vonderau 2009). This is particularly evident in the comments section located below each YouTube video, where "shout outs" to different highland Guatemalan towns coupled with the commentator's current place of residence creates a new mapping of Maya peoples that is inclusive of the diaspora. For example, many will mention they are from a specific Maya town in the Guatemalan highlands and now reside in places like Miami, San Francisco, Los Angeles, New York, Oakland, New Jersey, Kansas, and Georgia. Though diasporic communities in the United States tend to dominate the exchanges in the comments sections, other nontraditional places like Alberta, Canada, and Iraq are also mentioned. Maya Guatemalans in Mexico will frequently reference the specific state where they reside. This practice of naming places of origin and residence underscores the internal heterogeneity of Maya communities. Equally important, the comments illustrate the visible size and range of the Maya diaspora specifically in the United States. In this way, they produce awareness for Mayas in the diaspora about each other as well as a space for them to connect. And thus these virtual exchanges also aid in rethinking the ways Maya identities and communities are (re)constructed on the Internet.

The quasi-anonymity that online interactions create allows for undocumented migrants to step out of the shadows they are forced to live in the United States.[18] In doing so, migrants are able to write themselves into a public cyber Maya community through their reflections on the music produced by B'itzma and the videos they or other fans created and uploaded to YouTube. Many of the comments are written in the informal "vos" and use the Guatemalan vernacular, which provides a familiar tone to these exchanges. Among youth in Guatemala, words like "muchá," "chilero," and "calidad" are often used between friends, and thus these online exchanges virtually reproduce that closeness. In some cases, the Spanish in the comments section does not follow conventional grammatical rules and signals the user's limited access to a formal education. The writing of comments in Maya languages also creates another layer of intimacy and (re)connection to specific linguistic communities. Hence, the various styles, tones, and languages used to discursively articulate Maya identities stress their heterogeneity.

There are two principal themes that dominate the exchanges in the comments sections of the videos examined in this chapter. The first centers on the hardships faced by members of the diaspora in the United States, in which the writers note the loneliness and difficulties of living away from their families and communities "*en el otro lado* (on the other side)." The second and most common theme focuses on Maya cultural affirmation. Many express a feeling of empowerment after watching the videos and listening to B'itzma's music. For example, tziyaa notes below a video of B'itzma playing "El grito" at a community festival in San Sebastián Coatán, Huehuetenango, "*Orgullo de Ser Maya kakchiquel. Me Encanta!* (Proud to be Maya Kaqchikel. I love it!)."[19] These comments often express the ways B'itzma's music and the videos uploaded by fans root and reconnect the viewers to their Maya culture. In this way, the music, videos, and dialogues created on the YouTube platform virtually link Mayas across territories by emphasizing their cultural continuity. At the same time, they impart lessons on Maya histories, cultures, spirituality, and ancestral survival strategies.

B'ITZMA'S SURVIVAL AESTHETICS

While the Internet does not erase social inequalities, it does serve as part of several strategic tools employed by Indigenous cultural workers and activists that participate in local/hemispheric resistance movements. Over the past two decades, B'itzma Sobrevivencia and their "survival aesthetics," which fuses Maya ancestral knowledge and practices with a variety of non-Maya mediums, has formed part of an essential strategy to contest (trans)national power structures that erase and distort Maya histories and subjectivities. Additionally, as Stephanie Nohelani Teves suggests in her work on Hawaiian music, the fusion between traditional and modern instrumentation highlights the agency of Indigenous peoples' innovation and their abilities to retain their traditions while enduring the trauma of colonization, which includes forced displacement from their territories (2015, 260). In these efforts, B'itzma Sobrevivencia's music and videos have also produced essential bridges on the Internet for Mayas to (re)connect across geographical spaces through the videos their fans are inspired to create, as well as the varied dialogues they generate. These multiple mediums employed by B'itzma Sobrevivencia provide a space for both band members and their fans on the Internet to articulate historical and current struggles, to contest racism and erasures, and to publically and proudly affirm their Maya identity and assert in their own terms their place in the world (Wide Web).

NOTES

1. Sara Curruchich Cúmez's musical trajectory includes collaborations with B'itzma Sobrevivencia at local Guatemalan highland music festivals. Some of these participations have been video recorded and uploaded by fans to YouTube. See for example, https://www.youtube.com/watch?v=_x_ov41ohak. Since 2014, when the video for "Ch'uti'xtän (*Niña*/Girl)" was released on YouTube, Curruchich Cúmez has performed in France (2018), the United States (2016), and other Latin American countries. In 2015, she won the Artista Revelación award by the Fundación Dante Alighieri.

2. As Landzelius reminds us, "Indigenous populations, in general, are more likely to lack the basic physical resources to get connected, and less likely to be versed in the skills required to fully exercise connection [on the World Wide Web]" (2006, 8).

3. One of the group's initial efforts was through the use of the social network Myspace. Founded in 2003, Myspace was widely used between 2005 and 2008. By 2008 it was overtaken by Facebook, and many groups including B'itzma Sobrevivencia created pages on the new social network.

4. Maya migrants in Los Angeles founded the radio show *Contacto Ancestral* in 2003. The producers of the show use the Southern California airwaves and Internet to make the hemispheric struggles and resistance movements of Indigenous communities visible. On the show Indigenous scholars, cultural workers, activists, leaders, and community members are often interviewed. Audio archives of the show are maintained online by Pacific Radio (http://archive.kpfk.org). The program also has a Facebook page and website: http://www.kpfk.org/index .php/programs/68-contacto ancestral#.Wek_CUdrwlJ. For more on *Contacto Ancestral* see my articles "Ka Tzij: The Maya Diasporic Voices from *Contacto Ancestral*" (2013) and "The Maya Diaspora in Los Angeles: Memory, Resistance and the Voices of *Contacto Ancestral*" (2016) in *Indigenous Resistant Strategies* (http://scalar.usc.edu/works/resistant-strategies/index).

5. The founding members were Jorge Xulen Ortiz Sales and Eduardo Ramirez Ortiz. A year later, they were joined by Lorenzo Domingo Ortiz, José Gabriel Ortiz Ordoñez, Jaime Eduardo Ortiz Sales, and Samuel Ordoñez López. Over the course of the last two decades, the makeup of the group has changed with Jorge Xulen Ortiz Sales as the only continuing member. As part of what Ortiz Sales calls "cyclical changes," new generations have been incorporated. The current members are Jorge Xulen Ortiz, Lorenzo Domingo Ortiz (who after a few years of not participating returned), Rafael Morales, Samuel Ordoñez López, and Gabriel Ortiz Sales.

6. Unlike their other CD titles, their second does not provide a translation in Spanish.

7. Other Maya rock groups like Aj B'atz have also reproduced B'itzma Sobrevivencia's version of "El grito."

8. Itzep has other videos on YouTube including festivals from San Bartolo Aguas Calientes, Totonicapán, one of New York City's Empire State Building, and another titled "Invierno/Winter in New Jersey," where he records every day occurrences like walking, driving, and riding the bus on the snow-filled New Jersey streets. In the comments below his publication of Gardner's "El grito" video, Itzep enthusiastically tells other viewers using the Guatemalan vernacular "*personalmente, me cuadra esta música muchá*/personally, this music speaks to me, guys."

9. Since the colonial period in Guatemala, the term *Ladino* has referred to a variety of Indigenous and mestizo subject positions (Guzmán Böckler and Herbert 2002). Today, *Ladino* is often understood as the negation of Indigenous identity. While those who identify as Maya in Guatemala take part in a historically grounded and socially constructed collectivity—which is tied to common Indigenous ancestors, history, and culture (Bastos 1996; Fischer and McKenna Brown 1996).

10. Unless otherwise noted, all translations are mine.

11. Introduced in the sixteenth and seventeenth centuries by the Spanish clergy, the *chirimía* (*tzicolaj*) is a double-reed instrument. The *chirimía* and the *tunkul* (drum) are used during Catholic processions as well as in Maya dramas, dances, and ceremonies. The fusion of Maya ancestral musical instruments and cultural practices with those brought by the Spanish served as a survival strategy for Mayas.

12. *Kaq'ik* is a soup made with turkey. Its red broth is made of tomatoes, spices, and chilies. The soup is often accompanied with small white tamales. It originates from the Q'eqchi' region of Cobán, Alta Verpaz. In 2007, the Guatemalan Ministry of Culture and Sports declared the soup part of the country's Cultural Heritage.

13. A *morral* is a hand-woven fiber shoulder bag used by both women and men.

14. The Guatiendavirtual channel on YouTube is a virtual *tienda* (store) that sells music tracks by various Guatemalan musicians.

15. For more on *corridos* and migration see, for example, *Corridos in Migrant Memory* (2006) by Martha I. Chew Sánchez.

16. *Mecapal* is a tumpline, a leatherhead strap used for carrying loads on the back. The poem "Ri Patän/El mecapal/The mecapal" by Humberto Ak'abal (Maya-K'iche') posits the *mecapal* as a symbol of Maya oppression.

17. For more on Maya migrants in Florida see *Maya in Exile: Guatemalans in Florida* (1993) by Allan F. Burns as well as "'I Am Maya, Not Guatemalan, nor Hispanic'— the Belongingness of Mayas in Southern Florida" by Patrick Hiller and J. Linstroth (2009).

18. This quasi-anonymity also makes it difficult to know the gender of all the commentators, since names can vary from surnames to a nongendered word or phrase. Similarly, people who comment on YouTube do not always use profile photos. Yet the distinctions between generations are made evident by the words and references

stated on their comments. Similarly, the users often note their Maya identity in the comments section.

19. tziyaa's spelling of Kaqchikel differs from what is conventionally used.

REFERENCES

albeatman. 2011. "Soy Puro Guatemalteco–El Grito–sobrevivencia." YouTube video, 2:31, posted March 6, 2011, https://www.youtube.com/watch?v=FqX1CMviIRg.

Bastos, Santiago. 1996. "Los indios, la nación y el nacionalismo." *Espiral: estudios sobre estado y sociedad* 2 (6): 161–206.

Bastos, Santiago, and Manuela Camus. 2003. *Entre el mecapal y el cielo: Desarrollo del movimiento maya en Guatemala.* Guatemala: FLACSO.

B'itzma Sobrevivencia. 1999. *Twi' Witz: En la cima del cerro.* CD.

B'itzma Sobrevivencia. 2003. *Itz'x Qanq'ib'il.* CD.

B'itzma Sobrevivencia. 2016. "Al otro lado." *Dualidad.* CD.

Burns, Allan F. 1993. *Maya in Exile: Guatemalans in Florida.* Philadelphia: Temple University Press.

Carlson, Bronwyn. 2013. "The New Frontier: Emergent Indigenous Identity and Social Media." In *The Politics of Identity: Emerging Indigeneity,* edited by Michelle Harris, Martin Nakata, and Bronwyn Carlson, 1–9. Sydney: UTSe Press.

Chadwick, Andrew. 2006. *Internet Politics: States, Citizens, and New Communication Technologies.* New York: Oxford University Press.

Chew Sánchez, Martha I. 2006. *Corridos in Migrant Memory.* Albuquerque: University of New Mexico Press.

Contacto Ancestral. 2011. Produced by Manuel Felipe Pérez. KPFK Studios, North Hollywood, California.

Estrada, Alicia Ivonne. 2013. "Ka Tzij: The Maya Diasporic Voices from *Contacto Ancestral.*" *Latino Studies* 11 (2): 208–27.

Estrada, Alicia Ivonne. 2016. "The Maya Diaspora in Los Angeles: Memory, Resistance and the Voices of *Contacto Ancestral.*" In *Indigenous Resistant Strategies,* edited by Marcos Steuernagel and Diana Taylor, http://scalar.usc.edu/works/resistant-strategies/index.

Fischer, Edward F., and R. McKenna Brown, eds. 1996. *Maya Cultural Activism in Guatemala.* Austin: University of Texas.

Gardner, Matt. 2008. "Rock Maya." YouTube video, 6:31, posted August 25, 2008, https://www.youtube.com/watch?v=x_wGgzMpEpE&t=177s.

Guatiniendavirtual.com. 2010. "sobrevivencia-Gracias a nuestro creador." YouTube video, 3:52, posted October 8, 2010, https://www.youtube.com/watch?v=CdfwSahZNng&t=127s.

Guzmán Böckler, Carlos, and Jean-Loup Herbert. 2002. *Guatemala: Una interpretación histórico-social.* Guatemala: Cholsamaj.

Hilder, Thomas R. 2017. "Music, Indigeneity, Digital Media." In *Music, Indigeneity, Digital Media,* edited by Thomas R. Hilder, Henry Stobart, and Shzr Ee Tan, 1–28. New York: University of Rochester Press.

Hiller, Patrick, and J. Linstroth. 2009. "'I Am Maya, Not Guatemalan, nor Hispanic'—the Belongingness of Mayas in Southern Florida." *Forum: Qualitative Social Research* 10 (3): 1–23.

Itzep, Elias. 2009. "SOBREVIVENCIA—("El Grito")." YouTube video, 4:55, posted August 24, 2009, https://www.youtube.com/watch?v=ddtznmdɪv-M.

Kheshti, Roshanak. 2015. *Modernity's Ear: Listening to Race and Gender in World Music.* New York: New York University Press.

Kun, Josh. 2005. *Audiotopia: Music, Race, and America.* Berkeley: University of California Press.

Kyxhpi. 2009. "AMATITLAN by Sobrevivencia (imagenes del lago de ATITLAN)." YouTube video, 5:09, posted November 12, 2009, https://www.youtube.com/watch?v=DBTIwYC4gKM.

Landzelius, Kyra. 2006. *Native on the Net: Indigenous and Diasporic Peoples in the Virtual Age.* New York: Routledge.

McClintock, Anne. 1995. *Imperial Leather: Race, Gender and Sexuality in the Colonial Contest.* New York: Routledge.

Mérida López, Ronald Waldo. 2016. "ESTO SI ES ROCK CHAPIN." YouTube video, 6:41, posted June 18, 2016, https://www.youtube.com/watch?v=_x_ov4ɪohak&list=RD_x_ov4ɪohak.

Merrin, William. 2012. "Still Fighting 'the Beast': Guerrilla Television and the Limits of YouTube." *Cultural Politics* 8 (1): 97–119.

Mignolo, Walter. 1995. *The Darker Side of the Renaissance: Literacy, Territoriality, and Colonization.* Ann Arbor: University of Michigan Press.

Montero-Diaz, Fiorella. 2017. "YouTubing the 'Other': Lima's Upper Classes and Andean Imaginaries." In *Music, Indigeneity, Digital Media,* edited by Thomas R. Hilder, Henry Stobart, and Shzr Ee Tan, 74–94. New York: University of Rochester Press.

OTVO Ostuncalco TV. 2014. "Sobrevivencia gracias creador en mam sub español." YouTube video, 4:15, posted February 28, 2014, https://www.youtube.com/watch?v=4evYuyMl4T8&t=14s.

Proyecto Interdiocesano Recuperación de la Memoria Histórica et al. 1993. *Guatemala, Never Again!* Ossining, N.Y., and London: Orbis Books.

Quijano, Aníbal. 1993. "Modernity, Identity, and Utopia in Latin America." *Boundary 2: An International Journal of Literature and Culture* 20 (3): 140–55.

Ramirez, Junajbe. 2012. "Sobrevivencia." YouTube video, 4:26, posted July 8, 2012, https://www.youtube.com/watch?v=f2yzE4Mub6g.

Silko, Leslie Marmon. 1981. *Storyteller.* New York: Seaver Books.

Snickars, Pelle, and Patrick Vonderau, eds. 2009. *The YouTube Reader.* Stockholm: National Library of Sweden.

Taylor, Dianna. 2003. *The Archive and the Repertoire: Performing Cultural Memory in the Americas.* Durham: Duke University Press.

Teves, Stephanie Nohelani. 2015. "Tradition and Peformance." In *Native Studies Keywords,* edited by Stephanie Nohelani Teves, Andrea Smith, and Michelle H. Raheja, 257–70. Tucson: University of Arizona Press.

Vizenor, Gerald. 1999. *Manifest Manners: Narratives on Postindian Survivance*. Lincoln: University of Nebraska Press.

Wilson, Pamela, and Michelle Stewart. 2008. *Global Indigenous Media: Cultures, Poetics, and Politics*. Durham: Duke University Press.

YouTube. 2017. "Official YouTube Blog." September 4, 2017, https://youtube.googleblog .com.

5

TRAFFICKED BABIES, EXPLODED FUTURES

Jayro Bustamante's *Ixcanul*

DEBRA A. CASTILLO

Guatemalan Jayro Bustamante's mega-award winning 2015 opera prima, *Ixcanul*, is set in a coffee plantation on the skirts of a vaguely menacing active volcano. With dialogues almost entirely in Kaqchikel, except for a few phrases in Spanish, it tells the coming-of-age story of a young woman, María, as she tries to avoid her finally inescapable destiny of marriage to her father's foreman. Along the way, she gets pregnant by a reckless young man who has spent all his earnings on alcohol, not necessarily because she loves him, but rather because she sees him as a means to bribe her way into a trip north to the United States (and perhaps as a way to explore her own burgeoning teenage sexuality). María eventually loses her baby, in a confusing or sinister turn of events. Her father tries to console her that the child is better off in the north, where he surely has been adopted into a wealthy gringo home.[1] Yet behind this fate looms the unspoken specter of a far less optimal outcome, suggested by the police officer's reference to "el cuerpo" when he peruses the hospital's documentation attesting to the Mayan woman's release of her rights to the child.

In the context of a volume like this one, on contemporary Indigenous identities in dialogue with the forces of technology and globalization, a film like *Ixcanul* would seem necessarily tangential. The entire visual and ideological field seems bound up in a very conventional imaginary construct of indigeneity, featuring the community's distance from any of the conventional markers of modernity by highlighting the traditions that handicap them and the monolingualism that condemns them to second-class citizenship in a space that excludes them from participation or understanding. It is, in this sense, a story that could have been told in the nineteenth century—or the sixteenth—with almost no variation on the familiar shape and formulaic constructions of the indigenista[2] morality tale. The film further distances these coffee pickers and sharecroppers by situating them in the context of compelling landscapes that dwarf the humans, which loom large in their imaginations while also keeping them on the edge of disaster, whether by volcanic eruption or snakebite. Bustamante has been highly praised for the deployment of these spectacular landscapes, which serve as a convincingly remote, key spiritual/symbolic as well as physical site. That filmic landscape speaks to the viewer's romantic yearning for accessible, authentic exoticism. Certainly, it may surprise us to learn that the carefully curated camera images reflect a wholly imaginary distance from specific markers of Western modernity in the actual locality—the nearby McDonald's, for instance, that had to be carefully *not* included in the shots.

Almost all of the discussions of the film have focused on the central character, María, played by talented newcomer María Mercedes Coroy,[3] whose eminently photographable face and (especially) her clothing have cemented a furor around her—as in the April 2016 *LOOK* magazine cover photo highlighting her "mystique," another name for the fetishized quality of being-for-the-other that delivers her up to the readers of the magazine for our fascinated gaze. "Look" the magazine tells us, and she looks back, but only through a lush jungle setting, as she fades back into, or emerges from, an exotic natural background, the screen of an always already interpolated colonial history.[4] This mystique reinterprets the "tragic mysticism" embodied in the film, where the young woman is repeatedly equated with the much harsher landscape of the volcano, as if she is harnessing that inherent power to do . . . something.

In the narrative of the film, the posited, imaginary potential of the young woman, defined almost exclusively as her youthful beauty and presumed reproductive potential, abuts the filmic reality of the elder woman's powerlessness. Her vague, unruly power/mystique cedes to the frame tale of her helplessness as a victim of patriarchal oppression, but it is this same unruliness that detonates the fascination with Coroy's image (but not her words; most coverage of the film takes the form of interviews with Bustamante) as a commodity both within and outside the film.

Indeed, perceptive Indigenous commentators have taken issue precisely with this variant on colonialist nostalgia and liberal guilt: the heavy overreliance on stereotypical depictions of their countrypeople, in a highly praised film that comes from a national context in which Indigenous voices are seldom heard unless filtered through the perceptions and voices of Ladino interpreters like this one. Even more worrisome, fictional scenarios are taken by dominant culture audiences to reveal some fundamental "reality" that helps that broader audience "understand" the plight of the isolated Indigenous people (Xinico Batz 2016), in this case, the particular and grinding subordination of women by men from their own ethnicity, further exacerbated by the general discrimination against the majority of Guatemalan people by the ethnically whiter Spanish-speaking elites who hold the power in the country.

While not ignoring this context or these important debates, in what follows I want to take a different point of entry into the film. I suggest that passage into motherhood and the indeterminacy around María and Pepe's baby hint at a contemporary discourse about trafficked babies and trafficked body parts that allows me to bring together two very distant points in a single, long discussion about the differential impacts of modernity via new biotechnological practices. It is precisely the tension between what is strenuously kept outside the frame and the more obvious indigenista trappings held within the tightly contained space of the exotic setting, the incommensurability between the commodity and its recipient, that makes the film speak to other, very contemporary issues. These issues are represented within the film by encounters with Ladino technology (generally in the form of a Spanish-speaking official and a pile of papers or a clipboard). Outside the frame of the film, other technologies are very much in play in addition to the technopolitics of print, and these take on ever increasing importance in the crucial questions of what, how, by whom information is produced and accessed.

This has also been the most award-winning film in Guatemalan history, including major awards in Europe, Latin America, the United States, and even one from the Mumbai film fest 2015 (Golden Gateway Award); it was also Guatemala's entry for the U.S. foreign film Academy Award in 2016. The film seems to offer entry to a little known or hidden world, while also retaining a hint of its unknowability. This combination of access and exotic distance repeats itself over and over in international publicity about the film. As in the film, where her character spends almost all of her key scenes with her eyes lowered or closed (when being dressed as a bride, when she's walking through the snake-ridden field, delirious in the hospital), forbidding us entry, most of the many publicity photos of the actor are opaque in some way: her Mona Lisa smile, her colorful non-Western clothing make her hard to "read."

At the same time, like the bodies of the women, their visible markers of ethnicity, including their spectacularly beautiful clothing, tend to stand in for some kind of accessible authenticity that seems uncomfortably close to the much-critiqued aesthetics of *National Geographic*, with its infamous version of anthropology through high-resolution photographs of people in remote settings free from any contaminating contact with technology. They are goods come to market, and we consume their images. Yet we know that most viewers have no real way to reach these real/imagined remote spaces and people: we don't know the language, we don't know the customs, and we are also tripped up by our own colonial heritage that tells us that looking people in the eye is something equals do, and something for which an "indio igualado" can be punished or killed.

In festival appearances, Coroy is generally flanked by her co-star, veteran actor María Telón, an activist performer who focuses on social justice theater and was attracted to Bustamante's project precisely because of its important message about Indigenous rights. In the international festival photographs, both women are almost always overshadowed by much larger, much whiter men, who gather them in close to what can only be perceived as colonizer, ladino male bodies. In these photos, Telón generally looks even more serious than Coroy.

This combination of hypervisibility and (mostly) silence raises the old question first framed by Gayatri Spivak (1988) about how and when and where the subaltern speaks, and in what circumstances she can be heard. How bound up are these images with the well-meaning liberal pieties of the postcolonial oppressor, who speaks for her, asking her to remain a decorative doll at his side, under his hand, (re)producing for his market? How do marginalized voices and bodies gain access to the mainstream public within the contemporary structures of globalization, whether economic or cinematic?

This hypervisibility has another side, one that Édouard Glissant has theorized as the right to opacity, which we can perhaps intuit in these actors' serious faces, their half smiles: what authority does she hold, such that she can withhold herself, short circuiting commodification? Glissant writes: "If we examine the process of 'understanding' people and ideas from the perspective of Western thought, we discover that its basis is this requirement for transparency. In order to understand and thus accept you, I have to measure your solidity with the ideal scale providing me with grounds to make comparisons and, perhaps, judgments. . . . I admit you to existence, within my system" (2006, 189–90). Glissant concludes: "We clamor for the right to opacity for everyone" (194). Speech and opacity, then, operate as two different modalities for insuring subaltern presence in the mainstream consciousness, the first based on oral technologies, the second on a recognition that is visual. Within the context of the many interviews with the actors and director following the success of the film, this interplay of eloquent (to Western ears) voice and striking (to Western eyes) dress play off each other. Within the film, the long silences, the maliciously mistranslated exchanges between Kaqchikel and Spanish, the inadequate and even misleading subtitles create another interplay of voice and opacity.

Yet while both Spivak and Glissant have their relevance and could be productively employed in thinking about the workings of power and counterdiscourse in this film and the publicity furor around it, there is another factor as well, a methodological and theoretical blind spot precisely in the location of the Indigenous voice and Indigenous agency with respect to technocultural interaction. There are blindingly obvious reasons why many of the younger Maya activists these days are choosing radio, social media platforms like Facebook and Twitter, and alternative websites like the phenomenal online/DVD video news project Tz'ikin TeVé for sharing both fiction and nonfiction with their audiences. Older technologies, like the book, are much more recalcitrant for effective and timely sharing with the target audience. To choose, by way of illustration, perhaps the most commented example of an Indigenous Guatemalan woman's story, the hyper-familiar testimonio of Nobel Prize winner Rigoberta Menchú Tum, *Me llamo Rigoberta Menchú y así nació mi conciencia* (*I Rigoberta Menchú* 1982), is to also remind ourselves that within Guatemalan Indigenous communities there are almost no ideal readers for Menchú's book; it's a contradiction in terms, since the collective story has been more effectively shared in its entirety by other means, because books are expensive luxuries, and very few of her people can read, either Spanish or Kiché (this is not an original comment; Doris Sommer makes this point as well [1999, 130]).

Furthermore, as Doris Sommer commented long ago in her 1999 book, *Proceed with Caution*, not only are Latin America Indigenous voices constantly mediated—albeit often by well-meaning allies—but those allies tend to forget that the stories they hear are specifically shaped by deeply rooted colonial histories that define and overwhelm such asymmetrical collaborations. Thus, as Sommer writes: Menchú's "secrets stopped me then, and instruct me now in other contexts" (115), and she continues later in this meditation: "it is the degree of our foreignness, our cultural difference that would make her secrets incomprehensible. We could never know them as she does, because we would inevitably force her secrets into our framework" (122). In the twenty years since Sommer wrote this text, Rigoberta Menchú continues her activist work, through her foundation, her books, her speeches, and her video presence. Strikingly, she has traveled with Jayro Bustamante since the release of *Ixcanul*, to talk about the importance of this film and to celebrate its contribution to presenting powerful stories that echo the diversity of Mesoamerica.[5]

As he has commented in numerous interviews, Bustamante grew up in the area represented in this film, with his mother, who was a medical officer. There he learned Kaqchikel from his childhood nanny, who discouraged him from speaking that language in public. Much of the filming was done there, on his grandfather's coffee plantation near Lake Atitlán. The original María's story was among many he heard as a youth, told to him originally in Kaqchikel, then rewritten in French for a film school project, translated into Spanish, retranslated into Kaqchikel, then adapted by the actors (see the 2016 interview with Carolina A. Miranda). This story of the story behind the film has been repeated many times, giving rise to the commentary that this is an ethnographic film (something the filmmaker denies), while retaining a familiar, structured division between viewer and filmic subject familiar to most of us Northern/Western audience members to whom the ethnographer speaks; his subject/object provides the context and the local color.

The actors, in choosing to participate in this project and in cocreating the script with Bustamante, point to a more complex understanding. These Kaqchikel speakers are negotiating with a globalized, integrated, and technologically sophisticated network in which their exoticization can be seen as a necessary marketing tool for survival. As coscriptwriters for their own roles, in a film based on experiences that have happened to individuals from their community, these participants in *Ixcanul* demonstrate one way the subaltern speaks, and is heard, in a platform that has real and virtual technocultural agency. If their contribution has been minimized by interviewers and forgotten by the mainstream audience, it nevertheless does not eliminate their crucial formative role in setting out the terms of this interplay in local histories and literacies, where key issues of gender, reproductive rights, youth rights, labor rights, the right to immigrate or the right to stay home, the legacy of genocide, and the unresolved question of adoption and its relation to child and adult trafficking have become key talking points in many print publications, but also in Maya outlets like Tz'ikin TeVé's *Claro y pelado.*

I don't want to focus my discussion on this prestidigitation, however. Nor will I extend this discussion in terms of the film's plot and its central focus on María, whether in terms of a future in a legendary "north" she hardly knows how to imagine except as "on the other side of the volcano," or the predestination of her life, filmically evident when we realize the first sequence and the last create a frame, with her mother dressing her as the foreman's bride. Instead, this Kaqchikel history of relationships cannot be separated from another, sinister history associated with Indigenous Guatemalan women, of seeing them from outside as "breeders" for an international adoption/reproductive surrogacy/medical waste market.[6]

MOTHER LOVE

From the outset of the film, in their twinning and often silent companionship as they work, we see María's inevitable future of becoming her mother—where her mother's identity is consumed, and mother love is routed through abjection. This is first visible in the work-hardened hands that layer the bridal clothes and usher her daughter from her beautiful potential to her future nonentity as mother to the children of a man who has already exploited and threatened her family, and later in the film we see her love/helplessness in the mother's repeated pleading gesture, as she reaches out to beg for the return of her grandchild. Indeed, once the child is born, María's own agency reduces itself to the narrow frame of anguishing over her lost baby boy/girl.

What work does such sacrificial love do, ideologically? Jean Tan—whose work specifically focuses on Filipina migrant mothers and their surrogates—reminds us that motherhood, like all human exchanges, is a socially mediated practice, warning of the danger of universal theorizing, which tends to award dominant culture perspectives a paradigmatic status. Given the contested nature of claims about motherhood, she argues that we should take a dialectical approach, resisting the universalizing impulse as well as what she calls the "absolutizing tendency of particularism" (2012, 114). From the dominant culture side of this analysis, she traces out the cultural stickiness of the association of motherhood with the abject, in following Julia Kristeva's theorization of the iconography of the Virgin Mary and baby Jesus. Tan writes:

The metaphorics of separation and lost unity that organizes our understanding of maternity, as it focuses on the unique, irreplaceable relation between mother and child, is of a piece with the language of melancholic identification with the lost child. The longing "to experience within her own body the death" of her son is but the inversion of the anguish of delivering her child into the world and cutting off her union with him. . . . In identifying the mother with the womb, the woman (conceived as "the maternal body") is alternately figured as Mother Nature—a kind of infinite resource for the child's need—or as the abject body—the body that is risked and sacrificed by and for the child it shelters from as well as delivers to the world. (119–20)

Of course, abjection is also considered a virtue in many Latin American dominant culture frameworks; as is clear in the construction of "la madre abnegada," whose imaginary power perversely derives from her degree of silent suffering (Ladina Chiapanecan Rosario Castellanos wrote eloquently about this point).

In a dialectical swerve, Tan rearticulates maternity as "a segmented reality, with a series of phases and with a multiplicity of roles, in which we come to see that the mother is granted her subjectivity only when her subjectivity is allowed to slip away from—to differ from—her maternity, and when maternity itself is conceived as differing from itself, and thus opening itself to being performed by multiple agents" (120). Thus, motherhood in the first instance in Westernized culture is always already defined as loss, as in Kristeva's sense of a loss of an original unity, and framed through reference to an idealized distant/past, and a fascination with Othered cultures that seem to speak to this past. Tan proposes a different take on motherhood that would hold this Western idea in dialogue with contemporary experience of motherhood that includes separation from the child through the mother's migration to seek a better future for her child, and the distant mothering that ensues, via her agents. Tan explores the decomposition of traditional, limited notions of motherhood by looking at it longitudinally, thinking through the idea of surrogates who mediate the mother-child relation and take on a range of maternal activities. Thus, if one version of María's story has to do with the loss of her child, and her mother's frantic, ineffective efforts to have the child returned to them, another—via her father's insistence on the child's adoption into a northern family—would include maternity's negotiation with this other mother, and with surrogacy.

Internally, the film shows us two kinds of mothers and relations to motherhood, both holding fast to claims of men (both Indigenous and Ladino) over a Mayan woman's body as an exchangeable commodity. In the background of María's story is a parceling out of the process of reproduction into two distinct historical strands, one traditional and one more recent. *Ixcanul* highlights the tender connections between mother and daughter, as in the scenes in the *temazcal*, with the mother's loving cleansing of her adult daughter's pregnant body, as well as the tougher love manifested in her multiple efforts to get María to abort by drinking an herbal tea or jumping up and down.

THE TRAFFICKED CHILD

I want to turn to a key character that we never see, a character whose gender we don't know: the tenacious child that clings to life in María's womb. We never really learn if María and Pepe's child is a boy or a girl; we equally don't know if s/he is alive or dead, if the child was adopted into a rich family in the north (as her father imagines) or trafficked for other more sinister purposes, including the organ trade. As Gloria Chacón notes in comments on an earlier draft of this chapter, "María seems to know the unborn child's gender in a kind of 'ancient secret' way signaled by her mother's admonishment that she did not count her moons thereby getting pregnant and later learning that Maria's knowledge of the unborn child's gender is also about keeping count of the moon." In any case, our confusion at this crucial point matches that of the main characters, whose lack of knowledge of Spanish or reliable guidance to the Ladino medical and legal system leave them without any hope of recovering the child. By shifting focus to the trafficked child, I want to make a swerve that brings together two technologies that comment on the multiple and complicated ways that Guatemalans (or the idea of Guatemalan-ness) interact with northern systems of exchange, whether of excess labor, excess bodies, or humans seen as waste.

The original tale, as Bustamante recounts it, was both less and more shocking than its filmic version. Unlike the character in the film, his source for the María story did not marry; she did, however, go to prison for four months for child trafficking (a fate that the city police directly states would be the outcome if the film character María tried to get her child back). Xinico Batz writes, asking precisely about Bustamante's responsibility to his material and to the woman who shared this painful experience, and the evasion of responsibility implicit in his insistence that this is just a fiction, based on his free interpretation of an individual's story: "Why react to the movie? Because in the very words of the author, *Ixcanul* is based on the real story of a woman that he himself knew. . . . Would the film have had the same uptick without the Indigenous base that it uses? Of course, to accept that 'Maya culture' was the fundamental pillar upon which he erects his material would imply a great responsibility in a country as racist and unequal as Guatemala. In my opinion, this is a contradiction" (2016, Part II).[7]

The film internally posits its resolution of this contradiction in the juxtaposition of, and contrast between, stunning, starkly beautiful remote and unfamiliar landscapes with equally unfamiliar and aesthetically pleasing beliefs, customs, and daily practices, balancing an unfamiliar language (to most of the potential audience) and the long silences of companionable labor in the rural setting. This beauty and companionship is broken up by hints of violence both from nature and from outside humans: the snakes that make fieldwork dangerous and kill animals, the intrusion of Western poisons.

At the same time, the shock of the encounter with modern, legally enforced child trafficking practices in the city hospital reminds us that what we call "tradition" and what we call "modernity" cross each other continually and engage in direct or slipwise negotiations across a range of practices, which in this film are generally mediated through the material technology of print and the authority of paper. Midway through the film, María's father relaxes one evening while waiting for his dinner by leafing through a magazine that Ignacio gave him; this magazine later becomes his point of reference for how his grandchild must be living in the north. In the hospital, a bored employee encourages María's parents to expedite the paperwork by having them press their unconscious daughter's fingerprint on a form they can't read. Later, a police officer surrounded by paper indifferently tells María's parents that it was their obligation to see the child before signing the papers, that if they open a complaint about child theft, the first person to go to jail will be María, and her parents will follow her into custody. He then shoos them away, clearly uninterested in either the spirit or the letter or the law, or anything that looks like justice.

In fact, already on the mountain, we knew about the differential distributions of and access to modernity via official circuits of technopolitics, the biometrics of identification and citizenship, and how those practices are tied up with question of distance, ethnicity, and language. A government representative identifying herself in Spanish as coming from the Ministerio de Salud stops by for what she calls the collection of census data, and she conducts a cursory inspection of the family's circumstances (no electricity, no running water, no permanent address, she notes to herself), observations made without leaving the shadow of the pickup truck in which she arrived. The census taker with her checklist establishes a legal identity for the family with respect to the state, albeit a very tentative one, a process later reinforced by the thumbprint on the medical document and the threat of incarceration if the family pursues a formal legal complaint. In each case, these official maneuvers and documents are mediated by Ignacio, a highly self-interested and unreliable translator.

This Kaqchikel family does not know Spanish and has rarely left the region, but they *do* know that their exploiters come from this side of the mountain and live in the city. The other side of the volcano is where coffee, men, and trafficked babies go, and they have considerable lore built up about how people live in those remote places. They also know that the other side of the mountain is where snakes (and antivenom) come from, and the film hints at a rich storytelling practice that will account for the good and evil brought by these foreign ideas/beings. Their side of the volcano, in this structure, serves as a reservoir for goods, labor, and babies, all of which enter the transnational market, albeit in different ways.

Coffee can be discussed straightforwardly. The men work as coffee pickers and sell their labor locally for the meager wages that do not quite cover their families' needs (if they are responsible family men) or that pays for the liquor sold to them by the same foreman who has just exchanged the beans for a few tokens, keeping them locked in place as debt peons. There is an easy equivalency here: coffee for liquor, as if the alchemical exchange of these two commodities exhausts all possibilities of discussion. This is the first poison, and the theme of excess is graphically demonstrated by the men urinating away their income after consuming the alcohol.

As embodied by Pepe, the men who leave the plantation, seeking their fortune in the north, are already surplus population, bad workers, unattached, unwanted, teenaged human waste. We know that the north fears/demonizes Pepe as excess and excessive for different reasons and needs/solicits his labor (hers too, but he doesn't know that. He is needed in farms and construction, she is needed as a maid or a nanny). María tells him that if he wants to go to work in the north, he needs to learn Spanish first—a not unreasonable suggestion. He tells her that it is because of attitudes like hers that the country never progresses—his own imaginary engagement with futurity. He carelessly fathers a child while drunk, telling María the old wives' tale that she can't get pregnant the first time, and their child—unexpected but eventually wanted by the traditionally oriented small family of María and her parents—is also, and at the same time, a waste product, a problem that the foreman, Ignacio, needs to solve in order to bring about his desired goal of marriage to this nubile young woman, now even more valuable since she has been proven to be able to bear healthy children, but free of commitments.

Commentators who speak Kaqchikel say that it is a visual, conceptual language, so different from Western languages that the subtitles (in Spanish, English, and French)[8] offer interpretations rather than direct translations of the characters' dialogues.[9] We get a hint of this conceptual structure in the complexity of key images that guide the plot. The venomous (or sacred) snakes, for example, have come to infest the area, killing cattle, destroying lives and livelihoods. Their evil comes from outside the region and is a recent plague for the farmers. The foreman tries to control the plague, bringing in poison made in the United States, a place known for its superior technology, but the poison, for whatever reason, doesn't work in this mountain. As Jennifer Gómez Menjívar noted in her comments on an earlier draft of this chapter, "María's parents 'lose faith'/'pierden fe' in the manufactured chemicals. Their beliefs and hopes lead them elsewhere. Here, where first world solutions fail, the snakes' poison can—perhaps—be nullified by the power of a fearless pregnant woman. The snakes are, in some sense, the representation of the evils of capitalism that are elsewhere exemplified in the cycle of exploitation and debt around coffee and liquor. The snake is also a symbol for a more human and masculinist poison: Pepe and Ignacio, in the first instance, two snakes, no doubt about it. And the city police officer—another snake, out for his own interests and with no concern for protecting or defending the underdogs who come to him for help."

Contesting the snake, at some level, is the restless, revisionary, feminine energy embodied in María and echoed in the wisp of smoke from the volcano. Both images attach to a different understanding of nature and human relationships that does not entirely match up with the tradition of the European enlightenment, though the Kaqchikel understanding of their own history and land is necessarily shot through with the poisons of colonialism. The film's critique of imperialism and of Indigenous gender inequities is quite evident.

The scientific process of creating antivenom is a little like reproduction. It is made "by collecting venom from the relevant animal and injecting small amount of it into a domestic animal. The antibodies that form are then collected from the domestic animal's blood and purified" (Wikipedia, "Antivenom," n.d.). How does this scientific process map onto the social processes described in the film? The pregnant girl's body is supposed, by local religious belief, to serve as a kind of antivenom, purifying the fields and scaring away the poisonous snakes. María is let down three times in this brief moral tale: first by the ignorant boy, who told her she couldn't get pregnant the first time; then by her mother and the spiritual leader, who gave her the misleading information (or information she misunderstood) about the relation between pregnancy and snakes;[10] and then, once snake-bitten, by the ignorant social worker in the hospital, who either arrogantly presumed that Ignacio's translation was transparent, when all the time poison was being poured into her ear and the child was stolen, or was actively complicit in child trafficking herself.

The child then figures a certain kind of surplus reproductive material—living or dead, boy or girl—and this figure is at the heart of this plot, even as s/he is shunted to the side, never seen, the very epitome of a semiliving object. We know only scraps about the child's potential fate, through dialogues we overhear in medias res, unfaithfully translated by Ignacio, whose self-interest shapes what he tells María and her family. We know that there is some "service" offered to poor families; Ignacio says it is the cost of a coffin; we later learn María has signed away her maternal rights in a slipshod process in which culpability rests on her. The child moves mysteriously through the medical institution via a piece of paper marked with María's thumbprint taken while semiconscious and moves through the legal establishment as a potentially trafficked/legally adopted baby (or fragmented body parts). Thus, an adoptive child is imagined as a gift. And biomedical waste is a gift, perhaps the greatest of all gifts, giving life.

It is by way of this very indeterminacy, in this restriction of the child to the by-product of a series of paper maneuvers, that this "traditional" family is brought into contact with one of the most controversial aspects of high tech modernity, whereby brutality and profit are hidden under a language of a precious gift offered and moving freely from southern to northern participants: the tertiary biomedical industry that traffics in medical waste as the key building blocks for cutting-edge science. I am referring here to the "selective reductions" of implanted fetuses from assisted reproduction services, the nurtured stem cell lines, cancerous tumors, surplus of all sorts, profitably manipulated without consent—as revealed in the United States in Rebecca Skloot's important 2010 book, *The Immortal Life of Henrietta Lacks*—and as remains common practice worldwide. In the case highlighted in this film, too, consent is blurred and the lives of poor people of color are cannibalized to make northern lives more pleasant.

In a conversation between the father and daughter near the end of the film, both presume María's child is alive; her father tries to console himself and her with the story that the child is living a happy life, growing up in a garden, learning to speak English. María, more pragmatic, retorts that *she's* too young to speak. This is an old story, that echoes another story, that of Guatemala's years as the per capita adoption capital of the world, until 2007, when widespread abuse became so internationally notorious that almost all legal adoption was shut down following the ratification of The Hague Conventions (which were created largely in response to abuses in three countries, including Guatemala). That story, so familiar to rural Guatemalans, circulates through oral tales, like the one shared with Bustamante, and constitutes an important body of knowledge produced and circulated among people who have had little access to national or international technologies for wider distribution until very recently, but who—perhaps—can see the value of making these abuses known through the visual/aural technology of cinema.

Those were the years of baby factories, when Mayan women were perceived as marketable for their reproductive capacity, precisely because Ladino society saw them as having no other value, and where those women who objected were frequently treated by police as black marketeers who had changed their minds about selling their children (Rotabi and Bromfield 2014, 14–15). While Bustamante's film hints that the abuse of Mayan women's rights in this respect is ongoing, the question of the insertion of Mayan reproductive potential as a market value into economic discussions has taken a new turn, and one that makes the story even more urgent. It is the same logic of untapped reproductive potential that has spurred Guatemala's current interest in entering the ever-moving international reproductive surrogacy market as a viable alternative to the economies of adoption, as a way to take advantage of this same "wasted" womb space of women repulsively described as "breeders" (Rotabi and Bromfield 2014, 136). What seems to be currently holding Guatemala back from the booming industry in assisted reproduction surrogacy is the lack of the kind of clinical expertise associated with the notorious operations in India. The Central American actors who most profited from the adoption-era baby farm economic and structural model are ready to deploy their expertise once again.

María's baby, as adopted child or profitably sold body parts, urgently frames this discussion for today's global policymakers. Children are attractive loci for public policy statements since they are presumed to be valuable, presumed to be innocent, presumed to speak to our hopes for the future: the opposite of an unruly subject. Infants are considered especially vulnerable—and especially valuable, both ethically and economically—within this framework. Accordingly, "there is a large body of literature related to concerns about child sales into adoption—especially across international boundaries" (Smolin 2010, 453). In this context, it cannot surprise us that the 1989 Convention on the Rights of the Child is the most universally agreed upon and ratified human rights treaty (Grandinier 2010, xx). Likewise, the 1993 Hague Convention on Protection of Children and Co-operation in Respect to Intercountry Adoption has been signed by well over eighty nations, and its central principle is the best interests of the child, generally understood to include the child's right to be raised by their biological family, though without any provision to economically support that family in situations of dire deprivation.

It is this inconsistency in the concept of "best interests" that has long plagued legal scholars, who recognize that the concept is a universalizing frame. Whose authority determines "best interests"? In Guatemala, for instance, the irregular notarial adoption system has been taken to mean that Indigenous rights are unclear, while, in the context of this film, the Indigenous father can reasonably argue the right of the child to grown up in a U.S. house with a garden, speaking English rather than Kaqchikel or Spanish. These considerations, of course, however mediated, only obtain for the live, healthy, adopted child, and there is another, very unsavory alternative where the "gift" and the "best interests of the child" collide dramatically. At the same time as the adoption scandals were revealed, widespread rumors of traffic in children's organs have been circulating in Guatemala since the early twenty-first century, though independent international investigators have found no conclusive evidence either way. This form of child-trafficking—where infants bring the highest prices for adoption and may be sold for their organs—is the focus of international private law like The Hague Convention in its rulings since the 1990s. Thus, the Hague-sponsored investigations in Guatemala that found such rumors to be "without justification" also "attest to the existence of a large-scale traffic in children under the cloak of adoption," a more nebulous category. The van Loon report that led to The Hague Convention registers, without naming, this concern, attesting to "practices of international child trafficking either for purposes of adoption abroad, or under the cloak of adoption, for other—usually illegal—purposes" (Smolin 2010, 453). Those reports are "paper maneuvers," echoed in the film in all the various versions of official paper; what The Hague calls the rumors, and we might think of as the Kaqchikel oral histories, are precisely the kinds of stories shared with

Bustamante, reframed and rearticulated for wider distribution by activist actors like Telón, or, in other circles, articulated through exposés by powerful and eloquent young journalists like Andrea Ixchíu of Red Tz'ikin.

In that context, Guatemala's notoriously corrupt and highly profitable notarial system for intercountry adoption was put under intense scrutiny for its proven and widespread use of baby farms, child laundering, and abduction into adoption. It was clearly noncompliant with The Hague Convention, and vested interests in that country initially opposed Guatemalan ratification, which would close down a very profitable business that at its peak sent one in every one hundred Guatemalan children out of the country, mostly to the United States. Thus, when the United States ratified The Hague Convention, Guatemala lost its market, since the United States could no longer adopt from that country. This put pressure on their system and led to a change in Guatemalan policy. It was not, however, any abstract concept of "best interests" that drove U.S. policy, just as it was not a new-found concern for human rights in Guatemala: "anti-trafficking concerns apparently were far less central to Mr. Pfund and the United States than they had been to Hans van Loon and other nations. Indeed, it seems likely that the United States was focused, as a receiving nation, on maintaining access to children for intercountry adoption, and on protecting the role of private agencies and individuals as independent participants" (Smolin 2010, 457). Guatemala was getting just too messy, and widespread knowledge of human rights abuses was bad publicity.

María is identified with the volcano: she wants to erupt but her incipient rebellion is stifled, and it is clear that she won't. She yearns to find a different life but can't. In the context of the film she is limited to the role as bioreactor to the semiliving child (object for adoption or body parts for organ transfers), while she struggles against stereotypes that see her in terms of her labor value or reproductive potential. If she had accompanied Pepe on his trip north, there would have been an eight-in-ten chance of being raped on the way, and in the United States she would provide care work or sex work; in Guatemala her labor is likewise domestic and reproductive under a coercive, brutal structure, where loving parents make the best of a limited range of bad choices on her behalf.

Bustamante's film most directly references indigeneity via nostalgia, an old trope for Westerners who associate unfamiliarity with the past (of human race). Yet hidden in the interstices of the film, and lurking just outside the frame, are warning signs that implicate all our futurity,[11] and do so through the careful negotiations of local Indigenous agents who are making their story known, in their voices, through complicated negotiations with modern global structures.

CONCLUSION

Elisabeth Burgos-Debray is credited as author of the first edition of *Me llamo Rigoberta Menchú*, published by Casa de las Américas in Cuba in 1983. By the time it was published in English in 1984, Burgos-Debray slipped to the editor role. In the introduction to this book, she describes how she, a Venezuelan activist, met Menchú in Paris, where the recordings that became the core of the book were made. Of the many controversies surrounding this important document, the dialogic situation of the two women is one that has been comparatively less foregrounded. But the unconscious legacies of colonialism are breathtakingly apparent. Burgos-Debray writes, "The first thing Rigoberta did when she got up in the morning was make dough and cook tortillas for breakfast. . . . She did the same at noon and in the evening. It was a pleasure to watch her," a pleasure that Burgos-Debray compares to watching the maids in her childhood home make *arepas* (xv–xvi). Likewise, in another telling misstep, while Burgos-Debray's introduction begins, echoing a tradition of Western autobiography, "this book tells the life story of Rigoberta Menchú" (xi), Menchú herself insists that her story is not individual but collective: "it's not only *my* life, it's also the testimony of my people" (1). It is not important in this context to belabor the point: the breakthrough of Menchú's voice was mediated by Western social science, colonial histories, print culture, and textbook adoption throughout the global north that sparked an industry in testimonio studies, culminating in the 1992 Nobel Peace Prize and the controversy about the book's strict eyewitness attention to fact. Of course, like all contemporary activist figures, Rigoberta Menchú has continued to grow and thrive; she now maintains an active social media presence, with 18,810 Twitter followers as of January 2019 and more than 79,500 YouTube videos in her name.

Thirty years later, in a move not too dissimilar from that of Elisabeth Burgos-Debray a generation earlier, Jayro Bustamante evokes his nanny as his point of entry into the world of the Kaqchikel speaking community of his youth, and in his film—based on a true story, but not strictly ethnographic—also tells a tale that lingers between individual and collective, national and international. His medium, of course, is independent commercial cinema, and the film has been advertized as such, with all the publicity attending a well-oiled festival machine in the early twenty-first century, including a glossy webpage, Facebook site (currently with 23,962 likes), and a robust personal Twitter feed with 1,400 followers. Meanwhile, elsewhere in the rapidly changing technocultural landscape, young Guatemalan Mayans are taking charge of telling their own stories, their own way. Independent journalist, elected leader in her home community of Totonicapán, and self-described "K'iche Rebelde" Andrea Ixchíu has 9,426 Twitter followers, and the online Guatemala City-based media company most associated with her, Red Tz'ikin, has 11,553 Facebook likes. Episode 12 of their signature video newscast *Claro y Pelado*—available online or on DVD—touches on many of the issues raised in different ways by people like Menchú and Bustamante. The program is hosted by Ixchíu, who in Episode 12 (August 3, 2016) shares anchoring duties, and alternating languages, with Chana Mucú. Dedicated to the assassinated Indigenous Honduran activist Berta Cáceres, segments in the newscast probe the implications of the "Ley de juventud" for Indigenous communities; speak to activists from around the country in numerous languages (Q'eqchi,' Kaqchikel, Q'anjobál, Ixil, K'iché) about reproductive and sexual health; query Indigenous activists from countries ranging from Central America to Chile about respect for women's rights; talk to an Ixil mother about her daughter's migration to the United States; and feature a fictional short film, *Cantel/Candelaria* (38,149 YouTube views), created in 2015 through a Red Tz'ikin workshop in Chisec, Alta Veracruz. The film is about a girl who becomes pregnant very young through unprotected sex with an irresponsible partner and is expelled from her family home as a result. Alicia Roxana Mucu Choc, the protagonist and producer of the film, introduces the film in Spanish to the audience, though the film itself is in Q'eqchi,' with Spanish subtitles.

As connectivity rises and prices of cell phones come down, we see the growth of Indigenous networks throughout the Americas, linking Mapuches to First Nations in Canada and increasing the opportunity for conversation, visibility, and a celebration of linguistic pluralism. It is easy to become overoptimistic in the celebration of the changes cyberspace is making possible; Bustamante's film reminds us, among other things, to be sensitive to the many pockets in this world without electronic access of any sort except for the privileged few, where technology is still based in orality, and papers are unintelligible and to be feared. And Pepe, if he ever made it to the United States, needs to be wary of his social media usage, as would his trafficked son/daughter: U.S. Homeland Security now collects all immigrant Facebook and Twitter feed information.[12]

NOTES

1. María's father always refers to the baby as a boy; María consistently corrects him and says she is a girl. There is no basis in the film to decide either way.

2. The term "indigenista" or "indigenismo" points to a style of socially conscious narrative authored by non-Indigenous writers, focusing on Indigenous concerns.

3. As of this writing, Coroy was in New York City for the filming of *Bel Canto*, based on Ann Patchett's novel, playing the terrorist Carmen alongside Julianne Moore's opera singer. Vargas notes: "it seems Hollywood's traditional crossover standards have been shaken up in a big way" from the traditional bombshell image and the expectation that imported Latin American actors be "dark enough to be exotic, white enough not to offend 'mainstream' sensibilities" (2017).

4. I am grateful to Jennifer Gómez Menjívar, who in her reading of an earlier version of this chapter pointed me to an even more recent controversy in this same magazine, when a July 2017 cover featuring Francesca Kennedy surrounded by Indigenous women provoked a firestorm of critique. *Look* withdrew the original cover, replacing it with a solo image of the Guatemalan businesswoman (see López 2017).

5. See, for example, her remarks at Premios Platino 2016 (Madrid) and "La voz del inmigrante" (AFI Festival in Hollywood).

6. "The term 'breeders' has been used as a descriptive (Corea 1985), and for social workers, this is an inhumane term lacking in dignity and respect for persons. However, the activity uses technology that is systematized by animal husbandry practices, and the pejorative use of the term breeders underscores the emotionally provocative nature of the subject of surrogacy practices" (Bromfield and Rotabi 2014, 134).

7. "¿Por qué reaccionar ante la película? Porque en las misma palabras del autor, *Ixcanul* se basa en la historia real de una mujer que él mismo conoció. . . . ¿Hubiese tenido la película el mismo repunte sin la base indígena que utiliza? Claro, aceptar que la 'cultura maya' fue el pilar fundamental sobre el que se rige su material le implicaría una gran responsabilidad en un país tan racista y desigual como Guatemala. En mi opinión, esto es una contradicción."

8. The film credits translation from Spanish to Kaqchikel to María Elisa Orón Cuca and Justo Lorenzo. Spanish subtitles were done by Pilar Peredo, César Diez, and Jayro Bustamante; English and French subtitles are credited to Stéphane Levine.

9. The variety of Kaqchikel used in the film might have negative implications for the circulation among Kaqchikel speakers. Anthropologist Xinico Batz, in a much reprinted series of commentaries for *La Hora* on *Ixcanul*, notes that "La he visto en mi idioma, en kaqchikel, algo que me impactó, pues es mi idioma natal y a pesar de ello no la entendí, el kaqchikel utilizado en los diálogos me pareció inentendible, algo que corroboré con otras personas kaqchikeles que tampoco la

entendieron" (2016) [I saw it in my language, in Kaqchikel, something impacted me, because it is my native language, and despite that I didn't understand it. The Kaqchikel used in the dialogues seemed to me incomprehensible, something that I corroborated with other Kaqchikel speakers who didn't undestand it either]. Photographer Ajpu Nicho (https://www.facebook.com/ajpu.nicho) responds on Xinico Batz's Facebook page that "la variante del kaqchikel que se utilizó en la película es de Santa María de Jesus, Sacatepequez, que fue la que hablan las actrices por ser de ahí (yo si lo entendí bien). Los subtitulos estuvieron mal traducidos al español, habían cosas que no tenían sentido" [the variety of Kaqchikel that is used in the film is from de Santa María de Jesus, Sacatepequez, which is the one that the actresses speak because they are from there (I understood it well). The subtitles were badly translated into Spanish; there were things that made no sense]. Nicho's response is very similar to that of a native Kaqchikel speaker who saw the movie with me: he also said that the film's language was comprehensible, but the Spanish highly inadequate. Thus, the dialogue resists clear reading outside of the target linguistic community.

10. Jennifer Gómez Menjívar makes an apposite clarifying comment in her notes on an earlier draft: "Her mother admitted that her story was nothing but hyperbole, meant to convey spiritual strength, not to be taken literally. María believed— according to the film—what a Kaqchikel girl should have recognized as a story that is part of an ancestral tradition of storytelling for the purpose of spiritual/ intellectual growth. The spiritual healer, on the other hand, did encourage her walk through the snakes, but we can see him as subject to Ignacio's will, much like María's parents."

11. This is a reference to the idea that children are our collective future, but also that organ transplants allow fortunate individuals to have futures. Local Indigenous agents are working within the structure of commercial cinema, while making space for their voices and concerns despite those restrictions.

12. See, e.g., Novak 2017.

REFERENCES

"Antivenom." n.d. Wikipedia. Accessed November 1, 2018. https://en.wikipedia.org/w/index.php?title=Antivenom&oldid=864194208.

Bromfield, Nicole F., and Karen Smith Rotabi. 2014. "Global Surrogacy: Exploitation, Human Rights and International Private Law." *Global Social Welfare* 1: 123–35. DOI 10.1007/s40609-014-0019-4.

Burgos-Debray, Elisabeth, ed. and intro. 1984. *I Rigoberta Menchú: An Indian Woman in Guatemala*. New York: Verso.

Castellanos, Rosario. 1984. *Mujer que sabe latín . . .* Mexico: Fondo de Cultura Económica.

Corea, Gena. 1985. *The Mother Machine: Reproductive Technologies from Artificial Insemination to Artificial Wombs*. New York: Harper and Row.

Glissant, Édouard. 2006. *Poetics of Relation*. Translated by Betsy Wing. Ann Arbor: University of Michigan Press.

Grandinier, Meg. 2010. "Introduction: Why Should the United States Ratify the Convention on the Rights of the Child?" *Child Welfare* 89 (5): 7–13.

Hague Conference on International Private Law. 2012. *A Preliminary Report on the Issues Arising from International Surrogacy Arrangements*. The Hague, Netherlands: Hague Permanent Bureau. https://assets.hcch.net/docs/d4ff8ecd-f747-46da-86c3-61074e9b17fe.pdf.

Haimowitz, Rebecca, and Sinha Vaishali. 2010. *Made in India* (documentary film). http://www.madeinindiamovie.com.

Harvard Health Letter. 2012. "Putting the Placebo Effect to Work." April 2012. http://www.health.harvard.edu/mind-and-mood/putting-the-placebo-effect-to-work.

López, Esvin. 2017. "Revista Look Magazine retira polémica portada de este mes ante críticas." *Publinews*, July 5, 2017. https://goo.gl/859AVM.

Menchú, Rigoberta. 2015. "'Ixcanul' inspira sentimientos." YouTube video, 5:42, posted November 29, 2015, https://youtu.be/sjnRaSU2ehc.

Menchú, Rigoberta. 2016. "Premios PLATINO 2016—Rigoberta Menchú comenta Ixcanul." YouTube video, 3:28, posted June 22, 2016, https://youtu.be/FeKQPl8VM4w.

Miranda, Carolina A. 2016. "How 'Ixcanul' Director Jayro Bustamante Found a Feminist Tale on a Guatemalan Volcano." *Los Angeles Times*, January 6, 2016. http://www.latimes.com/entertainment/arts/miranda/la-et-cam-jayro-bustamante-ixcanul-guatemala-palm-springs-film-fest-20160106-column.html.

Novak, Matt. 2017. "US Homeland Security Will Start Collecting Social Media Info on All Immigrants October 18th." Gizmodo (website), September 26, 2017. https://gizmodo.com/us-homeland-security-will-start-collecting-social-media-1818777094?utm_medium=sharefromsite&utm_source=Gizmodo_facebook.

Perrin, David. n.d. "Ixcanul: An Interview with Director Jayro Bustamante." Berlin Film Journal (website). Accessed January 1, 2017. http://berlinfilmjournal.com/2015/02/ixcanul-an-interview-with-director-jayro-bustamante.

Rotabi, Karen Smith. 2014. "Force, Fraud and Coercion: Bridging from Knowledge of Intercountry Adoption to Global Surrogacy (Working Paper No. 600)." *International Institute of Social Studies*, September 2014. https://econpapers.repec.org/paper/emseuriss/77403.htm.

Rotabi, Karen Smith, and Nicole Footen Bromfield. 2012. "The Decline in Intercountry Adoptions and the New Practices of Global Surrogacy: Global Exploitation and Human Rights Concerns." *Affilia* 27 (2): 129–41. http://journals.sagepub.com/doi/abs/10.1177/0886109912444102?journalCode=affa.

Skloot, Rebecca. 2010. *The Immortal Life of Henrietta Lacks*. New York: Random House.

Smolin, David N. 2010. "Child Laundering and The Hague Convention on Intercountry Adoption: The Future and Past of Intercountry Adoption." *Louisville Law Review* 48: 441–98.

Sommer, Doris. 1999. *Proceed with Caution, When Engaged by Minority Writing in the Americas*. Cambridge, Mass.: Harvard University Press.

Spivak, Gayatri. 1988. "Can the Subaltern Speak?" In *Marxism and the Interpretation of Culture*, edited by Cary Nelson and Lawrence Grossberg, 271–313. New York: Macmillan.

Tan, Jean P. 2012. "Missing Mother, Migrant Mothers, Maternal Surrogates and the Global Economy of Care." *Thesis* 112 (1): 113–32.

Vargas, Andrew S. 2017. "Maya Actress María Mercedes Coroy of 'Ixcanul' to Star Alongside Julianne Moore in 'Bel Canto.'" *Remezcla*, March 1, 2017. http://remezcla.com/film/maya-actress-maria-mercedes-ixcanul-bel-canto.

Williams, Fiona, and Deborah Brennan. 2012. Special Issue: "Care, Markets and Migration in a Globalizing World." *Journal of European Social Policy* 22 (4): 355–450.

Xinico Batz, Sandra. 2016. "El síndrome de Ixcanul: ¿entre realidad y película?" Pts. 1, 2, and 3. *La Hora*, September 17 and 24 and October 1, 2016. http://lahora.gt/sindrome-ixcanul-realidad-pelicula-parte-i.

6

JOYSTICKS AND JAGUARS

Bribri-Inspired Games in Neoliberal Costa Rica

MAURICIO ESPINOZA

Despite Costa Rica's popularity as a tourist destination, the country's Indigenous population has remained largely unknown due to their relatively small numbers and the international focus on the much larger and influential Maya cultures in Central America. However, certain cultural aspects of Costa Rica's *indí-gena*[1] communities (words, visual elements, narratives, and myths) have found unprecedented public visibility during the twenty-first century—particularly in the discourses of marketing, ecotourism, social/environmental awareness, and new forms of media and popular culture. This explosion into the public realm appears to be connected to a wider effort to resist the negative consequences of neoliberal policies and globalization that have profoundly impacted Costa Rican society and culture in the past three decades. One salient example and productive case study is Ditsö (meaning "seed" in the Bribri language spoken mainly in southeastern Costa Rica), a nonprofit educational endeavor that involves *indígena* and non-*indígena* scholars and artists in an effort to promote and revalue Indigenous stories and knowledge. The project's main goal is "to increase awareness, not just among Costa Ricans but among people all over the world, about the great cultural heritage that our Indigenous peoples possess" (Mariño, personal communication).[2] Started in 2012, Ditsö has produced coloring books with information about Indigenous culture, trading cards with Native characters, a board game based on Bribri stories, and a new interactive video game, *El Camino del Useköl* (The Useköl's Way). This chapter analyzes Ditsö's products and discourses as examples of reterritorialization and alternative gaming, within the context of increased "visibilization" of Indigenous culture and issues throughout the Americas.[3] It also engages with the debate regarding *authenticity* and *appropriation* that typically arises from civil society or government efforts to promote Native culture globally.

MARKETABLE INDIGENEITY

The turn of the new millennium has ushered in an increase in the use of Indigenous words, images, and themes employed in the marketing of a variety of products, services, and organizations in Costa Rica.[4] One notable example was the selection of the Cabécar word *kölbi* (tree frog) by the state-owned telecommunications company (Instituto Costarricense de Eletricidad, or ICE)[5] as the brand name of its new mobile phone service in 2009. As ICE prepared to go up against powerful transnational brands such as Movistar and Claro in the highly profitable cellular market, it needed a way to convince Costa Rican clients that its services were competitive and that it had devised a fresh look to advertise them. ICE's choice of a tree frog and the Indigenous word kölbi to promote its products and services was not made at random. The combination of the Cabécar term and the stylized green frog represents a marketing strategy that seeks to differentiate a national service (of "all Costa Ricans") from those offered by foreign companies allied to the Central American Free Trade Agreement (CAFTA) and neoliberalism.[6] On the one hand, the Cabécar language (though unfamiliar to non-Cabécares) is exclusively Costa Rican, while the green frog immediately conjures up nature and is one of the symbols most commonly used to promote the country as one of the world's top ecotourism destinations.[7] In other words, ICE resorted to nationalism as a marketing strategy, configuring the competition for the mobile phone market as a battle between national heritage and autonomy and foreign invaders. That is why it is unsurprising that the hashtag at the bottom of kölbi's website is #somosdelosmismos (we are just like you). This nationalist recognition conveys that customers should trust ICE and kölbi—because they are Costa Rican and not Spanish or Mexican or some other nationality, as are their competitors.

While kölbi is a high-profile example of the use of Native words and iconography in the Costa Rican context, there are many other instances of small businesses and nonprofit organizations tapping into Indigenous culture to promote their products and causes. One of them is Sibö, a manufacturer of organic gourmet chocolates that chose the name of the main Bribri deity for its company, confections, and cafés.[8] The name Ditsö is also used by a political organization that works to protect the rights of the country's Indigenous communities.

This proliferation of Indigenous names, images, narratives, and digital products in the past few years attracts attention, first, for being so visible as well as for occupying such a diverse range of spaces in Costa Rica's public discourse and economy in the new millennium. A second point of interest is the counterintuitive nature of this phenomenon. In Costa Rica, Indigenous culture has been historically ignored and invisible in literature, film, official history, and school curricula. Likewise, Indigenous linguistic heritage (while present in Costa Rican Spanish and in the names of many towns and natural landmarks) has never been properly acknowledged or supported, let alone celebrated. There are a few exceptions, so few that they stand out exactly because of their peculiarity. Most Costa Ricans are familiar with the name *sukia* (shaman or healer from the country's Caribbean region) and the associated effigy employed by Labotorios Sukia, a local pharmaceutical company, to market its products since 1949. Costa Ricans and tourists alike would also recognize the name of marquee San José hotel Corobicí, established in 1976, which bears the name of a western Costa Rica cacique who lived during the time of Spanish conquest. And perhaps the most significant work of literature highlighting Indigenous culture and resistance is Tatiana Lobo's 1992 novel *Asalto al paraíso*, set during colonial times—but which obviously resonated with the quincentennial and the ongoing colonial situation of Indigenous peoples in Costa Rica.[9]

The question is, then, what motivated this sudden burst of interest in and use of Indigenous language and other cultural elements of the nation's original inhabitants? Why did the signs of indigeneity become more visible and less unusual in twenty-first-century Costa Rica? While there may be several answers to this question, my argument rests on the following factors. The noticeable "indigenization" of Costa Rica's public and cultural discourses represents one of various responses—from the government as well as from civil society—to the fast-paced and sometimes crippling impact of globalization and the neoliberal project that have transformed the country's (and the region's) society and economy in the past three decades. While this indigenization is brandished as a sort of weapon in the midst of this unequal and contingent battle, it also reveals the contradictions inherent to its display. In other words, the growing visibility of all things *indígena* as the banner of a Costa Rican-ness that feels threatened by foreign forces outside of its control makes even more salient the inequalities that still exist (and have in some cases increased) in the country, and which ironically disproportionately affect Indigenous people and other marginalized groups.

Most often, the initiatives to make Indigenous culture more visible are external, carried out without consultation with Native communities. Additionally, the use of images and legends that fuse Indigenous culture and nature has the effect of highlighting the contradictions that exist between Costa Rica's ecological reputation and its environmental protection policies, which routinely allow for the destruction of precious natural resources and even for the murder of environmentalists.[10] In this sense, it is a deceiving visibilization. If one does not critically explore what is behind the names and logos and narratives, one might end up assuming that the increase in the use of Indigenous culture elements in Costa Rica's public discourse points to a greater acceptance of Native heritage as part of the country's cultural fabric. Even worse, one might mistake it for a sign of greater equality. In reality, this growing visibility has the power of invisibilizing Indigenous people further: that is, it masks the harsh reality that hides behind the stylized and colorful slogans and brand names.

What does the increased visibilization of certain aspects of Costa Rican Indigenous culture mean for the country's Indigenous communities? Are these efforts capable of translating into the empowerment of Indigenous culture and language as national patrimony? Or are these just examples of cultural appropriation whose actual impact on Native lives will not go beyond marketing slogans and pretty graphics? Finally, are there any alternative models that can offer Indigenous communities more say in how they are made visible by the state? I will return to these questions after the analysis of Ditsö in the context of Costa Rican Indigenous culture and alternative gaming.

COSTA RICA'S INVISIBLE INDIGENOUS HISTORY

The history of Costa Rica's Indigenous peoples is marked by the country's position as a cultural bridge. The small territory that became known as Costa Rica sits on the frontier between two different cultural traditions. Its land includes people of Mesoamerican extraction (the Chorotegas of the northwestern province of Guanacaste, who migrated from Mexico between the sixth and seventh centuries), along with other ethnic groups of Chibchan origin who came from the lower parts of the Andes and possibly the Amazonian region (Ferrero 2000, 51–55). That Costa Rica served as a place of cultural confluence and interaction during pre-Columbian times should not come as a surprise. The country is part of a geographical and biological bridge that united North America and South America approximately three million years ago, although recent studies have suggested that the Central American Seaway that separated both land masses may have vanished ten million years earlier ("North and South America" 2015, n.p.). It is known that some twelve thousand to ten thousand years ago there were hunter-gatherers who lived in the region of Turrialba, between Costa Rica's Central Valley and the Caribbean slope. However, some Costa Rican archaeologists have hypothesized that the territory may have been settled much earlier, as recent research has suggested the presence of humans in the Central American isthmus at least thirty thousand years ago (Guevara and Chacón 1992, 14).

For thousands of years, these peoples developed a complex and original process of sociocultural evolution, domesticating crops such as maize and cassava and creating complex societies organized in *cacicazgos*. When the Spaniards arrived in the 1500s, there were around four hundred thousand Native inhabitants in Costa Rica, divided among at least fourteen *cacicazgos* (Guevara and Chacón, 14; Boza Villarreal 2014, 42). The Spanish conquest of this colonial province began in the 1560s. By the end of the sixteenth century, most of the Indigenous communities from the Central Valley (where a majority of Costa Ricans live today) had been reduced to Indian towns, subjected to the *encomienda* system and to tribute collection. Around the same time, Spanish presence had also consolidated along the Pacific and Caribbean coasts. During the remainder of the colonial period, the Spanish only managed to add a few more Indian territories under their control. However, the mountainous region of Talamanca in the eastern and southern parts of the country (home to the Bribris and Cabécares) as well as the northern plains (inhabited by the Malekus) completely escaped colonial control (Boza Villarreal, 44). The Talamanca region was the main site of resistance against the Spaniards, and numerous confrontations and rebellions have been recorded in history books. The town of Santiago de Talamanca was established in 1605 on the Caribbean slope along the current Costa Rica-Panama border, but the Indigenous population destroyed it five years later and halted Spanish expansion in the region (Rojas Conejo 2009, 5). The most significant rebellion in the Talamanca region took place in 1709, when all the Caribbean towns joined under the command of the cacique Pablo

Presbere to destroy in only a few days all Spanish missionary and military out-posts in their lands (Guevara and Chacón, 21–22).

Spanish conquest and colonization took a tremendous toll on Costa Rica's Indigenous population due to disease and slavery. By the late 1500s, the Span-iards had controlled 120,000 *indígenas* in the Central Valley, but by 1661 this population had been reduced to only about 10,000 people (Boza Villarreal, 44). The first census of Costa Rica's population took place in 1864. However, it only counted the Indigenous population of the Talamanca region, which was estimated at 10,500 to 12,500, or 8.7 to 10.4 percent of 120,449 total inhabitants for the entire country (Boza Villarreal, 59). Almost 150 years later, the 2000 national census counted 63,870 Indigenous people, or 1.7 percent of the country's population. Most of them (60.5 percent) were living within or near the country's twenty-two Indian reservations that existed at the time (Boza Villarreal, 41).[11] According to the 2011 national census, the country's Indigenous population is 104,143 (2.4 percent of the total population). This number includes 78,073 people who belong to specific Indigenous peoples and 26,070 who didn't report belonging to a specific Indigenous group. Of the total number of Indigenous people living in Costa Rica, only 48,550 reside within Indigenous territories (Instituto Nacional de Estadística y Censos 2013, 34). While the reservation system was established to protect Indigenous rights, particularly to land, this has not always occurred. In 1990, reservations encompassed 320,650 hectares, or 6.3 percent of the country's territory. However, conservative numbers esti-mate that only 60 percent of that land was actually in the hands of Indigenous people, with the rest having been invaded by migrant settlers or landowners throughout the years (Guevara and Chacón, 12). Today there are twenty-four "territorios indígenas" belonging to eight distinct ethnic groups: Bribri, Brunca or Boruca, Cabécar, Chorotega, Huetar, Maleku or Guatuso, Ngöbe or Guaymí, and Teribe or Térraba.[12]

The historical and demographic presence of Indigenous cultures in the Costa Rican territory—both past and present—is undeniable. However, the invisi-bilization of these peoples throughout the country's history is not a matter of numbers—but of racist attitudes. For example, many nineteenth-century Costa Rican scholars were certainly aware of the existence of Indigenous people in the country during that time, but in the few occasions that they mentioned them in their writings would be to clarify that they were reduced in numbers and completely isolated from the "true" Costa Rican population, which was "white, homogenous, healthy and robust" (Calvo 1887, 34).[13] Educational policies reflected this general attitude; for example, a school text from the 1940s taught that Costa Rica was "effectively the Caribbean's white nation" (León 1943, 33). Luis Demetrio Tinoco, who was the minister of education and first rector of the University of Costa Rica, explained the situation of Indigenous people in these terms in 1942: "Regarding these [aboriginal] individuals, there only remain a few groups in Talamanca, Boruca, Térraba and Guatuso, who live miserable lives and are decimated at an extraordinary pace, without having any influence on the progress and development of the country, just as they did not have any effect on its formation" (qtd. in Yglesias Hogan 1942, 1).[14] As we can see from these statements, official attitudes regarding Indigenous people in Costa Rica portrayed them as an insignificant portion of the country's population and historical development, emphasizing whiteness as the essence of Costa Rican-ness.

In fact, Costa Rica has represented itself through the reproduction of myths that emphasize its whiteness, equality, democracy, and security in contrast with other Latin American countries, Marcos Guevara and Rubén Chacón explain. As part of this mythologization, official history has long (and erroneously) stated that the few Indians who inhabited the country embraced all the developments brought by the Europeans and only a few foci of resistance took place in isolated regions. This official discourse also states that today, the few Indigenous communities that remain are on their way toward progress, assisted by the state's social programs, the system of reservations, and laws that guarantee their rights. However, reality shows that many Costa Ricans (Indigenous and non-Indigenous alike) still face a profound social inequality despite the country's democratic tradition, that the myth of peacefulness has led to conformism, and that the supposed "whiteness" of the population is no more than an image used by the tourism industry to attract visitors and financial or foreign investment (Guevara and Chacón 1992, 11). Furthermore, Guevara and Chacón summarize the Indigenous population's contemporary reality by stating that: "Costa Rica houses an Indian population not so numerous but qualitatively as important as that of other Central American isthmus countries; and despite having enjoyed a considerable indigenist legislation (comparatively), this is seldom carried out. Even worse: In other places, Indian populations plead for legally recognized rights. Here, those rights are recognized legally but violated in practice" (11).[15] What the authors describe is something Indigenous leaders and allies frequently criticize: the usurpation of land from Indigenous territories that are supposed to be protected and chronic failure by the National Commission on Indigenous Affairs and other governmental institutions to truly represent their interests.

Anthropologist Karen Stocker aptly summarizes the reasons for this systematic invisibilization and exclusion of Indigenous people from the Costa Rican national imaginary—and the impact this has had on their material reality. Stocker identifies three discourses (historical, legal, and anthropological) that "simultaneously create both an absence and an ambiguous presence of Indigenous peoples in Costa Rica" and which have "constructed a vision of the nation that ostensibly aims to assimilate and define Indigenous peoples but that in practice results in excluding them from the nation as a whole" (2005, 47). History, Stocker explains, has erased Indigenous people from the modern nation, whereas legal discourse has "officially declared their existence and enclosed them in reservations with the goal of acculturation"; and finally, anthropology "has evaluated each reservation according to a constructed hierarchy of perceived authenticity or legitimacy in each community's merit of reservation status" (47). In fact, most Costa Ricans' understanding of the country's Indigenous presence has been conditioned by the creation of the reservation system, which served to classify them and enclose them in "legitimate" areas where they could exist specifically as *indígenas*. Stocker sees the reservation system as an attempt by the Costa Rican government to promote assimilation and "cultural improvement" (i.e., through expansion of mandatory public schooling in Spanish and with approved national curricula and through implementation of Western medicine practices via the country's universal healthcare system), as "Indianness was something to be contained and eventually eradicated" for the ultimate goal of creating a homogenous nation (48). Even though reservations were meant to serve an assimilationist project, Stocker observes that in some instances they had the opposite effect: "[B]eing set apart promoted instead (among some members) an increased sense of ethnic difference. Thus, in some cases the imposition of a given identity, through the establishment of the reservation system, could lead to a reaffirmation of ethnic distinctiveness" (48).

It is precisely this "ethnic distinctiveness" (particularly through preservation of languages and a variety of cultural traditions) that has translated into the recent phenomenon of increased visibility of *lo indígena* in Costa Rican public discourses and popular culture, as exemplified by kölbi, Sibö, Ditsö, and other brand names or cultural products. It is also telling that the cultures represented in these discourses are predominantly the Cabécar and the Bribri—that is, those with the highest populations of Indians in the country (63.8 percent of the total), those who live in remote areas away from non-Indigenous Costa Ricans, those who have most successfully resisted assimilation by retaining their languages and traditions, and those with a well-documented history of resistance against Western incursion (Rojas Conejo, 1; Instituto Nacional de Estadística y Censos, 34). Employing Cabécar and Bribri language and culture transmits ideas of resistance (important for nationalist discourses), authenticity and connection with nature (important for social justice and fair-trade discourses), and difference and peculiarity (crucial for the fantastical and visually rich environments portrayed in games). While these characteristics seem admirable and work well for the purpose in which they have been employed, their implementation has so far done little to improve the material realities of Indigenous communities or even increase awareness of their plights.

EL CAMINO DEL USEKÖL: BETWEEN RETERRITORIALIZATION AND ALTERNATIVE GAMING

Videogames have not been a fertile ground for cultural or ethnic diversity, to say the least. A 2009 study of games released between 2005 and 2006 found that the most popular games had a greater percentage of white male characters than even the general U.S. population, and that Native Americans and Hispanic leading characters were nonexistent (Burgess 2011, et al.).[16] Even a decade later, Indigenous people or their cultures seldom appeared in the world of videogames, which follows the pattern of underrepresentation of Natives in popular culture and mainstream media (Newman 2012, n.p.). Native American video game characters are particularly rare. And when they do appear—for instance, Nightwolf from *Mortal Kombat* or Tal'Set from *Turok: Dinosaur Hunter*—they are often boiled down to generic, spiritual people, with all their cultural nuances lost in their depictions (Newman 2012, n.p.).

A few video and mobile games, however, have made efforts to avoid essentializing and stereotyping Native characters. For example, *Assassin's Creed III* (released in 2012) features a half-Mohawk, half-British assassin named Connor, who plays the role of an outsider during the game's American Revolution setting. The team at Ubisoft Montreal, which created the character, hired a Mohawk cultural consultant with the goal of avoiding stereotypes and factual errors (Newman 2012, n.p.). North American Indigenous game developers have also sought to bridge the representational gap in this industry. One noteworthy example is Elizabeth LaPensée, who is well-known for creating Indigenous characters (particularly strong female characters) for online gaming and ani-mation. Her games include *Invaders* (2015), *Honour Water* (2016), and *Thunderbird Strike* (2017). Against all odds, Latin American Indigenous cultures have actually been featured in a number of popular videogames. In *Crusader Kings II: Sunset Invasion* (2012), players have the option of staging an Aztec invasion of Western Europe, which effectively evokes discourses of *reconquista* and decolo-nialism. The games *Age of Empires II: The Conquerors* (2000) and *Age of Empires III: The War Chiefs* (2006) feature the Aztecs as a playable civilization, as well as Mayan and Inca armies. Additionally, *Medieval II: Total War* (2006) also features the Aztecs. A more interesting example is Ubisoft's *Theocracy* (2000), a game completely set in Mesoamerica in which various tribes from Mexico and Cen-tral America must prepare for the Spanish invasion.[17] Games featuring Indige-nous characters or culture developed in Latin American countries are rare. One example is *Tejo World Tour*, a smartphone application created by Bogotá-based Big Teeth Media in 2011. This game allows users to play the Colombian sport of *tejo*, of preconquest origin, in settings from around the world. There is also a new game, *Mulaka*, just released in 2018 by Mexico-based studio Lienzo. In this game, players become a Tarahumara shaman from northern Mexico who calls upon the powers of demigods (Joho 2017, n.p.). We can easily see from this brief listing that *El Camino del Useköl* is a rarity when it comes to games based solely on Indigenous culture and developed in Latin America.

   El Camino del Useköl is the latest and most ambitious project carried out by Ditsö (http://www.mcomunicacionvisual.com/ditso.htm), a project conceived by Costa Rican artist and graphic designer Jonathan Mariño and his wife Nancy Camacho. A self-described "geek" with an affinity for comics, videogames, and historical narratives, Mariño first learned about the wealth of stories and charac-ters contained in Costa Rican Indigenous cosmogony during his university years in the early 2000s. "I met a group of Indigenous students and then began to do research on my own, and became captivated by the stories and the characters. It was like an awakening, like opening your eyes to something new but which at the same time felt like your own. And I asked myself, 'How come I'm just now learning about this?'" (Mariño, personal communication).[18] After college, and before founding Ditsö, Mariño first developed an educational concept based on Costa Rican Indigenous characters that he and his design partners pitched to a local snacks company. "The idea was to include these collectible cards in their products. The company initially liked the idea, but then they asked for too many changes to the characters' depictions and descriptions, to the point that

I felt it negated the educational purpose of the cards. They paid good money, but I refused" (Mariño, personal communication). In 2011, Ditsö won the "Best Social Innovation" award from the University of Costa Rica's Foundation for Research. With the $1,000 from this award plus $2,000 in personal savings from Mariño and Camacho, the company produced the Ditsö board game, which was presented at the 2012 Costa Rican International Arts Festival. In 2014, Ditsö conceived the idea of a videogame, which received close to $40,000 in funding from the Ministry of Science and Technology. *El Camino del Useköl*, currently in its beta stage, was developed 100 percent in Costa Rica by the Omar Dengo Foundation.

The *useköl* is the highest figure of authority among the Bribris, combining spiritual and political powers that go beyond those of the *awa* (shaman) and the *cacique* (chief) (Castro, qtd. in Mariño 2016, "Investigación," 11–12). The characters and storyline of the game were created based on research about the figure of the *useköl* and shamanistic practices of the Bribri conducted by Mariño. For example, the *useköl* can be either a man or woman; he or she must go on a "journey of discovery" that allows him or her to acquire the necessary knowledge and skills to achieve his or her objectives; and he or she carries and wears distinctive objects, including a wooden stick that possesses special powers, amulets made from jaguar teeth and colorful bird feathers, and sacred stones for healing and seeing the future, among others (Mariño, 17–18). These characteristics and special objects are represented in the game, as players can choose either Siarke (male character) or Tanú (female character) to face the game's obstacles and try to become *useköl*. The characters, both primary and secondary, are also taken from Bribri cosmogony and legends. They include Sibö (the creator), Tsirú (cacao, Sibö's wife), the *awapa* (shamans), Dikum (the jaguar), Bi (evil spirits), and Sul (good spirits). The game also features places that are of particular importance for the Bribri, such as Ará (the Talamanca region where the Bribri live), Alto Lari (place where creation took place), Sulayöm (a sacred mountain located in Alto Lari), and Suré M (spiritual world that lies beyond the sun). The game's backgrounds include recognizable artifacts, buildings, and landmarks that are significant to Indigenous culture of southern Costa Rica, including *metates*, cone-shaped thatched-roof houses, and the iconic stone spheres of the Diquís Valley, which UNESCO declared a World Heritage Site in 2014.

The game begins with Bribri creation stories that introduce key characters, concepts, and locations. In general, *El Camino del Useköl* follows the familiar narrative and playing strategy[19] of mainstream games, but objects, powers, friends, foes, and other features have been replaced with elements from Bribri culture and stories. For example, players collect cacao seeds (the equivalent of coins in *Super Mario Brothers*), are confronted by antagonists such as the mischievous and scary Arabru (goblins), are aided by friends such as Kua'kua (butterfly spirit), and must overcome a number of challenges to collect valuable objects such as a jaguar teeth necklace. For Mariño, the main challenge in developing the game (particularly from a visual perspective) was to create a product that incorporated the conventions and playability of videogames to which people are accustomed while being as accurate and respectful as possible with the way Bribris and their cosmogony are represented:

> We have conducted extensive bibliographic and visual research, consulted with Indigenous and non-Indigenous experts, and worked with people from Indigenous communities. However, the information that's available is incomplete, because most stories have been transmitted orally and the visual record is limited. So, in order to create a congruent visual universe, sometimes we need to take certain liberties, but always doing our best to infer from available information. For example, no one knows for sure what the Arabru look like. We know that some Indigenous people did use scarifications, so we decided to portray these characters as being scarified to highlight their gruesome appearance. Other times we play a bit with fantasy: gold and jade artifacts are from different historical periods, but some of our characters wear both of them together. (Mariño, personal communication)

As is to be expected, some issues arose during the design of the game because of conflicting Westernized and Indigenous representational concepts. Alí García (Bribri), Director of Indigenous Languages at the University of Costa Rica and one of Ditsö's consultants, complained that the women in the game were "too skinny." García explains, "We see women differently. The tapir (Sibö's sister) is one of our most significant symbols of beauty, and so these ideals of people who are too skinny do not fit within the Indigenous culture's aesthetic ideals" (qtd. in Mariño 2016, 25).[20]

Ditsö's products, particularly *El Camino del Useköl*, can be viewed as an example of the phenomena of cultural reterritorialization and alternative gaming. Globally mediated resources (including video games) are being constantly adopted by new actors all over the world and reworked in specific local contexts. As James Lull explains, individuals culturally reterritorialize images, texts, and objects from the flow of global culture and make them their own in distinct ways: "Reterritorialization [. . .] is a process of active cultural selection and synthesis drawing from the familiar and the new. But creative construction of new cultural territories also involves new ways of interpreting cultural icons in processes of resignification. The entire cultural milieu [. . .] become symbolic resources to be used in ways that differ radically from their original meanings and functions" (1995, 161). In the case of *El Camino del Useköl*, reterritorialization works in multiple avenues. First, gaming is a concept first developed in industrialized nations such as the United States and Japan and then reterritorialized by developing nations (such as Costa Rica, which has a nascent video game industry). Mariño encountered Indigenous culture as something new and incorporated it into something that was familiar to him: video games and geek culture. Along these lines, many individuals who have played Ditsö's board game and video game approached them through their familiarity with these platforms. However, they were surprised by the newness of Indigenous themes. In the end, they realized that such newness actually represents something very close (though previously unknown) to their Costa Rican cultural heritage, in contrast with the common video game themes of medieval Europe, warfare, or other foreign influences. In this regard, the creation of *El Camino del Useköl* takes global symbolic resources and uses them in ways "that differ radically from their original meanings and functions" (Lull 1995, 161) in at least two ways: it gives a central role to local knowledge from a traditionally underrepresented and marginalized community that has been typically excluded from the flow of global culture; and it turns video games, which are generally created for entertainment and financial gain, into an educational tool.

The two reterritorialization functions just mentioned above directly connect with the concept of alternative gaming. Nick Dyer-Witheford and Greig de Peuter have posited that popular video games (particularly those that promote consumption and war) are "a paradigmatic media of Empire" (2009, xv), following the concept of Empire developed by Michael Hardt and Antonio Negri, whose two pillars are the market and the military. While most mainstream video games support the goals of Empire, Dyer-Witheford and de Peuter indicate that there are also forces within the world of gaming that challenge this purpose and seek to construct an alternative to Empire (xv). Following the slogan, "Don't hate the media, become the media," some examples of this alternative use of gaming include: "polity simulators," which involve players in issues of public policy formation, "serious games," which promote diverse social applications of gaming, and "Games for Change," which encompass social awareness mini-games "aim-ing to educate players about a variety of international political, ecological, and health crises" (Dyer-Witheford and de Peuter 2009, 200). Because its main purpose is educational and because it gives center stage to a culture ignored and invisibilized in contemporary media and popular culture, *El Camino del Useköl* fits within this concept of alternative gaming. Moreover, the fact that the game has been produced in Central America (where the gaming industry is still in its infancy) about a little-known Indigenous culture makes its alternative and potentially resistant nature even more pronounced and radical. This is because the game chooses to positively represent the Bribri culture as belonging to and representing the nation in a region where Native populations have been his-torically marginalized and have also been the target of bloody state repression.

That being said, several questions remain to be explored when analyzing the use of Indigenous visual and narrative elements in non-Indigenous-created brands and educational games: (1) Who benefits from increased visibility of Indigenous culture in new media and popular culture products? (2) Who is driving such portrayals and why? and (3) Are these products merely additional examples of the rampant appropriation of Indigenous culture by international clothing, crafts, tourism, art, music, food, and other industries? Cultural appro-priation impacts many subaltern groups, but it's often associated with Native communities and their heritage in literature about the topic. Following Eliza-beth Burns Coleman, I view cultural appropriation here as the process by which one non-Indigenous people take, use, and/or benefit from Native knowledge and/or depictions of their culture (2016, n.p.). In Costa Rica, the answer to the first question is a mixed bag that leans toward the side of negative appropriation. In the case of the kölbi mobile phone brand, there is no indication that ICE asked for permission from Indigenous communities to employ the Cabécar term in the creation of its for-profit brand and prominent advertisement cam-paigns, or that it consulted with them to find out their opinions on the matter. What can be gathered from ICE's way of proceeding in this case is that certain aspects of Indigenous culture (just like natural elements such as the tree frog that complements the kölbi brand) are part of the larger and "common" Costa Rican cultural heritage—and thus are free for the taking. In the case of Ditsö, the question of who benefits is less clear-cut. Mariño's enterprise is not-for-profit and has made a clear effort to develop its educational products in con-sultation with Indigenous scholars. It could be argued that the success of the kölbi brand is a positive step in vindicating the value of Indigenous language, which ICE has made ubiquitous throughout the country. However, the benefit to Indigenous communities is only symbolic, and just marginal and superficial at that. Another question arises here: should Indigenous words be protected under some kind of copyright law to guarantee their fair use and monetary compensation in consultation with native communities, regardless of its commercial or educational purpose? Such discussion goes beyond the scope of this chapter, but it is one that resonates well beyond the Costa Rican context.

The question about who is driving Indigenous portrayals in new media and popular culture brings the issue of authenticity to this discussion. What counts as Indigenous in this age of almost unrestricted access to knowledge, increased technological capability to produce and distribute content, and a renewed push to create more diverse and inclusive representations of minorities in our overwhelmingly visual and virtual reality? In an effort to try to parse this thorny subject, let us consider the examples of two developers of Indigenous-themed games mentioned in this chapter: Elizabeth LaPensée and Jonathan Mariño. Of Anishinaabe, Métis, and Irish descent, LaPensée identifies as a Native woman and as an artist and researcher "whose work addresses the development and evaluation of Indigenous media including games, comics, and animation" (LaPensée n.d., n.p.). In other words, her ethnic identity and her interests in Indigenous media and video gaming coincide. It would be hard to argue against the assertion that LaPensée is an authentic Indigenous game developer working from a culturally relevant Indigenous perspective. This is not the case of Mariño, who is not of Indigenous ancestry. Even though he has endeavored to learn as much as possible about Bribri culture from books, consultation with Indigenous experts, and interviews with members of the Bribri community, his knowledge and access are limited by his condition as an outsider to the community and his radically different upbringing as a mestizo urbanite.

This does not mean, of course, that Mariño's aim to educate fellow citizens on the wealth of local Indigenous cultures and their struggles is not as well-intentioned as that of LaPensée. Mariño's games may be as "authentic" as LaPensée's in terms of their attention to iconographic detail and cultural accuracy. However, the difference resides in the location of agency: in the case of LaPensée and other native game developers, agency is exercised by Indigenous individuals, who conceive and guide the process of game creation—becoming a contestatory process because the gaming industry is dominated by non-Indigenous people. In the case of Mariño and others like him, agency is inevitably taken away from Indigenous communities, despite the artist's good intentions. The problem is not so much that Mariño is making Indigenous-themed games but that no Indigenous Costa Ricans have had the opportunity to participate in this industry directly, making their voices and cultural perspectives heard and seen. This is an area where educational and culture-promoting institutions could make a positive intervention, devising programs that train and work with Indigenous youth on the production of games, video, and other twenty-first-century digital platforms.

This takes us back to appropriation. First, it is clear that as a non-Indigenous individual, Mariño has appropriated and modified aspects of Cabécar and Bribri Indigenous culture through the process of representation involved in his artistic renditions. At the same time, as a Costa Rican, he has simply worked with aspects of the culture that are already present in his own country, despite the fact that they belong to an ethnic minority and are virtually unknown to most of that country's population. Without trivializing cultural appropriation, a better way to look at this issue, in the Costa Rican context, is through the lens of the creator's *intent*. Is the purpose of Ditsö to exploit and profit from Indigenous culture or to take advantage of it in any way? It is not. The goal of the project remains educational: "The original idea was to promote Indigenous culture among non-Indigenous people, because the more they know about it, the easier it will be for them to empathize with the problems facing Indigenous communities" (Mariño, personal communication). Nor is the project a moneymaker. Funded by awards, government grants, personal savings from Mariño and Camacho, and in-kind resources from Mariño's design company, "so far the project has just broken even" (Mariño, personal communication). Intent, of course, could be defined in many different ways to fit a variety of agendas. Here, intent refers specifically to educational efforts that are respectful of Indigenous people and culture. There is a long and problematic history in Latin America of nation-states appropriating Indigenous cultures for different ends that are not educational, such as tourism promotion and the advancement of nationalist agendas.

Closely tied to appropriation is the issue of how Indigenous people and culture are portrayed in media and popular culture. Are the representations of Indigenous people and culture found in *El Camino del Useköl* and other Ditsö products respectful or stereotypical? In speaking with Mariño, going through the extensive bibliographic and visual research he has conducted, and looking at the finished products against the backdrop of their meticulous process of development, Ditsö does a commendable job of balancing historical and cultural accuracy with the constraints and expectations imposed by the conventions of board games and video games (which emphasize playability, enjoyment, and some form of competition). According to Matthew Kapell and Andrew Elliott, digital games that re-create the past have great potential for making history less boring and allowing people to actually enjoy learning by interacting "with a past that, if not wholly accurate, is at least *authentic*" (2013, 13). As Mariño explains, his choice of platforms for this project is dictated by his target audiences and the most effective strategies for reaching them:

We are trying to reach children and adolescents in a language that they know. The idea is that they will learn from trading cards and games while enjoying themselves, not just through textbooks that sometimes bore them, but through something they can and want to interact with. [. . .] Kids today are used to dealing with images. So, what we are trying to do is take some key concepts of Indigenous culture, visually work them into characters that are attractive to these youngsters, and that they can relate them with other characters and stories they are familiar with. (Mariño, personal communication)

Mariño makes a powerful statement here about the importance of engaging learners with the technologies with which they are most familiar and are more likely to interact. Indigenous culture is not ecstatic—and certainly not a thing of the past, but ever evolving as all living cultures are. For that reason, it makes sense that it should dialogue with modern technologies and expand its reach among new audiences.

Finally, it is important to bring attention to two areas in which Ditsö has made a positive impact for Costa Rican Indigenous communities. In addition to non-Indigenous people who have been exposed to the trading cards, board game, and video game, Ditsö's products have been received positively by the Indigenous community and could benefit educational efforts on reservations as well. Mariño states that several Indigenous groups have approached him and told him that his products might be helpful for the children of their communities, as many of them are no longer interested in learning about their own language and culture: "We donated several coloring books and board games to a Cabécar school, and the teacher told us the kids were fascinated because they saw in the materials their own stories and recognized the things she had taught them" (Mariño, personal communication). Seeing yourself and your culture represented in a respectful and uplifting way—contrary to centuries of racist attitudes and policies aimed at devaluing native culture—can indeed be a powerful tool. Another important intervention made by Ditsö is that it challenges the idea of a white, homogenous, and monolingual nation by elevating ancient Indigenous stories to the status of "epic Costa Rican mythology."

CONCLUDING THOUGHTS

The two examples of twenty-first-century usage of images and themes from Costa Rican Indigenous communities introduced in this chapter represent opposite poles in the way native cultures have been translated into contemporary discourses of marketing, new media, and popular culture. On the one hand, the Costa Rican Electricity Institute's (ICE) decision to use a Cabécar word, kölbi, to name its new and profitable brand of mobile telephony without consultation with Indigenous communities points to a long and problematic practice by Latin American states of appropriating native knowledge and imagery for their agendas. At the same time, there is a powerful contestatory element in the selection of an Indigenous word to represent a Costa Rican state-owned enterprise in the midst of a battle for survival against powerful transnational telecoms such as Claro and Movistar. ICE chose the name kölbi and the green frog that harks back to nature (a staple of Costa Rica's "green" identity) as part of a nationalist marketing strategy that sought to push back against the forces of globalization and neoliberalism that resulted in the liberalization of the telecommunications market in the late 2000s. The logic here is that Indigenous culture and nature represent "pure," unadulterated forms of authentic Costa Rican identity, and that the elements employed in the kölbi brand would operate as symbols of resistance to these predatory market forces. As noble as this strategy may seem for the state-owned company and the national pride it represents for Costa Ricans, the country's Indigenous people have not benefited in the least from this usurpation of their linguistic heritage. Indeed, ICE is the same entity that plans to build the Diquís hydroelectric dam (the largest in Central America) on mainly Indigenous territory in southern Costa Rica—a project that Native communities have vehemently opposed with little recourse.

On the other hand, Ditsö represents an educational, nonprofit effort to promote Indigenous culture among non-Indigenous Costa Ricans through the creation of coloring books, board games, video games, and other popular culture products. It shares with kölbi the fact that it was created by non-Indigenous individuals. However, Mariño made from the beginning every effort to investigate about local Native cultures from knowledgeable sources and consult with Indigenous scholars and community members. While clearly appropriating Indigenous culture, Ditsö does so for educational purposes and in a respectful manner—attempting to strike a balance between preserving cultural authenticity and appealing to younger generations, Indigenous and non-Indigenous alike, through ludic platforms and technologies with which they are most likely to engage and learn. Both kölbi and Ditsö have in their own ways helped to make Costa Rican Indigenous culture more visible in the public sphere, contesting a centuries-long insidious process of invisibilizing their existence and ignoring their contributions to national culture. However, kölbi's visibilization does nothing to improve the material conditions of Indigenous communities. To the contrary, Ditsö has already made meaningful (though small in scale) contributions to educating non-Indigenous youth about native culture and inspiring Indigenous youth to revalue their cultural heritage through the power of representation. Important next steps to promote positive and culturally significant portrayals of Indigenous life and knowledge would include the development of initiatives aimed at training Native youth in marketing, new media, and videogame creation—so that they can lead the next generation of Indigenous-centric cultural products across a variety of platforms and channels.

ACKNOWLEDGMENTS

Research for this chapter was partly funded by a travel grant from the University of Cincinnati's Charles Phelps Taft Research Center.

NOTES

1.   The word *indígena* is commonly used in Costa Rica to refer to the country's Native population as well as aspects of their culture.

2.   Interview originally conducted in Spanish and translated by the author.

3.   By "visibilization" I refer to the actions undertaken by both educational projects and commercial enterprises (such as tourism) to make various aspects of Indigenous culture more known among non-Indigenous people. It is a priori a problematic term, as it encompasses largely positive efforts to raise awareness about Native culture and issues, as well as the often controversial use of Indigenous culture for profit that does not necessarily benefit native communities.

4.   A discussion of this phenomenon was presented at the 2016 Symposium on Indigenous Languages and Cultures in Columbus, Ohio.

5.   ICE is one of Latin America's most profitable state-owned companies and an enterprise that inspires trust among Costa Ricans due to its successful power infrastructure projects ("The Costa Rican Electricity Institute" 2013, n.p.).

6.   After decades of democratic socialism, welfare state policies, and governmental control of economic activity beginning in the 1940s, neoliberalism led to a deep transformation of Costa Rica's social, economic, political, and cultural constitution. This new neoliberal reality reached full consolidation in 2007, when Costa Ricans passed by a small margin a contentious referendum that ratified the Central American Free Trade Agreement (CAFTA). The vote, and the intense campaign that preceded it, revealed the deep divisions that existed within Costa Rican society back during the 2000s and that remain in place today. The free-trade deal led to the liberalization in the early 2010s of the telecommunications and insurance markets, previously controlled by state monopolies.

7.   Costa Rica often leads Latin America in several ecotourism and tourism rankings, including the Global Tourism Monitor Survey (see Dyer 2014).

8.   According to George Soriano, co-owner of Sibö Chocolates, the name was chosen "to give cultural reference and Costa Rican identity to chocolate, which originates in Central America. And it was to celebrate the natural connection. Sibö gives us all of nature, all that is good, and cacao is so special to Sibö that he marries cacao, Tsirú. So it's about environmental commitment, deep cultural roots, and reclaiming the story of chocolate for Costa Rica and Central America" (Personal communication, August 12, 2016).

9.   Born in Chile in 1939, writer Tatiana Lobo is an outsider to Indigenous communities but also a transplant to Costa Rica, having moved to the country in 1966. However, she is considered a Costa Rican writer, as all her works have been published in her adopted homeland.

10.   A highly publicized recent case was the 2013 killing of Jairo Mora, a sea turtle conservationist working near the Caribbean port city of Limón. Four men were found guilty of this crime in 2016. The judges in the case said the murder's motive was revenge by poachers operating in the area.

11.   The first seven of Costa Rica's twenty-four reservations were created in 1956, with the rest established after Congress passed the Ley Indígena 6172 in 1977. This law sought to protect the Indigenous communities' cultural heritage, right to self-determination, and property. Its main goal was to assign land to native populations within the legal structure of the reservations and to protect it from outside interests. Previously, in 1973, Congress created the National Commission on Indigenous Affairs (CONAI), a government entity tasked with advocating on behalf of Native communities, providing services, and managing resources assigned by the state for various initiatives.

12.   The twenty-four current reservations or territories are Cabagra, Këköldi, Salitre, Talamanca Bribri (Pueblo Bribri), Boruca, Curré (Pueblo Brunca or Boruca),

Bajo Chirripó, China Kichá, Chirripó, Nairi Awari, Talamanca Cabécar, Tayni, Telire, Ujarrás (Pueblo Cabécar), Matambú (Pueblo Chorotega), Quitirrisí, Zapatón (Pueblo Huetar), Guatuso (Pueblo Maleku or Guatuso), Abrojo Montezuma, Altos de San Antonio, Conteburica, Coto Brus, Osa (Pueblo Ngöbe or Guaymí), and Térraba (Pueblo Teribe or Térraba).

13. Quote translated by the author. Original Spanish: "blanca, homogénea, sana y robusta."

14. Quote translated by the author. Original Spanish: "En cuanto a los individuos [aborigines], solo quedan algunos grupos en Talamanca, Boruca, Térraba y Guatuso, que llevan una vida miserable y se diezman con extraordinaria rapidez, sin ejercer influjo alguno en la marcha y desarrollo del país, como tampoco lo ejercieron en la formación de éste."

15. Quote translated by the author. Original Spanish: "Costa Rica alberga una población india no tan numerosa pero cualitativamente tan importante como la de otros países del istmo centroamericano, que a pesar de haber sido objeto de una considerable legislación indigenista (comparativamente), esta casi no se aplica. Peor: en otras partes las poblaciones indias claman por derechos legalmente reconocidos, aquí se reconocen legalmente tales derechos y se violan en la práctica."

16. A content analysis of games from around the same time period (Williams et al. 2009) found that minority male characters were portrayed as more aggressive than whites, and were often relegated to athletic or violent roles.

17. The presence of the Aztecs in mainstream video games is discussed at length by Joshua D. Holdenreid and Nicolas Trépanier 2013.

18. All interviews with Mariño conducted in Spanish and translated into English by the author.

19. Popular games like *Super Mario Brothers* involve a hero who must overcome a series of obstacles to reach an end goal (such as rescuing a princess or defeating an enemy), aided along the way by special items and allies.

20. Translated from the original Spanish by the author.

REFERENCES

Boza Villarreal, Alejandro. 2014. *La frontera indígena de la Gran Talamanca: 1840–1930*. Cartago: Editoriales Universitarias Públicas Costarricenses.

Burgess, Melinda, et al. 2011. "Playing with Prejudice: The Prevalence and Consequences of Racial Stereotypes in Video Games." *Media Psychology* 14: 289–311.

Calvo, Joaquín Bernardo. 1887. *República de Costa Rica. Apuntamientos geográficos, estadísticos e históricos*. San José: Imprenta Nacional.

Coleman, Elizabeth Burns. 2016. *Aboriginal Art, Identity and Appropriation*. New York: Routledge.

"The Costa Rican Electricity Institute (ICE): An Exceptional Public Enterprise in an Atypical Social Democracy." 2013. TNI (website), July 11, 2013. https://www.tni.org/es/node/13522.

Dyer, Zack. 2014. "Costa Rica Named Top Tourism Destination in New Global Survey." *The Tico Times* (website), June 11, 2014. http://www.ticotimes.net/2014/06/11/costa-rica-named-top-tourism-destination-in-new-global-survey.

Dyer-Witheford, Nick, and Greig de Peuter. 2009. *Games of Empire: Global Capitalism and Video Games*. Minneapolis: University of Minnesota Press.

Ferrero, Luis. 2000. *Costa Rica Precolombina: Arqueología, Etnología, Tecnología, Arte*. San José: Editorial Costa Rica.

Guevara Berger, Marcos, and Rubén Chacón Castro. 1992. *Territorios indios en Costa Rica: Orígenes, situación actual y perspectivas*. San José: García Hermanos S.A.

Holdenreid, Joshua D., and Nicolas Trépanier. 2013. "Dominance and the Aztec Empire: Representations in Age of Empires II and Medieval II: Total War." In *Playing with the Past: Digital Games and the Simulation of History*, edited by Matthew Wilhelm Kapell and Andrew B. R. Elliott, 107–19. New York: Bloomsbury.

Instituto Nacional de Estadística y Censos. 2013. *Territorios Indígenas: Principales Indicadores Demográficos y Socioeconómicos*. San José: Instituto Nacional de Estadística y Censos. http://www.inec.go.cr/sites/default/files/documentos/inec_institucional/estadisticas/resultados/repoblaccenso2011-02.pdf.pdf.

Joho, Jess. 2017. "An Indie Game That Aims to Preserve an Indigenous Culture and Its Mythology." *Mashable* (website), September 29, 2017. http://mashable.com/2017/09/29/mulaka-switch-tarahumara-digital-preservation/#upBVTHGsAEqq.

Kapell, Matthew Wilhelm, and Andrew B. R. Elliott. 2013. *Playing with the Past: Digital Games and the Simulation of History*. New York: Bloomsbury.

LaPensée, Elizabeth. n.d. Elizabeth LaPensée (website). Accessed November 2, 2017. http://www.elizabethlapensee.com/about.

León, Jorge. 1943. *Nueva Geografía de Costa Rica*. San José: Soley y Valverde Editores.

Lull, James. 1995. *Media, Communication, Culture, a Global Approach*. New York: Columbia University Press.

Mariño, Jonathan. 2016. Investigación documental: Fundamentos para desarrollo del prototipo de videojuego Ditsö, *El Camino del Useköl*. Unpublished.

Newman, Jared. 2012. "*Assassin's Creed III's* Connor: How Ubisoft Avoided Stereotypes and Made a Real Character." *Time*, September 5, 2012. http://techland.time.com/2012/09/05/assassins-creed-iiis-connor-how-ubisoft-avoided-stereotypes-and-made-a-real-character.

"North and South America Came Together Much Earlier Than Thought: Study." 2015. *NBC News*, April 5, 2015. http://www.nbcnews.com/science/science-news/north-south-america-came-together-much-earlier-thought-study-n338826.

Rojas Conejo, Daniel. 2009. *Dilema e identidad del pueblo Bribri*. San José: Editorial de la Universidad de Costa Rica.

Stocker, Karen. 2005. *"I Won't Stay Indian, I'll Keep Studying": Race, Place, and Discrimination in a Costa Rican High School*. Boulder: University Press of Colorado.

Williams, Dmitri, et al. 2009. "The Virtual Census: Representations of Gender, Race, and Age in Video Games." *New Media and Society* 11 (5): 815–34.

Yglesias Hogan, Rubén. 1942. *Nuestros aborígenes. Apuntes sobre la población precolombina de Costa Rica*. San José: Editorial Trejos Hermanos.

PART III

INDIGENIZING SOCIAL MEDIA

7

DIGITIZING ANCESTRAL MEMORY

Garifuna Settlement Day in the Americas and in Cyberspace

PAUL JOSEPH LÓPEZ ORO

The reenactment [Garifuna Settlement Day] is really hard for me to watch. It is something I enjoy watching, but it is something deep for me. It goes deeper than just a reenactment. It is my people asking for a home, my people searching for a home, and trying a land where they are not wanted. So it is very emotional for me to watch it. It is very important to keep Garifuna alive, because it is a rich culture. We are a minority so we have to fight hard to keep our culture alive. We can't allow it to die so especially in Orange Walk [Belize] you know it's like Garifuna, so what? But it's a big deal to us, I'm proud to be a Garifuna.
—NELITA SAMBULA, INTERVIEW, 2015

Ancestral memory is sacred. Ancestral memory is political. Ancestral memory is an embodied archive passed on transgenerationally to and through the flesh vis-à-vis oral traditions. Within the Garifuna political imagination, ancestral memory is conjured into the present through remembering and reenacting the past. Garifuna Settlement Day is a public act of remembering, reenactment, a performative space to embody ancestral memory. Garifuna are Black Indigenous peoples whose ethnogenesis on the lesser Antillean island of St. Vincent, born out of the mixture of shipwrecked enslaved West Africans and Carib-Arawak Indians, is memorialized and invoked as an act of resistance to enslavement and European colonialism. In Belize, November 19, 1823, is recognized as the date of arrival of the Garínagu to Dangriga, the largest Garifuna community in the country.[1] The very first Garifuna Settlement Day celebration in the Americas took place there on November 19, 1941, as a political project of remembrance and ethnoracial recognition in the face of land encroachment and antiblack racism forty years prior to Belize's independence on September 21, 1981. In the present day, Garifuna Settlement Day is commemorated throughout the Americas, specifically within the Garifuna diasporas in the United States and Central America's Caribbean Coasts. However, the origins of Garifuna Settlement Day are distinctively Central American and Caribbean, marking a time and space of arrival from St. Vincent. St. Vincent marks a discursive and geographical nostalgia as a birthplace of Garifunaness. While the historical origins of Garifuna Settlement Day merit much more in-depth attention, especially as it informs a larger contemporary Garifuna political imaginary, this chapter concentrates on the performative act of Garifunaness vis-à-vis embodied ancestral memory in the public space of Garifuna Settlement Day in Central America's Caribbean Coasts and New York City.[2] Importantly, this chapter interrogates the digital space of social media as a medium for archiving Garifuna ancestral memory through the venues of YouTube, Instagram, Facebook, and Brooklyn-based blogs, as alternative spaces for diasporic mobilization of Garifuna ancestral memory.

GARIFUNA SETTLEMENT DAY IN CENTRAL AMERICA

The reenactment of ancestral arrival from St. Vincent to Central America on Garifuna Settlement Day illustrates the complexities of the racialized geographies of Central America's Caribbean Coasts. Blackness in the Central American imaginary is ascribed and conceptualized as always being present only on the Caribbean Coasts of the isthmus, removed from the interior of mestizo governance. Blackness is therefore alien, marginal, and foreign to the mestizo Central American national subject, which in turn sustains the erasure and negation of Black history and presence in the region. Garifuna in Central America face a multi-sited complexity and negotiation with Blackness and Indigeneity, as Garifuna peoples are racialized and interpellated as Black (*morenos* or *negros*) by mestizos and the nation-state. Yet Garifuna articulation as Black Indigenous through their enactment of their ancestors to Central America during Settlement Day is fundamental to their sense of indigeneity, especially within a multicultural paradigm. Here Central American multiculturalism fashions what Christopher Loperena refers to as the "double-bind of Garifuna ethnopolitics," the simultaneous commodification and hypervisibility of Garifuna cultures and bodies. Therefore, Garifuna communities engage in a complex choreography with the mestizo nation-state that benefits from UNESCO's (United Nations Educational, Scientific, and Cultural Organization) 2001 proclamation of Garifuna language as a "Masterpiece of the Oral Intangible Heritage of Humanity" and a growing cultural tourism economy driven by foreign investment. Loperena argues that "Garifuna political expression through cultural performance reproduces folkloric representations of Garifuna subjectivity, but it also makes visible nonnormative political desires that cannot be accommodated by simple legal recognition of difference as enshrined within multicultural legislations" (2016, 519). It is important to highlight this double-bind, especially since for Garifuna communities Garifuna Settlement Day is a sacred act of ancestral memory but is also a central tourist attraction for the region at the local and national level.

While Garifuna's Blackness is visibly demarcated onto their bodies, Indigeneity becomes an ethnic signifier performed and negotiated vis-à-vis rituals, oral traditions, and invocations of St. Vincent and Arawak Caribness. Mark Anderson has written extensively on the conceptual orientation toward Blackness and Indigeneity not as mutually exclusive categories but as modalities of identity formation that can overlap with each other. Furthermore, he notes:

> The Garifuna case illustrates that subjects interpellated as Black and who identify as Black can assert Indigenous status, and not merely because they can claim Indian descent. Indigenous status here refers both to the broadest sense of being native born and the legal sense of bearing an Indigenous condition as a culturally distinct people. This case thus suggests that assertions of Indian heritage may not be necessary for the production of Indigeneity. Garifuna produce forms of Black Indigeneity that partially disrupt a conceptual-political grid that links Indigeneity with Indians and Blackness with displacement. (2009, 21)[3]

Anderson's attention to the ontological disruptions Garifuna embody and engage with as Black Indigenous peoples is useful to analyze the diasporic processes that reinscribe the multiple meanings of what it means to be Garifuna, Black, and Indigenous; in this sense also, we can further problematize an ongoing opposition between Indigeneity and Blackness commonly found in scholarship. Moreover, St. Vincent as a site of ethnogenesis homeland becomes central in the ways in which Garifuna political imagination is constructed diasporically and routed/rooted onto an ancestral memory of a nostalgic geography that is Black Indigenous for the Garínagu.

Settlement Day in Dangriga highlights the act of arrival/arriving as a central role in the performance of Garifuna Settlement Day in Central America, which begins on a crowded beach with Garifuna men drumming and Garifuna women singing an ancestral *parranda* titled "Yurumein," which is Garifuna for St. Vincent. The song depicts the bravery of Joseph Chatoyer's bloody journey from St. Vincent to Central America and his nostalgia for freedom and prosperity on St. Vincent. The performance of arrival to the Caribbean shores of Central America is reenacted on three small speedboats (*pangas*). As crowds grow on the beach, mostly locals and tourist onlookers, a Garifuna flag waves ferociously and reenactors hold in their hands the main crops in Garifuna cuisine, such as cassava, plantains, coconuts, and palm tree branches. These crops are symbolic of an ancestral memory as they are commonly understood to have sustained the ancestors on their dreadful exile from St. Vincent to the Bay Islands of Honduras (fig. 7.1). This reenactment of arrival is mobilized by a collective ancestral memory embodied in the songs, drumming, attire, dancing, and speedboats. The symbolic meaning of the ship in the form of a speedboat here carries the collective memory of the transatlantic slave trade, however it is used as a site of reenacting the warrior-like mutiny that ignited Garínagu maroonage and marking Garifuna ethnoracial nationalism as a distinct marker from other Black and Indigenous communities in the region and throughout the Americas. It is a common invocation that this reenactment is what the ancestors did upon their arrival to the shores of the Honduran island of Roatan. Beyond historical accuracy, what continues to be significant here is the political mobilization of the ancestors and their memory—Garifuna Settlement Day as a performative public site of ancestral memory, as an embodied archive reenacted onto the flesh: a conjuring of the past into the present. I turn to Black Performance theory to think through the ways in which Garifuna Settlement Day as an embodied archive of ancestral memory is a manifestation of Garifuna epistemologies. E. Patrick Johnson's pioneering work offers us a blueprint grounded in the praxis of Black Performance as "a knowing made manifest by a 'doing'" (2003, 446). Doing here for Garifuna communities is one that conjures ancestral knowledges through dance, songs, drums, and the Atlantic Ocean. Water and land on Central America's Caribbean Coast are central to the performance of ancestral memory in this geopolitical project of remembrance and restoration into claiming land rights and ethnoracial rights within a multicultural paradigm in Central America.

FIGURE 7.1. Garifuna Settlement Day in Dangriga, Belize, on November 19, 2016. Photo by Amber Edwards.

Social media opens up an alternative digital diasporic self-making as Garifuna political imaginary travels, mobilizes, and is performed throughout Central America's Caribbean Coasts and the United States, specifically in New York City.[4] The notion of arrival and settlement is a hallmark to Garínagu ethnogenesis narrative of hybridity, marronage, and alterity as Black Indigenous peoples. Social media aids in dispersing those complex narratives throughout the Americas, especially as second- and third-generation U.S.-born Garifuna engage in a process of self-making. More importantly, social media is foundational to the archiving of Garifuna traditions, language, and history in ways that bridge a hemispheric political project of restoration and preservation that reaches to the corners of New York City and back and forth to the shorelines of Central America's Caribbean Coast.

YURUMEIN: DIGITIZING ANCESTRAL MEMORY

Ancestral memory is multi-sited as it can manifest in multiple spaces and forms such as dreams, oral traditions, storytelling, visions, spiritual possessions, and reenactments of passed-on generational rituals. As I have indicated in my dis-cussion of Settlement Day in Central America, Garifuna ancestral memory is embodied knowledge lived and experienced through and onto the flesh. Further-more, ancestral memory serves as an embodied archive for Garifuna in their polit-ical processes of subject-making and is a significant articulation and invocation. M. Jacqui Alexander's conceptualization of "marking on the flesh" as inscriptions, processes, ceremonial rituals through which practitioners become habituated to the spiritual and Diana Taylor's (2003) analyses of the body in performance as a vehicle for political claims, transmission of memory, and a tool for forging cultural memory are both of notable value to this analysis. Working from the premise that the body is a site of memory, I engage with questions about how Garifunaness is consumed and exported by Garifuna. I ask, how is ancestral memory mobilized, politicized, and imagined among Garifuna New Yorkers as a sacred act of remem-brance? How do they embody, archive, and perform ancestral memory across their multiple diasporic communities, from Central America's Caribbean Coasts and St. Vincent through social media and digital spaces?

Sarah England notes that the Garifuna are members of three diasporas: the African diaspora, the Garifuna diaspora, and the Central American diaspora: "Garifuna occupy an ideological border zone between four racial/ethnic identi-ties: Black, Indigenous, Latino, and Garifuna: expressed differently in each of the nation-states within they live" (2006, 218). Garifuna are thus simultaneously Black, Indigenous, and Latino; they are Honduran, Belizean, Guatemalan, Nicaraguan, and North American; they are part of Central America and part of the Caribbean. As an ethnic group, they share a common language and culture, as well as histories of colonialism, displacement, and transnational migration that unite them across nation-state borders (England, 8). However, Garifuna subjectivity and lived expe-riences are not uniformly universal, there are variations on how Garínagu engage with land rights, politics of cultural preservation, and ethnoracial identity forma-tion. England's and Johnson's (2007) studies are the only extensive ethnographic texts to date on Garifuna New Yorkers. England's contribution on Garifuna New Yorkers as constitutive of a "transmigrant" community through circular migrations in which boundaries of collective identity are continually refashioned at the con-fluence of racial and ethnicising processes vis-à-vis differentiated nation-states is a useful analytical blueprint for this analysis.

England footnotes the invocation of the ancestors by her participants that, as I have found, continues to be central to contemporary Garifuna youth's cultural and political mobilization. Take for example Trevan Castillo. Castillo was at the time of our interview a sixteen-year-old Garifuna from Dangriga, Belize.

He lit up immediately when speaking about how his participation in Garifuna Settlement Day was an act of remembering his ancestors and living what they lived: "I chose to be a part of Yurumein because my ancestors did it. And so I want to take up that habit of doing it because I don't want my culture to be lost. I want to uplift my culture really" (Trevan Castillo, interview, 2015). This notion of young descendants living what their ancestors lived is quite telling of the aesthetic and feeling of Garifuna Settlement Day, as the dancing, drumming, attire, and arriving on shore all choreograph a calling to the ancestors for lived memory—an ancestral lived memory that has become increasingly dispersed via social media, particularly Facebook, YouTube, and Instagram. Social media continues to be a growing and crucial space for Garifuna folks to engage one another throughout the multiple spaces in Central America's Caribbean Coasts (Belize, Guatemala, Honduras, and Nicaragua) as well as in the largest urban metropoles in the United States (New York City, Chicago, Houston, Los Angeles, Miami, and New Orleans). Jared L. Johnson and Clark Callahan closely examine social media by Garifuna communities in Honduras and the United States. Their findings highlight how Garifuna communities are using social media to create a "supraterritorial cyberspace" (2013) as newer forms of social media are creating virtual cultural cyberspaces that extend Garifuna culture. Johnson and Callahan's coinage of supraterritorial cyberspace is worthwhile as Garifuna social media transcend the multiple geographies of the localities and ethnoracial practices and reenactments, just as Garifuna Settlement Day bring these social media spaces into conversation with each other.

Facebook, Instagram, and YouTube are central to the ways in which Garifuna New Yorkers and Garifuna Central Americans maintain multiple social networks of Garifuna history, language, traditions, cuisine, and music, which reinforces the larger diasporic project of Garifuna revitalization and restoration. One of the most popular Brooklyn-based blogs by Teofilo Colon Jr. also known as "Tio Teo" is a significant cyberspace platform to open an alternative digital conversation on Garifunaness throughout its diaspora. "Being Garifuna" emerges as an online archive to document Garifuna life in the United States, as Teofilo is a first-generation U.S.-born Garifuna of Honduran descent whose upbringing in East New York, Brooklyn, in the company of African Americans, West Indians, Latinx Caribbean, and Black Caribbean communities ignited his passion to preserve his Garifuna subjectivity. A significant element of the "Being Garifuna" blog is its explicit intent in documenting Garifuna history, culture, and language as it is expressed throughout the United States and Central America (figs. 7.2 and 7.3).

Our Story

 BEING GARIFUNA · TUESDAY, DECEMBER 5, 2017

Founded by Teofilo Colon Jr (a.k.a Tio Teo or Teofilo Campeon) in February 2010. BEING
GARIFUNA is a media platform that uses photos, videos and articles to document the
culture, arts, politics, sports, spirituality & social lives of people who identify as Garifuna.

The Garifuna people are people of mixed ancestry (Carib Indian, Arawak Indian and African)
who are originally from St. Vincent. After losing a war to the British, they were exiled to
Roatan Honduras in 1797. They now reside in villages/towns on the Caribbean coasts of the
Central American countries of Honduras, Belize, Guatemala and Nicaragua. Some have
migrated to the United States and live in cities like New York City, Chicago and Los Angeles.
I can be reached at: PHONE (646) 961-3674. EMAIL: teo@beinggarifuna.com

FIGURE 7.2. "Being Garifuna: Our Story" Facebook page, created by Teofilo Colon Jr.
Used with permission.

While Teofilo is based in Brooklyn, New York, his blog that is linked to
Twitter, Instagram, YouTube, and Facebook intentionally posts on Garifuna cuisine, community-based organizations, community events, language workshops,
and additional educational planning coordinated by U.S.-based and Central
American Garifuna organizations. Garifuna cyberspaces disrupt mainstream
social media dealing with U.S. Central Americans. U.S. Central Americans
are racialized as non-Black and the dominant presence in social media cele-
brates a regional nationalism to mark a distancing from mestizo Mexicanidad.
Building on their alterity to U.S. Latinidad, Central Americans deeply engage
ethnic signifiers that mark their distinctive identities from other U.S. Latinx
communities, but simultaneously disengage from critically interrogating race
and racism in the isthmus and its diasporas. Therefore, Garifuna cyberspaces
become an important space for Black Indigeneity to be archived, honored, and
articulated. The hashtags #CentralAmericanTwitter and #IAmCentAm serve a
much-needed political visibility for U.S. Central Americans, but they are predominantly mestizo centered. Garifuna folks are invisibilized by these hashtags

FIGURE 7.3. Brooklyn-based blog "Being Garifuna" home page, created and updated by Teofilo Colon Jr. Used with permission.

and only make appearances when Central American ethnicity is called upon. Twitter has generated a growing discussion among Garifuna in response to these hashtags for the ways in which they do not critically engage Black Indigeneity to interrogate the complexities of land rights, antiblack racism, and state-sanctioned violence. #GarifunaTwitter, on the other hand, engages in a politics of visibility that centers Garifuna culture, language, and history as an embodied archive of knowledges led by ancestral memory.

The archive of Black diaspora is, as Hartman suggests, "a death sentence, a tomb, a display of a violated body, an inventory of property, a medical treatise . . . an asterisk in the grand narrative of history" (2008, 2). Therefore, ancestral memory offers us the theoretical space to reimagine alternative multi-sited archivings that do not adhere to colonial governance of documentation, namely ancestral memory as an archive of resistance and survival in the afterlife of the Middle Passage and slavery. Garifuna epistemology is grounded in maroonage, a freedom from plantation slavery through heroic acts of shipwrecked mutiny, an exceptionalism that problematically divorces itself from other Black Atlantic communities. The invocation of ancestral memory on Twitter (figs. 7.4 and 7.5) nourishes the transnational Garifuna political imaginary of resistance to enslavement and the preservation of a Black Indigenous culture and language.

FIGURE 7.4. Tweet by @BeeAnnaNicholle sharing image from the 2018 Garifuna Settlement Day celebration in Honduras. Used with permission.

FIGURE 7.5. Tweet by @insanely_made in response to the 2018 Garifuna Settlement Day celebration in Honduras. Used with permission.

Garifuna Settlement Day is a day burned into the ancestral memory of Garinagu across nation-state borders. Remembering is a crucial way of teaching and preserving traditions, and recalling the people (elders) who created customs is one way of keeping them alive. Memory refers both to what has been written and to what has been transmitted through rituals, practices, symbols, and other unwritten aspects of Garifuna culture. As Manigault-Bryant suggests in regard to ancestral memory among Gullah/Geechee communities, a creole community in coastal South Carolina, memory "also encompasses the features of the past that are very much a part of the present. Understanding the aspects of memory as they are ritualized, (re)appropriated, and performed is significant because it provides a means of understanding the social, cultural, and religious perspectives of a given community" (2014, 173).

GARIFUNA SETTLEMENT DAY AND DIASPORIC GARIFUNANESS

Garifuna communities throughout Central America and the United States disrupt notions of who, what, and where Blackness, indigeneity, and mestizo Latinidad is to be situated. St. Vincent as an ancestral homeland is an important social memory that marks diasporic Garifunaness, because it anchors a site of belonging, remembering, and maroonage to colonialism and slavery. St. Vincent continues to be a sacred ground for thinking on how Garifuna New Yorkers position their cultural and racial exceptionalism, as Afro-descendant Indigenous peoples whose liberation from plantation slavery and hybridity in the Americas constructs their exceptionalism. St. Vincent is not just a site of archival fact checking but rather an ancestral source on diasporic Garifuna imaginary, "a production which is never complete, always in process, and always constituted within" to borrow from Stuart Hall (1990, 222). Diasporic Garifunaness is not static but is an ongoing production, a performance that places multiple spaces into play with each other, and it is a negotiation with multiple subjectivities of Blackness, Indigeneity, and Latinidad in relation to ancestral memory.

Belizean-based Garifuna cultural activist Joshua Arana (2018) reminds us in his TEDx Talk in Belmopan, titled "How Drumming Made Me a Feminist," of the necessity to seek our ancestors as spiritual guides as we walk in our lives. As he states, "We look to our ancestors' guidance and knowledge. They expect that we will never forget them through our rituals. They also expect that we will nurture the culture passed on, that we will leave it as pristine as possible, and in some cases, even build upon it and before passing it onto the future generation. Our future generation will be expected to do the same and also look up to us for guidance." Ancestral invocation is a political act of Garifuna spirituality that is embodied onto and through the flesh, which has been archived and digitized into the cyber-space. Ancestral memory is diasporic, embodied knowledge, archival materiality. Garifunaness is marked by the contingencies of long histories of displacements and genealogies of dispossession, entangled by racialized histories of colonialism, imperialism, and modernity, echoing the work of the late Richard Iton. Diaspora is a site of dislocation where multiple and dissident maps and geographies of Blackness are living and working across, within, and against, nation-states (Iton 2008, 201). Online as well as offline, Garifuna Settlement Day is a radical invest-ment on the ancestral memory that keeps the community connected across vast distances that might result from geographic and generational differences. Dias-pora and ancestral memory serve as a conceptual space to unearth the liminal spaces where the multiplicity of Garífuna subjectivities live/survive.

Garifuna Settlement Day is ritualized throughout all spaces within the Gar-ifuna diaspora; they are sacred spaces where ancestors are conjured through offerings such as hudutu, gifiti, singing, and dance. Drumming invites for spirit possession to be invoked as an inscription of ancestral memory onto the body, providing guidance, memory, and future plans. The performance of ancestral memory in Garifuna Settlement Day, and its echoes in virtual spaces, in effect mobilizes an embodied archive that relies on kinship as a mode of returning to home: a home that is not located on the Caribbean Coast of Central America but at Yurumein, a site of maroonage, self-governance, and traditions. Settle-ment Day is thus fueled by an urgency to restore and preserve Garifuna culture, language, and history in ways that "save" young people from becoming discon-nected from their ancestors, which could, in turn, lead to the loss of Garifuna culture itself. As Mita Guerrero reminded me as we walked through New York City together one afternoon in 2015, "The ancestors are our memory. They give us our memory." Indeed, they do.

ACKNOWLEDGMENTS

I thank the Department of African and African Diaspora Studies, John L. War-field Center for African and African American Studies, and the Department of

Mexican American and Latina/o Studies at the University of Texas at Austin for their intellectual and financial support. I am indebted to my interlocutors for their deeply critical and generous feedback: Juliet Hooker, Jennifer Gómez Menjívar, Christen Smith, Edmund T. Gordon, Yomaira Figueroa, Tacuma Peters, Omaris Z. Zamora, Daisy E. Guzman Nuñez, and Traci-Ann Wint-Hayes.

NOTES

1. Greene Jr. 2014, 173.
2. López Oro 2016, 251–53.
3. Anderson 2009, 22.
4. The origins of Garifuna Settlement Day are rooted in the public act of performing ancestral memory from St. Vincent to the new site of arrival in a diasporic mapping onto the Caribbean Coast(s) of Central America. As Garifuna Settlement Day grew in annual presence and multiple communities along the Caribbean Coast of Belize began to enact them, Garifuna Honduran civil rights activist, Thomas Vincent Ramos, led a national campaign to pressure the Belizean nation-state to recognize November 19 as a national holiday. Thomas Vincent Ramos is a fascinating political figure whose multiple ties to Honduras and Belize highlight the fluidity of nation-borders on the Caribbean Coast(s) of Central America for Garifuna, Creole, and Indigenous communities whose ascription of Blackness and Indigeneity make them perpetual alien citizens by the national imaginary of these mestizo nation-states.

REFERENCES

Alexander, M. Jacqui. 2005. *Pedagogies of Crossing: Meditations on Feminism, Sexual Politics, Memory, and the Sacred.* Durham: Duke University Press.

Anderson, Mark. 2007. "When Afro Becomes (like) Indigenous: Garifuna and Afro-Indigenous Politics in Honduras." *The Journal of Latin American and Caribbean Anthropology* 12 (2): 384–413.

Anderson, Mark. 2009. *Black and Indigenous: Garifuna Activism and Consumer Culture in Honduras.* Minneapolis: University of Minnesota Press.

Arana, Joshua. 2018. "How Drumming Made Me a Feminist." YouTube video, 18:15, posted January 23, 2018, https://www.youtube.com/watch?v=K1sm1WCcY6o.

Byrd, Jodi A. 2011. *The Transit of Empire: Indigenous Critiques of Colonialism.* Minneapolis: University of Minnesota Press.

England, Sarah. 2006. *Afro-Central Americans in New York City: Garifuna Tales of Transnational Movements in Racialized Space.* Gainesville: University Press of Florida.

González, Nancie L. 1979. "Garifuna Settlement in New York: A New Frontier." *The International Migration Review* 13 (2): 255–63.

González, Nancie L. 1988. *Sojourners of the Caribbean: Ethnogenesis and Ethnohistory of the Garifuna*. Urbana-Champaign: University of Illinois Press.

Gordon, Edmund T. 1998. *Disparate Diasporas: Identity and Politics in an African Nicaraguan Community*. Austin: University of Texas Press.

Gordon, Edmund T., and Mark Anderson. 1999. "The African Diaspora: Toward an Ethnography of Diasporic Identification." *The Journal of American Folklore* 112 (445): 282–96.

Greene, Oliver N., Jr. 2002. "Ethnicity, Modernity, and Retention in the Garifuna Punta." *Black Music Research Journal* 22 (2): 189–216.

Greene, Oliver N., Jr. 2014. "Celebrating Settlement Day in Belize." In *Sun, Sea, and Sound: Music and Tourism in the Circum-Caribbean*, edited by Timothy Rommen and Daniel T. Neely, 179–212. New York: Oxford University Press.

Gudmundson, Lowell, and Justin Wolfe. 2010. *Blacks and Blackness in Central America: Between Race and Place*. Durham: Duke University Press.

Hale, Charles R. 2005. "Neoliberal Multiculturalism: The Remaking of Cultural Rights and Racial Dominance in Central America." *PoLAR: Political and Legal Anthropology Review* 28 (1): 10–28.

Hall, Stuart. 1990. "Cultural Identity and Diaspora." In *Colonial Discourse and Post-Colonial Theory: A Reader*, edited by Patrick Williams and Laura Chrisman, 222–37. London: Harvester Wheatsleaf.

Hartman, Saidiya. 2008. "Venus in the Two Acts." *Small Axe* 26: 1–14.

Henderson, Mae G. 2014. *Speaking in Tongues and Dancing Diaspora: Black Women Writing and Performing*. New York: Oxford University Press.

Hintzen, Percy C. 2001. *West Indian in the West: Self-Representations in an Immigrant Community*. New York: New York University Press.

Hooker, Juliet. 2005. "Indigenous Inclusion/Black Exclusion: Race, Ethnicity, and Multicultural Citizenship in Latin America." *Journal of Latin American Studies* 37: 285–310.

Hooker, Juliet. 2010. "Race and the Space of Citizenship: The Mosquito Coast and the Place of Blackness and Indigeneity in Nicaragua." In *Blacks and Blackness in Central America: Between Race and Place*, edited by Lowell Gudmundson and Justin Wolfe, 246–77. Durham: Duke University Press.

Hooker, Juliet. 2014. "Hybrid Subjectivities, Latin American Mestizaje, and Latino Political Thought on Race." *Politics, Groups, and Identities* 2 (2): 188–201.

Iton, Richard. 2008. *In Search of the Black Fantastic: Politics and Popular Culture in the Post-Civil Rights Era*. New York: Oxford University Press.

Jimenéz Román, Miriam, and Juan Flores. 2010. *The Afro-Latin@ Reader: History and Culture in the United States*. Durham: Duke University Press.

Johnson, E. Patrick. 2003. *Appropriating Blackness: Performance and the Politics of Authenticity*. Durham: Duke University Press.

Johnson, Jared L., and Clark Callahan. 2013. "Minority Cultures and Social Media: Magnifying Garifuna." *Journal of Intercultural Communication Research* 42 (4): 319–39.

Johnson, Paul Christopher. 2007a. *Diaspora Conversions: Black Carib Religion and the Recovery of Africa*. Berkeley and Los Angeles: University of California Press.

Johnson, Paul Christopher. 2007b. "On Leaving and Joining Africanness Through Religion: The 'Black Caribs' Across Multiple Diasporic Horizons." *Journal of Religion in Africa* 37: 174–211.

Jones, Omi Oshun Joni L. 2015. *Theatrical Jazz: Performance, Àse, and the Power of the Present Moment*. Athens: Ohio University Press.

Kerns, Virginia. 1983. *Women and the Ancestors: Black Carib Kinship and Ritual*. Urbana: University of Illinois Press.

Loperena, Christopher. 2016. "Radicalize Multiculturalism? Garifuna Activism and the Double Bind of Participation in Postcoup Honduras." *The Journal of Latin American and Caribbean Anthropology* 21 (3): 517–38.

López Oro, Paul Joseph. 2016a. "'Ni de aquí, ni de allá': Garífuna Subjectivities and the Politics of Diasporic Belonging." In *Afro-Latin@s in Movement: Critical Approaches to Blackness and Transnationalism in the Americas*, edited by Petra R. Rivera-Rideau, Jennifer A. Jones, and Tianna S. Paschel, 61–83. New York: Palgrave Macmillan.

López Oro, Paul Joseph. 2016b. "Ramos, Tomas Vicente." In *Dictionary of Caribbean and Afro-Latin American Biography*, edited by Franklin W. Knight and Henry Louis Gates Jr., 251–53. New York: Oxford University Press.

Manigault-Bryant, James A., and Manigault-Bryant, LeRhonda S. 2016. "Conjuring Pasts and Ethnographic Presents in Zora Neale Hurston's Modernity." *Journal of Africana Religions* 4 (2): 225–35.

Manigault-Bryant, LeRhonda S. 2014. *Talking to the Dead: Religion, Music, and Lived Memory among Gullah/Geechee Women*. Durham: Duke University Press.

McKittrick, Katherine. 2006. *Demonic Grounds: Black Women and the Cartographies of Struggle*. Minneapolis: University of Minnesota Press.

Morris, Courtney Desiree. 2016a. "Becoming Creole, Becoming Black: Migration, Diasporic Self Making, and the Many Lives of Madame Maymie Leona Turpeau de Mena." *Women, Gender, and Families of Color* 4 (2): 171–195.

Morris, Courtney Desiree. 2016b. "Toward a Geography of Solidarity: Afro-Nicaraguan Women's Land Activism and Autonomy in the South Caribbean Coast Autonomous Region." *Bulletin of Latin American Research* 35 (3): 355–69.

Perry, Marc. 1999. "Garífuna Youth in New York City: Race, Ethnicity, and the Performance of Diasporic Identities." Master's thesis, University of Texas at Austin.

Scott, David. 1991. "That Event, This Memory: Notes on the Anthropology of African Diasporas in the New World." *Diaspora* 1 (3): 261–84.

Scott, David. 2008. "Introduction: On the Archaeologies of Black Memory." *Small Axe* 26: v–xvi.

Taylor, Diana. 2003. *The Archive and the Repertoire: Performing Cultural Memory in the Americas*. Durham: Duke University Press.

Tinsley, Omise'eke Natasha. 2008. "Black Atlantic, Queer Atlantic: Queer Imaginings of the Middle Passage." *Gay and Lesbian Quarterly* 14: 191–215.

8

IN A TIME OF WAR AND HASHTAGS

Rehumanizing Indigeneity in the Digital Landscape

GABRIELA SPEARS-RICO

Mexico has entered the new millennium as a metaphorical and physical mass grave of unidentified Indigenous and mestiza/o bodies. Ironically, for a population that engages in a conscientious effort to remember and honor their dead, we have not done enough to count, name, or bring justice to the unidentified casualties of the Drug War. This is particularly true for the Indigenous victims of Felipe Calderón's and Enrique Peña Nieto's campaigns against drug cartels. Indigenous death haunts digital landscapes, as the names and photos of Indigenous people who have been tortured, murdered, and disappeared as a result of Mexico's Drug War and the Mexican government's targeted efforts to crush Indigenous autonomy are released online.

Recent incidences of territorial infringement and resource extraction on Indigenous communities demonstrate that Indigenous people and Indigenous lands are the drug cartels' new targets while Mexican officials and the Mexican government play a part in the anti-Indigenous violence. This is a moment of both symbolic and high-intensity warfare; it is another genocidal moment in Mexican history. Yet the stories of Indigenous hauntings and Indigenous death from cartel violence have seldom been framed as integral to the legacy of Mexico's colonial violence. In what follows, I explore how Mexican Indigenous people and their allies willfully address the haunting caused by this social materiality with the use of hashtags that grant visibility to Indigenous death in social media platforms.

HAUNTING AND DISPOSABILITY IN MEXICO

In Mexico, Indigenous social haunting is palpable. It is present in every pyramid and yácata,[1] in artifacts trapped in a museum, in the codices written by Indigenous historians, in the statues honoring heroes like the final Aztec emperor Cuauhtémoc[2] and the revolutionary historical figure Emiliano Zapata.[3] It is visually manifest in every Mesoamerican relic and mural that tells Mexico's story, as well as in the *pasamontañas* (ski masks) shielding the faces of *comandantes* (commanders) of the EZLN.[4] These reminders of the past remind us of what sociologist Natividad Gutiérrez has termed Mexico's ultimate contradiction: the tendency to glorify the Indigenous past while marginalizing contemporary Indigenous communities and, consequently, denying them the right to an autonomous future (Gutiérrez 1999, 98). These spaces and relics manifest ghosts that not only speak of the violence committed against Indigenous bodies in the past but also demand that "something be done" as Mexico faces its future.

Sociologist Avery Gordon posits that haunting is present in the material production of things as well as in the social relations between people. History is, for Gordon, always a site of struggle between the living and the dead and the ghostly manifestations in the materiality of everyday life demand a "something-to-be-done" (Gordon 1997, xvi), particularly in situations where injustices have ensued. The casualties of mass acts of violence may be trapped in a constant state of remembrance where they are bound to develop ghostly haunts and must call for an official inquiry into their deaths.[5] Ghosts implore that we be accountable to the people who were not counted. This query demands the reinscription of the marginalized and racialized into the writing of history by the public who passively bore witness to or benefitted from the deaths; it calls that those who share social group status or nationality with the ghosts view themselves as agents who can critically question their amnesia and/or acknowledge their roles and responsibilities for the atrocities committed.

While theories of social haunting speak to the contemporary relevance of colonial violence, they do not reflect on the contemporary disposability of Indigenous peoples, nor do they explore how mass violence against Indigenous bodies create ghostly hauntings. Disposability has informed the racialization of Indigenous peoples since the inception of colonial violence in the Americas.[6] In her book *Dying from Improvement*, Shireen Razack argues that Indigenous bodies are disposable to settler societies because settler colonialism relies on the trope of the disappearing Indian, and violently evicting Indigenous bodies from the land is normalized to appease settler fantasies. Even when they are victims of homicide, Indians are typically blamed for their own deaths. Alcoholism, dysfunction, and poverty are named as contributing factors because Indigenous people are framed as "incompletely modern" or unable to survive modernity (Razack 2015, 12). Tanya Talaga (Ojibwe) draws similar conclusions from an analysis of the inquest into seven missing and/or deceased aboriginal students attending high school in Thunder Bay, Ontario, in the early 2000s. These children's mysterious disappearances or drowning deaths in rivers surrounding Lake Superior are blamed on alcohol and suicide, despite the presence of cuts on some of the bodies and the students' experiences of severe anti-Indigenous racism in their schools and in the community (Talaga 2017, 285).[7]

The framework of disposability and/or what scholar Lisa Marie Cacho has termed "social death" applies to the treatment of Indigenous lives and deaths in Mexico. Mexican Indigenous people, too, experience state violence and murder with impunity because they are "ineligible for personhood" before the state (Cacho 2012, 6). Relegated to the past and/or viewed as premodern, Indigenous people in Mexico have been denied their humanity by the majority of the mestiza/o population and the Mexican government. This is evident in the ongoing atrocities committed against Indigenous bodies today and in the Mexican government's apparent war against Indigenous autonomy. Within this context, Indigenous autonomy is viewed as contradictory because according to the state backward people do not know how to govern themselves or how to manage their resources or land. Anti-Indigenous racism has been cemented into Mexican society since the Spanish *encomiendas* treated Indigenous people as exploitable and Indigenous women, specifically, as rapeable. Marked by poverty and marginality and viewed as speaking unintelligible languages, Indians in Mexico are socially dead. As Cacho states, "Racism is a killing abstraction. It creates spaces of living death and populations 'dead-to-others.' It ensures that certain people will live an 'abstract existence' where 'living is something to be achieved and not experienced'" (Cacho 2012, 7).

In *Dying from Improvement*, Razack states, "In pursuing the official story about Indigenous death in custody, this book does not expand upon how Indigenous communities live with disappearances" (2015, 7). In other words, her analysis does not extrapolate to ghostly hauntings, to querying how Indigenous absences impact the communities themselves and what they demand from Canadian society at large. In this chapter, I weave the framework of disposability with the theory of social death to propose that Indigenous hauntings in Mexico extend from physical structures that present Indigenous people as "remnants of the past" to the Indigenous bodies that have become casualties to the Drug War and to the Mexican government's repression of autonomy movements. I will then argue that Indigenous journalists, activists, and movement participants document the killing of Indigenous people and create hashtags to answer the dead's desire to be named, the disappeared's need to be found, and to encourage the Mexican public to bear witness to the violence when the government is invested in censure and silencing. Indeed, in bearing witness by capturing the violence with smartphones and then posting horrific footage on social media, Indigenous and mestiza/o journalists and activists are answering the ghostly haunting's desire to "go viral" in order to demand the "something-to-be-done" from the interfaces of the Internet, an audience of fellow *mexicanos* and members of the international community who may be invested in learning about genocidal moments impacting Mexican Indigenous people.

INDIGENOUS SOCIAL HAUNTINGS IN THE AGE OF THE INTERNET

As technological advances ensue, Indigenous lives are considered superfluous to modernization and to capitalist growth and are therefore subject to exclusion from the official story (ineligible for humanity) and to digital social death. Indigenous people, however, have been engaging with technology since the pre-Cuauhtémoc period, when the Americas enjoyed technological advances that surpassed those in Europe. As communications scholar Marisa Elena Duarte (Yaqui) reminds us, despite the digital divide and inequality that has impacted Indigenous people, we have been engaging with the Internet since its beginnings, using it as a platform to promote our causes, to preserve our culture, and to build what she terms "network sovereignty" (2017, 115–16). Our engagement with these interfaces, indeed, is part of our timeless tradition to record our histories, tell our stories, and I propose bear witness to the changes and fluctuations in loss of life that affect us. Duarte summarizes it best when she contextualizes the EZLN's use of the Internet in a long Maya tradition of textuality and inscription: "The difference between, for example, Mayan ancestors inscribing prophetic histories on a rock face and Zapatista Subcomandante Marcos issuing cyber communiques via airwaves is in the choice of media and in the desired impact. Across centuries, however, the drive toward Maya autonomy is the same. The philosophies are resilient, explanatory, and intact. The peoples are connected and waiting for the messages" (2017, 27). Although Duarte doesn't explicitly name them, the EZLN's efforts to expose genocidal moments like the Acteal massacre, an instance in December 1997 when Mexican paramilitaries killed forty-five Tzotzil people attending a prayer meeting in the small village of Acteal, countered the looming threat of narratives of extinction and inferiority that have been applied to Indigenous people since the pre-Cuauhctémoc period. Whether denouncing NAFTA and neoliberalism or sharing photos of the victims of Acteal, the Zapatistas made Indigenous death visible using the Internet.

Today, more than ever, Indigenous death haunts the digital world. The War on Drugs has turned into a civil war between corrupt politicians and drug cartels, and the primary casualties have been thousands of innocent Mexicans, many of them from Indigenous communities. Since December 2006, when President Felipe Calderón deployed more than 6,500 Mexican soldiers to Michoacán to fight drug traffickers (followed by a deployment of an additional 20,000 troops throughout Mexico two months later), more than 26,000 Mexicans have gone missing[8] and more than 138,000 people have been killed. This stands without accounting for the deaths and disappearances of thousands of Central Americans en route to the United States, many also victims of the Drug War. The majority of those atrocities are accredited to organized crime.[9] The United States has been complicit in the Mexican War on Drugs by providing $2.3 billion in aid since 2008 to purchase equipment and to train police and K9s while America's citizens continue to be the primary consumers of drugs imported from Mexico.[10] In a short decade, Mexicans have been slaughtered to support a multibillion-dollar business that largely benefits drug cartels and the politicians on their payroll.

In the digital age, the deaths of Mexicans have become public spectacle. A quick Google search of these and related key words results in gory images of decapitated heads, tortured nude bodies, and lines of men with AK-47s pointed at them. Mexican death is consumed without context of the violence on the Internet, via snuff videos produced by drug cartels shared on social media, the proliferation of an obsession with narco-culture on video-streaming services like Netflix and Hulu, and through the distribution of black-and-white photos of missing young people on various platforms. There is a paradox here between the immediate access to spectating the graphic deaths of Mexicans involved in or affected by the Drug War and the Indigenous haunting that transpires in Mexico. The men being targeted by the Drug War whose deaths and mutilated bodies we consume in these images and videos are primarily uneducated, impoverished mestizo men feeling disenfranchised by the hetero-patriarchal demands of a failing Mexican economy. Their deaths are treated like statistics in a war that takes no prisoners; they are viewed as "getting what they deserve" with mentions of their pre-cartel lives mostly erased. Their disposabil-ity, however, is different than the disposability of Indigenous people targeted by the cartels and the state. While their ghosts may desire to be named, many of these men are also the ones responsible for committing injustices in a war that most violently impacts women and Indigenous communities. They became disposable *after* the carnage turned their bodies into nonhuman matter, whereas, as the most marginalized, the disposability of women and Indigenous people was presumed *before* death. Their bodies were targeted for gory hate-motivated violence displayed online before the Drug War. The haunting of Indigenous people then demands political action and accountability, a call to end injustice targeting specific communities. The Indigenous nameless must come to light during this moment of pronounced violence because their lives are in increased danger as they fight for autonomy in territory being encroached upon by the cartels. In an age where the death of the nameless can be instantly shared online and when naming the nameless can result in death for those living in the eye of the hurricane, then how can online platforms be used to name the dead and bring justice to those most marginalized by the Drug War? How can the very platform that homogenizes and spectacularizes Mexican death be used to bring justice to the ghostly hauntings of the victims demanding answers?

MAKING INDIGENOUS SOCIAL DEATH AND HAUNTING VISIBLE ON THE WEB

The Internet has grown as a space to organize against Mexican government corruption and drug cartel violence since the Drug War erupted. Hashtags have been particularly useful in naming the Indigenous casualties of today's violence in Mexico, though the use of hashtags to build social movements around racial, economic, and social justice is not unique to Mexico or to Indigenous com-munities.[11] Indigenous communities in different states and municipalities have responded to the government's collusion with the cartels by forming *autode-fensas* (self-defense armies) to take up arms in order to defend themselves from drug cartels. Following in the footsteps of the EZLN, autodefensas currently operate in more than thirteen states and sixty-eight municipalities.[12]

#YOAMOCHERAN: ORGANIC AUTONOMY-BUILDING IN MICHOACÁN

One of the first autodefensas was born in Cherán K'eri, Michoacán, where P'urhépechas began organizing against illegal logging coordinated by drug cartels as early as 2008. After being victimized by drug lords, who were taxing communal famers and orchestrating illegal logging operations that led to the deforestation of 70 percent of Pakua Karakua (Cherán's forest), Cherán K'eri's *comuneros* (inhabitants) collected weapons and took up arms. Cherán K'eri's declaration of autonomy became official in April 2011 after P'urhépecha women were almost killed by a truck of illegal loggers as the women attempted to block their exit with the forest's booty. The community then organized able-bodied men into armed patrols while the women held watch over *fogatas* (bonfire barricades) in order to stop the pillaging of Pakua Karakua. When Cherán K'eri's comuneros realized that their local government was complicit in the illegal logging of their forest, they turned to *La Relación de Michoacán*, the account of P'urhépecha origins and pre-Conquest history orated by P'urhépecha historians to Spanish friars circa 1540, for instructions on erecting an autonomous government modeled after pre-colonial P'urhépecha governance.[13] Campaigns and politicians affiliated with Mexican political parties are no longer allowed in Cherán K'eri. A general counsel of community elders was elected and the municipal authorities ejected. The council's demands include safety, justice, and the reforestation of their territory—all goals that the community actively works toward as they organically build autonomy against the constant threat of drug cartel violence.[14] There have been more than twenty murders and kidnappings of P'urhépecha activists from Cherán K'eri and of journalists who covered the story after a government-sanctioned media blackout.[15] These murders and disappearances remain unsolved as Indigenous people's lives continue being undervalued in the current wave of mass violence in Mexico.

In the midst of the violence in Chéran K'eri, P'urhépecha activists and their accomplices created and released their own media, popularizing the hashtags #CheranMichoacan, #YoAmoCheran, and #CheranSeLevanta to proliferate their message and counter the media blackout. P'urhépecha journalist Pedro

Victoriano Cruz created a series of documentaries and posted them on You-Tube, later sharing them via Facebook with the hashtags #CheranMichoacan and #CheranSeLevanta. These productions were liked and shared hundreds of times and led to P'urhépecha migrants in the United States organizing efforts to fundraise in support of autonomy-building in Cherán K'eri and soliciting letters of support for the movement from entities in the United States. Additionally, the Facebook group Yo Amo Cherán was created by mestiza/o allies with the movement. The group posts prominent updates about the happenings in Cherán, including clandestine reporting via smartphone recordings as violence erupts on the ground. It has been the primary source of information on social media about what became an internationally known movement for P'urhépecha autonomy covered by outlets like Al Jazeera, the BBC, and Univision. Currently, the group enjoys more than 42,500 Facebook likes and more than 40,000 followers (this may not seem extensive, but it has made a great difference for a movement that suffered a state-sanctioned media blackout). Together, the hashtags and Facebook page brought visibility to the dozens of disappeared and murdered comuneros from Cherán K'eri, including Urbano Macías Rafael and Guadalupe Gerónimo Velasquez, whose tortured bodies were discovered in a forest near Zacapu.[16] In January 2018 the community was shocked by the discovery of the Guadalupe campaneur's nude body in Chilchota. "Lupita" was a young thirty-two-year-old P'urhépecha woman who had been active in Cherán K'eri's movement since its birth. Unlike the high-profile cases of disappeared and mutilated mestizas in places like Mexico City, Lupita's death has not been labeled a femicide although her body showed signs of strangulation.[17] Her death barely garnered media attention. The community and, more specifically, P'urhépecha women have taken to the streets and to social media to demand #JusticiaParaLupita.[18] Justice continues to evade the P'urhépechas murdered for protecting their resources from outside extraction and their families from violence.

#NOSFALTAN43 AND NAMING DISAPPEARED INDIGENOUS YOUTH

In September 2014, forty-three Me'phaa, Nahua, and Mixtec *normalistas* (student-teachers) from Ayotzinapa, Guerrero, disappeared in Iguala after the group of students claimed three government-owned buses to transport them to a protest in remembrance of the 1968 massacre of student demonstrators in Tlatelolco. In their efforts to name the victims from the massacre in Tlatelolco, the student-teachers were kidnapped by the "Guerreros Unidos" drug cartel and reportedly shot and burned. The case sparked national outrage against the Mexican government after suspects revealed that María de los Ángeles Pineda Villa, the spouse of the mayor of Iguala, ordered the students' disappearance. The hashtags #NosFaltan43 and #AyotzinapaSomosTodos emerged as rallying cries for the disappeared students, who were presumed dead. In this case, university students in urban centers popularized the hashtags as they identified themselves with the young student-teachers. The popularization of the search for the missing normalistas through the hashtags gave the case international coverage and led to international media outlets and celebrities like Puerto Rican singer "Residente" from the band Calle 13 covering the disappearances as serious casualties of the Drug War. The parents of the disappeared students mobilized online and on the ground, urging authorities to uncover the events that led to the kidnapping of their sons, employing the hashtags as rallying cries. Although not immune from threats and violence, activists continued to demand the unearthing of the bodies of the student-activists. In their searches, Mexican law enforcement ultimately found mass graves of more unidentified victims from the Drug War.[19] And, adding unimaginable insult to injury, the body of Miguel Ángel Jiménez Blanco, the activist prominently leading search efforts for the missing normalistas, was found riddled with bullets in August 2015.[20]

The cry for justice for Ayotzinapa via #NosFaltan43 continues today. The hashtag is used to both call for justice for the disappeared students and to shame the politicians and officials who have not cooperated with the investigation. An example of the extended use of this hashtag transpired in May 2015 when a video of Lorenzo Córdova, the president of Mexico's National Electoral Institute, was leaked on YouTube. In the video, Córdova insulted the parents of the missing student-teachers after meeting with them to discuss voting barriers impacting Indigenous people. In the leaked footage, Córdova can be heard openly mocking the speech of the normalistas' parents, claiming they are unintelligible because Spanish is their second language. At one point he says, "I almost thought the guy was going to say, 'Me Great Chief Sitting Bull, Leader of the great Chichimec Nation'" (2015, n.p.).[21] Córdova's tone and language demonstrated his complete ignorance of linguistic complexity and utter disrespect toward Indigenous people. His racist comment poured salt on the wounds of a nation still mourning the disappearance of the student-teachers;

people took to Twitter to call him an incompetent racist and to demand that he be removed from his post. Córdova released a video with a nonapology where he expressed more preoccupation with the way the footage was obtained and leaked than with the feelings of those he offended.[22] Córdova's attitude toward Indians like the normalistas and their parents echoed that of other Mexican officials: the backward Indian normalistas were disposable, their bodies having been allegedly incinerated and dumped in a trash can by Guerreros Unidos.[23] Their lives were inconsequential to Mexican political life. They were marked by social death as racialized and impoverished and thereby ineligible for humanity, and the unworthiness attributed to their remains projected unto their parents, who as Indians were always already unworthy of dignified treatment or answers.

The kidnappings and killings of these poor rural Indigenous student-teachers and of Miguel Ángel Jiménez Blanco, like those of the missing comuneros from Cherán K'eri, demonstrate the devastating effect that Mexico's Drug War has had on Indigenous people. Further, the hashtags associated with Ayotzinapa have opened up conversations about racism and anti-Indigenous attitudes in Mexico on Twitter and other Internet forums. During a time when "race" continues to be taboo in Mexican society, these hashtags have served to open up conversations about power, privilege, and inequality in Mexico.[24]

#TODOSSOMOSARANTEPACUA AND THE CONTINUANCE OF INDIGENOUS DEATH

The most recent violence in Michoacán has taken place in the communities of Caltzontzin and Arantepacua. Both conflicts have arisen out of P'urhépechas' call for honoring original land grants. Both communities were inspired and supported by Cherán K'eri and both have been met with government bullets and repression. In December 2016, Cherán K'eri hosted the first Gathering of Indigenous Peoples of Michoacán. Communities like Pichataro, Aranza, Caltzontzin, and Arantepacua became inspired to organize their own community patrols to defend their resources with the end goal of building autonomy. The comuneros of Caltzontzin decided to reclaim the territory that the community was evacuated from after Paricutin erupted in 1943. They claim that they never ceded that land to the Mexican government and in February 2017 demanded a meeting with Silvano Aureoles, the governor of Michoacán. Their demands for a meeting or public hearing were shut down by a governor with an anti-Indigenous track record. The community responded by blocking the highway and roads going into their town. Auroles ordered the deployment of one thousand policemen to Caltzontzin to terrorize the townspeople. Many were wounded and seventeen were arrested.[25] Although media outlets did not extensively cover the repression in Caltzontzin, the hashtag #Caltzontzin recalls testimonies from the violence and demands freedom for the P'urhépechas who were imprisoned without just cause.

Arantepacua took arms to defend 520 acres of forest territory granted to them in a 1941 treaty. The land in question is rich in pine trees and was given to the nearby community of Capacuaro in 1986 by presidential decree. Although this land dispute is between two P'urhépecha communities, the violent outbreak has been a result of government repression rather than provoked by the P'urhépecha intra-conflict. Michoacán's government claims that thirty-eight P'urhépechas from Arantepacua were arrested on April 4, 2017, because they defiantly captured a government-owned bus after their request for a hearing to resolve the land dispute between the two communities was denied. Comuneros in Arantepacua responded to the arrests of their comrades by capturing twenty government-owned vehicles and holding them in their community. Aureoles's government then deployed four hundred policemen to recapture the vehicles, and officers tear-gassed residents upon entry into the community without explaining why they were there. They then forced their way into homes without warrants, stole jewelry, and terrorized women and children. Police killed three comuneros in Arantepacua, including unarmed high school student Luis Gustavo Hernández Cuente, who died after police shot into the barbershop where he was getting a haircut.

Underresourced and vulnerable, more than 80 percent of Arantepacua's residents are classified as living in dire poverty. Community members claim that they offered to give up the vehicles to the police but were met with violence and gunfire.[26] Using the hashtags #TodosSomosArantepacua and #Arantepacua, comuneros hold Aureoles's government solely responsible for the violence and murders; they do not point the finger at Capacuaro, which received their own repressive violence at the hands of the government for their involvement in the land conflict. To add insult to injury, it was later revealed that hours before the attack on Arantepacua, Governor Auroles dissolved Michoacán's Office of the Secretary for Indigenous Communities, a social service agency that provided some of the limited resources that the state was funneling to Michoacán's Indigenous populations.

The repression that Indigenous communities in Michoacán face is not new. The events in Arantepacua were denounced by well-known Indigenous rights proponents and agencies because the government can no longer hide its repression. In the age of smartphones and other handheld devices, the crimes of policemen and state-sanctioned violence are more likely to be documented and shared online. Shortly after terrifying video footage was released documenting the siege of a poor unarmed P'urhépecha pueblo, entities like the EZLN and the National Indigenous Congress released statements condemning the actions of Aureoles's government, naming the community's decision as a choice to "not allow themselves to be killed, dispossessed, or bought" (qtd. in Pavón-Cuellar 2017, n.p.).[27] These national entities and Michoacán's Indigenous organizations including the Council of Cherán K'eri and Michoacán's Supreme Indigenous Council identify the violence against Michoacán's Indigenous communities as part of a legacy of conquest and colonization that began with Hernán Cortés's arrival to Mexico in 1521. Meanwhile, Arantepacua identifies their divine right to self-determination using the Mexican government's own constitution as well as international accords that recognize Indigenous communities' rights to autonomy. The climate in Michoacán is one of repression and racist violence that first and foremost targets Indigenous insurgency.

Journalist David Pavón-Cuellar's poignant analysis speaks to the connection between Governor Aureoles's attitude and that of common colonizers: "This attack must be understood as just another link in the series of actions and decisions against Indigenous communities, especially against those which have had the gall to resist the destruction orchestrated by the governments of Peña Nieto and Silvano Aureoles, men who are fitting heirs to the likes of conquistadors Hernán Cortés and Cristóbal de Olid"[28] (2017, n.p.). The colonial violence targeting Indigenous communities appears to be similar, although the forces infringing on Indigenous lands and resources have changed. Today, instead of conquistadores and their accompanying dogs, it may be drug cartels, what the EZLN has called "el mal gobierno" (poor governance) and multinational corporations, but the new wave of repressive violence is still undoubtedly driven by notions of Indigenous disposability and inferiority (anti-Indigenous racism) and by the capitalist desire to exploit Indigenous people and Indigenous resources. Mexico, like Canada and the United States, is imagined as landscape where the real Indians have perished and their remnants are inconveniences to settler and neoliberal desires (Razack 2015, 8).

The social haunting of the past is ever-present during these turbulent and bloody times when Mexicans are being slaughtered and are slaughtering each other. While Mexicans are desperately turning to each other to ask, "Where do we go from here?" Gordon's work calls forth the question, "What do ghosts demand that we do?" Accustomed to making their own humanity visible, Indigenous people have addressed both of these questions. For Indigenous communities invested in controlling their natural resources and educational institutions and in preserving their languages and defining their own identities, autonomy is an important means of guaranteeing their fully achieved destiny as human beings.[29] For these communities, the ghost demands visibility and so they organize; they organize to make Indigenous haunting visible through accessible platforms on low budgets (such as social media). *Se los agarran a twitazos!*[30] They use hashtags to counter notions of Indigenous disposability and invisibility, to demand that the dead are named, counted, and found. They stash weapons and organize community patrols against cartel violence and they work toward what Victoriano Cruz calls "digital sovereign territory" (qtd. in Taylor 2017, n.p.) and what María Teresa Duarte terms "network sovereignty" (2017, 5), building international networks of sympathizers through the interfaces of the World Wide Web. The question of "What is to be done," however, continues to haunt Mexicans during a time when, engulfed in civil war replete with indiscriminate carnage and human rights violations, the country feels as though it escapes us. "Where do we go from here" as a collective may not become clear until the injustices and atrocities committed against Mexico's disenfranchised are addressed. In that spirit, I will conclude by exploring how Mexican mestizos can concretely demonstrate solidarity with Mexican Indigenous communities.

#UNMUNDODONDEQUEPANMUCHOSMUNDOS AND #CAMINANDOJUNTOS

Despite the paralyzing fear driven by staggering drug violence, Mexican society is not mute or complicit. This is apparent in the social movements that persist and continue to demand justice for all those murdered and disappeared under Mexico's current conditions. Millions of Mexicans took to the streets after results of the 2012 election were announced. Mexicans have strategically relied on social media to mobilize people into social action. The movement

#YoSoy132, led by mestiza/o college students, organized protests against the election of Enrique Peña Nieto and provided a platform to voice the concerns of disenfranchised young people. The success of #YoSoy132 successfully sparked other Twitter hashtags, such as #MexicoMeDueles and #YaMeCanse, platforms that gave everyday Mexicans an international platform to denounce political corruption. Additionally, #TodosSomosAutodefensas and #AyotzinapaSomosTodos allowed Mexicans to demonstrate solidarity with Indigenous people affected by the Drug War. The kidnappings and killings of the forty-three student-teachers in Ayotzinapa received international attention by notable news outlets, thanks to Mexican journalists and everyday Mexican citizens who have continued to leak information. This campaign of outrage transmitted via social media has been largely fueled by mestiza/o solidarity (members of what the EZLN terms "*la sociedad civil*"). Importantly, the parents of the missing forty-three student-teachers have been at the forefront of the movement as leaders and speakers, while Mexican mestizas and mestizos have shown up by the hundred thousands on social media and in-person to protest the disappearances. The fact that Mexicans have not shied away from framing the killings as violent acts fueled by anti-Indian sentiment and prejudiced racism is also noteworthy. Ayotzinapa activism and #AyotzinapaSomosTodos are prime examples of Mexican mestizos' meaningful solidarity for a timely and important Indigenous cause.

The most interesting result, perhaps, of Mexicanos' use of Twitter hashtags to express political outrage is that these hashtags have sparked discussions about race in Mexico in a way that analog forums did not. As an example, people tweeted against Liliana Sevilla, director of Tijuana's Municipal Women's Institute, using the hashtags #LadyEuropa and #LadyIndigena after she posted an anti-Indian comment on Facebook: "What if all that is mine is in Europe and here I am suffering amongst these Indians?"[31] The tweets led Sevilla to publish an empty apology (blaming the post on humor) and to quit her public office just days after her racist comment was denounced by other mestizos on social media.[32] In an age when Indigenous deaths must be accounted for, it is important that anti-Indigenous racism be denounced and that public shaming results in consequences for the racists. Indigenous mobilizations have demonstrated that Indigenous lives must be respected, and that, against the frameworks of invisibility and disposability, Indigenous peoples be seen as contemporary political subjects. Additionally, decolonizing models created by Mexico's Indigenous peoples have provided clear courses of action.

In the absence of hashtags, the EZLN reached the Mexican and international population in 1994 by posting their declarations online. The EZLN
indeed became pioneers in their use of technology and engaging the international community and international media to call attention to Mexican Indigenous communities and to Mexican Indigenous social movements. They devised
catchphrases that were not hashtags at the time but functioned nonetheless as
effective calls for solidarity—particularly from mestiza/o "civil society." In their
Cuarta Declaración de la Selva Lacandona (1996; "Fourth Declaration from the
Lacandon Jungle"), the EZLN calls for Mexicans to build "a world where many
worlds fit."[33] The EZLN insisted from its inception that autonomy-building
should not rely on one universal model or on the belief-system of one people.
Rather, EZLN leaders advocated for the coexistence of different worldviews
within a movement for social justice. This meant that there would be room for
mestizos in the EZLN's vision for a just world for Indigenous people, and that
mestizos should fight for a "world where many worlds fit."

In their *Sexta Declaración de la Selva Lacandona* (2005; "Sixth Declaration
from the Lacandon Jungle"), the EZLN called for a model of "*caminando
juntos,*" or walking alongside each other. "La Sexta" called upon all oppressed
sectors of Mexican society, including women, the poor, the disabled, Indigenous communities, and LGBT people to walk alongside each other, to work
toward their shared vision of a Mexican government that will deliver justice to
the oppressed.[34] The EZLN, however, defined "caminando juntos" as building
autonomy according to one's own local context. "Caminando juntos" does not
necessarily call for allies to join the EZLN army or to move to Chiapas. After
all, remaining autonomous means that Indigenous people should be able to
define and lead their own movements rather than take cues from outsiders.
Instead, the EZLN calls for people to struggle for autonomy within their local
contexts and to build autonomy according to their own desires and rules.

The EZLN is intent on Indigenous movements being Indigenous-led and
so solidarity from mestizos would mean "walking alongside each other" without intruding on Indigenous sovereignty. Indigenous communities in Michoacán articulate the same objectives of solidarity while remaining autonomous.
This is an important lesson: Indigenous communities are not looking to be led
into freedom by mestiza/o saviors. Meaningful solidarity implies a respect for
the centuries of struggle that Indigenous peoples have endured and the sociocultural context that informed Indigenous modes of organizing. Being led by
Indigenous people (rather than attempting to consume Indigenous identities)

and allowing (and supporting) Indigenous people's quest for their own liberation is an effective way to respond to Mexico's Indigenous hauntings and to address the ghosts' imploring that "something-to-be-done."

PARTING WORDS

If we understand Zapatista/Maya/Mesoamerican engagement with technology as part of a continuum that dates back to the pre-Cuauhtémoc era, we can conceptualize the building of network sovereignty in Mexico as one of the many means that Mexican Indigenous communities have accessed to protect Mother Earth, their territory, their resources and wellness, to wage war (albeit currently metaphorical) against forces attempting to obliterate their existence, to communicate in their languages and across borders and nations, to build community and engage in diplomatic negotiations, to promote their cultures and identities, to talk to each other and to build strategic alliances with other Indigenous tribes and nations. The major difference between using technology in the pre-Cuauhtémoc era and doing so today is that Indigenous people face the challenge of defining their peoplehood in the face of colonization. I have discussed the use of smartphones to document the Mexican government's and the cartels' slaughter of Indigenous people as an immediately accessible means to bear witness to atrocities. The resultant use of hashtags, then, becomes a means to encourage Mexican "civil society" and the world to also bear witness to the disposability of Indigenous bodies. In this way, demanding that Indigenous death be seen in social media is a means to challenge Indigenous social death and a call to rehumanize Indians. It is a way for the ghost of Indigenous hauntings to materialize in the interface of the Internet so that the "something-to-be-done" is addressed.

Since the Zapatista revolt, Indigenous autonomy has taken on an array of meanings; it has been theorized from the landscapes of Indigenous women's bodies thanks to the demands of the EZLN's Revolutionary Law for Women, it has been articulated in literal terms attached to land rights and in abstract terms attached to intellectual property rights and Indigenous identities, it has meant cutting ties with political parties and reimagining how to practice decolonial governance, it has called for economic self-determination in the face of ongoing neoliberalism, it has meant stashing and taking up arms when necessary. Autonomy has taken shape in the right of Indigenous peoples to defend themselves:

as autodefensas. On- and offline, autonomy is the antonym for Indigenous disposability and invisibility. Autonomy is a declaration of Indigenous life in the face of death.

NOTES

1. Yácatas: pyramid structures built by P'urhépecha people in precolonial times.
2. Cuauhtémoc was the Aztec leader (tlatoani) of Tenochtitlan from 1520 to 1521.
3. Emiliano Zapata was the leader of the Mexican Revolution from 1909 to 1919 and is known to be of Nahua descent.
4. The EZLN (Ejército Zapatista para la Liberación Nacional) is a militarized Indigenous organization made up of Maya communities based out of the Lacandon Jungle in Chiapas, Mexico. They declared war on the Mexican government on January 1, 1994, agreed to a cease-fire twelve days into the war, and continue building autonomous communities called *caracoles* (snails) in the territory they control. Italics used followed by parentheses as we have done with chapter 9.
5. Gordon contends that ghosts have their own desires, which may speak to addressing the consequences of institutional violence such as the long-term impacts of slavery, or to naming invisible entities (such as racialized/gendered capitalism). For example, the monuments that recall the slave trade address the silencing of people who were excluded from the historical record (Gordon 1997, 139).
6. Historian Andrés Reséndez has extensively researched the paramount number of cases of enslavement and sex trafficking impacting Indigenous people in the Americas. For further reading with statistical data and historical accounts of Indigenous disposability, see his book *The Other Slavery: The Uncovered Story of Indian Enslavement* (Reséndez 2016).
7. Both Razack 2016 and Talaga ("Inquiry" 2017a) also write about the pandemic of missing and murdered Indigenous women in Canada in a similar vein; a culture of impunity surrounds the rapes and murders of Indigenous women because their sexual assaults, disappearances, and deaths are seen as natural occurrences attributed to their impoverished "lifestyles" rather than to the settler rapist pathologies of their (typically white male) perpetrators.
8. "Mexico Drug War Fast Facts" (CNN 2018).
9. Heinle, Molzahn, and Shirk 2015.
10. See Gómez 2015 and Associated Press 2009.
11. For further scholarship on hashtag activism, see Taylor's analysis of the growth of Black Lives Matter from a hasthtag to a social movement (2016) and Rambukkana's book *Hashtag Publics* (2014) where he elaborates how hashtags contribute to building political discursive networks. Kuo 2018 and Sharma 2014 are also relevant.
12. Espach and Asfura-Heim 2013.
13. The Fault Lines Digital Team 2014.
14. Sedillo 2013.
15. Pacheco 2014.

16. Martínez, Pérez, and Pérez 2012.

17. Linthicum and McDonnell 2018.

18. Nobiss 2018 features a picture of P'urhépecha women and girls holding poster-size photos of Lupita Campaneur. One poster features the hashtag #JusticiaParaLupita demonstrating that P'urhépecha women and girls participated in large public demonstrations (including the Women's March in Seattle referenced in this article) to bring awareness to Guadalupe Campaneur's death.

19. Lankhani 2015.

20. Jenkins 2015.

21. El Economista 2015. My translation; original quote, "Ya nada más le faltó decir, 'yo Gran Jefe Toro Sentado, líder de gran nación chichimeca.'"

22. El Financiero 2015.

23. Mosso 2016.

24. Godoy 2015.

25. Olvera 2017.

26. Pavón-Cuellar 2017.

27. Pavón-Cuellar 2017.

28. Pavón-Cuellar 2017. My translation; original quote: "Este ataque tan sólo resulta comprensible como un eslabón de la serie de acciones y decisiones contra las comunidades indígenas, especialmente contra aquellas que se han atrevido a resistir contra la estrategia destructora orquestada por los gobiernos de Peña Nieto y de Silvano Aureoles, dignos herederos de los conquistadores Hernán Cortés y Cristóbal de Olid."

29. Mexican sociologist Rudolfo Stavenhagen defines autonomy according to these specific terms in the introduction to the book *Indigenous Autonomy in Mexico*, edited by Aracely Burguete Cal y Mayor (Stavenhagen 2000).

30. This is a colloquial expression used by Mexican youth to describe public online shaming of corrupt politicians. It roughly translates into "they beat them with tweets."

31. My translation, original quote: "Qué tal si lo mío está en Europa y yo aquí sufriendo con estos indígenas?"

32. Salinas 2015.

33. Comité Clandestino Revolucionario Indígena-Comandancia General del Ejercito Zapatista para la Liberación Nacional 2015.

34. Comité Clandestino Revolucionario Indígena-Comandancia General del Ejercito Zapatista para la Liberación Nacional 2005.

REFERENCES

Associated Press. 2009. "U.S. Drug Habits Help Finance Mexican Cartels." *NBC News*, May 26, 2009. http://www.nbcnews.com/id/30946730/ns/us_news-crime_and _courts/t/us-drug-habits-help-finance-mexican-cartels/#.VcvjloX2im4.

Cacho, Lisa Marie. 2012. *Social Death: Racialized Rightlessness and the Criminalization of the Unprotected*. New York: New York University Press.

Castellanos, Laura. 2017. "The Feminist Indigenous Candidate Running for President of Mexico." *Vice*, November 13, 2017. https://www.vice.com/en_us/article/9kqbqd/the-feminist-Indigenous-candidate-running-for-president-of-mexico.

CNN Library. 2018. "Mexico Drug War Fast Facts." Updated July 16, 2018. http://www.cnn.com/2013/09/02/world/americas/mexico-drug-war-fast-facts.

Comité Clandestino Revolucionario Indígena-Comandancia General del Ejercito Zapatista para la Liberación Nacional. 1996. "Cuarta Declaración de la Selva Lacandona." January 1996. http://palabra.ezln.org.mx/comunicados/1996/1996_01_01_a.htm.

Comité Clandestino Revolucionario Indígena-Comandancia General del Ejercito Zapatista para la Liberación Nacional. 2005. "Sixth Declaration of the Lacandon Jungle." June 2005. http://enlacezapatista.ezln.org.mx/sdsl-en.

Duarte, Marisa Elena. 2017. *Network Sovereignty: Building the Internet Across Indian Country*. Seattle and London: University of Washington Press.

El Economista. 2017. "Lorenzo Córdova sobre indígenas y padres de Ayotzinapa." June 4, 2017. http://eleconomista.com.mx/sociedad/2015/05/19/lorenzo-cordova-sobre-indigenas-padres-ayotzinapa.

Ejercito Zapatista para La Liberación Nacional. 2017. "Comunicado Conjunto del CNI y del EZLN Denunciando la Represión Contra la Comunidad P'urhépecha de Arantepacua, Michoacán." Enlace Zapatista. April 6, 2017. http://enlacezapatista.ezln.org.mx/2017/04/06/comunicado-conjunto-del-cni-y-el-ezln-denunciando-la-represion-contra-la-comunidad-purepecha-de-arantepacua-michoacan/.

Espach Ralph H., and Patricio Asfura-Heim. 2013. "The Rise of Mexico's Self-Defense Forces: Vigilante Justice South of the Border." *Foreign Affairs Magazine*, July/August 2013. https://www.foreignaffairs.com/articles/mexico/2013-06-11/rise-mexico-s-self-defense-forces.

The Fault Lines Digital Team. 2014. "How a Mexican Town Toppled a Cartel and Established Its Independence." *Al Jazeera*, May 1, 2014. http://america.aljazeera.com/watch/shows/fault-lines/FaultLinesBlog/2014/5/1/how-a-mexican-towntoppledacartelandestablisheditsindependence.html.

El Financiero. 2015. "Lorenzo Córdova se disculpa por comentarios discriminatorios." May 19, 2015. http://www.elfinanciero.com.mx/nacional/lorenzo-cordova-se-disculpa-por-comentarios-discriminatorios.html.

Godoy, Emilio. 2015. "Missing Students Case Highlights Racism in Mexico." *Mint Press News*, January 31, 2015. http://www.mintpressnews.com/missing-students-case-highlights-racism-in-mexico/201719.

Gómez, Alan. 2015. "After Years of Drug Wars, Murders Decline in Mexico." *USA Today*, April 30, 2015. https://www.usatoday.com/story/news/world/2015/04/30/mexico-drug-war-homicides-decline/26574309.

Gordon, Avery F. 1997. *Ghostly Matters: Haunting and the Sociological Imagination*. Minneapolis: University of Minnesota Press.

Gutiérrez, Natividad. 1999. *Nationalist Myths and Ethnic Identities: Indigenous Intellectuals and the Mexican State*. Lincoln and London: University of Nebraska Press.

Heinle, Kimberly, Cory Molzahn, and David A. Shirk. 2015. "Drug Violence in Mexico Special Report." Justice in Mexico Project of the University of San Diego, April 2015.

Jenkins, Nash. 2015. "The Mexican Activist Who Led the Search for Missing Students Has Been Killed." *Time*, August 10, 2015. http://time.com/3990126/mexican-activist -missing-students-miguel-angel-jimenez-blanco.

Kuo, Rachel. 2018. "Racial Justice Activist Hashtags: Counterpublics and Discursive Circulations." *New Media and Society* 20 (2): 495–514.

Lankhani, Nina. 2015. "Search for Missing Mexican Students Turns Up 129 Bodies Unrelated to the Case." *The Guardian*, July 27, 2015. https://www.theguardian.com/world/ 2015/jul/27/mexico-search-missing-students-129-bodies.

Linthicum, Kate, and Patrick J. McDonnell. 2018. "She Fought Back Against Illegal Loggers, Now She's Been Found Strangled on a Highway in Mexico." *Los Angeles Times*, January 23, 2018. http://www.latimes.com/world/mexico-americas/la-fg -mexico-activist-killed-20180123-story.html.

Martínez, Ernesto, Ciro Pérez, and Matilde Pérez. 2012. "Torturan y matan comuneros de Cherán, dejan cuerpos en Zacapu." *La Jornada*, July 11, 2012. http://www.jornada .unam.mx/2012/07/11/estados/034n1est.

Mosso, Ruben. 2016. "Guerreros Unidos atacó a normalistas por toma de buses en Iguala." *Milenio*, August 6, 2016. http://www.milenio.com/policia/caso_Ayotzinapa -caso_Iguala informe_Ayotzinapa-normalistas_Ayotzinapa_0_752325041.html.

Nobiss, Christine. 2018. "Missing and Murdered Women Need Your Attention This International Women's Day." *Bustle*, March 8, 2018. https://www.bustle.com/p/ missing-murdered-Indigenous-women-need-your-attention-this-international -womens-day-8439882.

Olvera, Al-Dabi. 2017. "Caltzontzin: la represión contra indígenas en México de la que nadie está hablando." *Actualidad*, March 14, 2017. https://actualidad.rt.com/ actualidad/233274-caltzontzin-represion-indigenas-mexico.

Pacheco, Juan. 2014. "Exigen aclarar 18 asesinatos y desapariciones de comuneros en Michoacán." *Quadratin Oaxaca*, July 27, 2014. https://oaxaca.quadratin.com.mx/ Exigen-aclarar-18-asesinatos-y-desapariciones-de-comuneros-en-Michoacan.

Pavón-Cuellar, David. 2017. "Porque murieron los comuneros de Arantepacua?" *Michoacán Tres Punto Cero*, April 9, 2017. http://michoacantrespuntocero.com/por-que -murieron-los-comuneros-de-arantepacua.

Rambukkana, Nathan. 2014. *Hashtag Publics: The Power and Politics of Discursive Networks*. New York: Peter Lang.

Razack, Shireen. 2014. "'It Happened More Than Once:' Freezing Deaths in Saskatchewan." *Canadian Journal of Women and the Law* 26 (1): 51–80.

Razack, Shireen. 2015. *Dying from Improvement: Inquests and Inquiries into Indigenous Deaths in Custody*. Toronto: University of Toronto Press.

Razack, Shireen. 2016. "Gendering Disposability." *Canadian Journal of Women and the Law* 28 (2): 285–307.

Reséndez, Andrés. 2016. *The Other Slavery: The Uncovered Story of Indian Enslavement*. New York: Houghton Mifflin Harcourt.

Salinas, Arturo. 2015. "Renuncia funcionaria que posteo 'yo aquí sufriendo con estos indígenas.'" *Periódico Excélsior*, March 3, 2015. http://www.excelsior.com.mx/nacional/ 2015/03/03/1011323.

Sedillo, Simon. 2013. "Self-Determination and Self-Defense in Cherán, Michoacán." *El Enemigo Común*, January 4, 2013. http://www.elenemigocomun.net/2013/01/self -determination-defense-cheran.

Sharma, Sanjay. 2014. "Black Twitter: Racial Hashtags, Networks and Contagion." *New Formations* 78 (2): 46–64.

Stavenhagen, Rudolfo. 2000. "Introduction." In *Indigenous Autonomy in Mexico*, edited by Aracely Burguete Cal y Mayor, 10–21. Copenhagen: International Work Group for Indigenous Affairs.

Talaga, Tanya. 2017a. "Inquiry into Murdered and Missing Indigenous Women Set to Begin Hearings in May." *The Toronto Star*, March 29, 2017. https://www.thestar.com/ news/canada/2017/03/29/inquiry-into-murdered-and-missing-Indigenous-women -set-to-begin-hearings-in-may.html.

Talaga, Tanya. 2017b. *Seven Fallen Feathers: Racism, Death, and Hard Truths in a Northern City*. Toronto: House of Anansi Press.

Taylor, Keeanga-Yamahtta. 2016. *From #BlackLivesMatter to Black Liberation*. Chicago: Haymarket Books.

Taylor, Roy. 2017. "Interview with Pedro Victoriano Cruz." *Indigeniety Rising*. Minneapolis: KFAI, October 18, 2017.

9

TWEETING IN ZAPOTEC

Social Media as a Tool for Language Activism

BROOK DANIELLE LILLEHAUGEN

Social media is used by speakers of languages big and small. For languages
with a small number of speakers, social media may offer opportunities not easily available elsewhere, such as low-cost publishing and distribution of text.
Furthermore, smaller languages are often devalued by surrounding communities—in these situations, the use of language in global media, such as Twitter,
can have additional layers of impact and can be a form of language activism
in itself. Not all speakers of a language may want to write their language, and
not all who want to write their language may want to do so on social media. In
some cases, there may be groups or individuals who do not wish to share their
language with those outside their speech community at all.[1] This chapter is
written from the point of view of a linguist ally for speakers who want to write
their language on social media. One such speaker, Zapotec writer and activist @
BnZunni, expresses his motivation: "When I speak my language, I want to tell
other people how I view the world" (@BnZunni, February 2, 2016).

This chapter focuses on social media as a resource for those who are curious
about using their language in such a context, those who are already doing so,
and those who are supporting others who are using social media in this way
or who wish to. It provides context on social media and digital language activism before looking specifically at digital language activism in the context of
Latin American Indigenous communities. It then presents a project centered

on writing in Zapotec on Twitter and examines ways that Twitter can be used as a tool for language advocates, drawing on examples from the Zapotec Twitter project. Finally, it offers additional context and concludes that writing language on Twitter can be an effective and powerful way for speakers to make space for their language, to write their language (often for the first time), and to present/ perform their language globally, pushing back against discriminatory ideologies that assert that Zapotec has no relevance outside the pueblo or in the modern world.

This work contributes to the growing literature on the use of small and marginalized language varieties in social media, which includes work on the following languages on Facebook: nonstandard Breton (Davies-Deacon 2018), Éton (Rivron 2012), Low German (Reershemius 2016), Kenyah (De Falco and Cesarano 2016), Luxembourgish (Wagner 2013), Welsh (Honeycutt and Cunliffe 2008 and Cunliffe et al. 2013), and Yucatec Maya (Cru 2015). Beyond Facebook there are papers on the use of Puerto Rican Spanish on MySpace (Carroll 2008) and Lakota on a proprietary social media platform (Arobba et al. 2010), as well as Sámi (Cocq 2015), Welsh (Johnson 2013), and Zapotec (Lillehaugen 2016) on Twitter. In addition, Jongbloed-Faber et al. (2016) provides information about the use of Frisian in social media more generally (WhatsApp, Facebook, and Twitter) and Scannell's Indigenous Tweets Project provides data on a large range of Indigenous languages used on Twitter (Lee 2011).

SOCIAL MEDIA AND DIGITAL LANGUAGE ACTIVISM

Nearly two decades ago, Laura Buszard-Welcher reflected on the growing number of endangered languages making use of the Web. She opens by noting the recent dramatic increase of "web sites on endangered languages," stating: "Five years ago [1996] there were only a few sites; now there are more than one could visit in the course of a week" (2001, 331). The rest of the article is dedicated to exploring what role such sites could play in language maintenance and revitalization. Her conclusion is optimistic: "My position in this discussion has been that we are only beginning to realize the potential of the Web for language maintenance and revitalization. As new technologies develop and more people access and use the Web to do more things, the importance of the Web in creating and maintaining community can only grow" (2001, 343). Her cautious tone throughout the article is well justified, as mass media—electronic and otherwise—has oft been named a factor in language shift away from a smaller language to a larger, often colonial language.[2]

Similarly, Dorian notes more generally that "The broadcast media challenge the survival of small languages . . . since broadcast media . . . can invade even the strongest small-language sanctuary—the home" (1991, 134). She goes on to point out that as of 1991, broadcast media had primarily been used for "serious and usually educational" purposes for small languages, and argues that this focus misses out on the actual strengths of these languages, namely local knowledge and expression of tradition (1991, 134). Social media presents opportunities for sharing and interacting with local knowledge, tradition, culture, images, and experiences in a small-language context. In fact, the nature of the tweet allows for both more serious and more educational content, as well as more informal and entertaining uses. The fact that individuals can contribute content to mass social media without the gatekeeping of a small group of (potentially highly educated) individuals was probably unimaginable in 1991, but it addresses Dorian's concern about an elite class gatekeeping the material made available through mass media (1991, 135).[3]

Given the new opportunities presented by modern social media, can speakers of small languages use digital media to the advantage of their language? Some scholars remain skeptical, pointing out that new media may in fact be a threat to smaller languages. Cormack, for example, states: "However much minority languages may use new media, such media were not developed with these languages in mind. Indeed, it could be convincingly argued that the main thrust of new media, as far as language is concerned, is to consolidate the power of the globally dominant languages" (2013, 255). However, the inventor of the World Wide Web, Tim Berners-Lee, is quoted as saying, "I hope we will use the Net to cross barriers and connect cultures" (King and Berners-Lee 2005, 1), and Kevin Scannell, the director of Indigenoustweets.com, stated, "I view things like Twitter and social media as an opportunity for smaller languages" (qtd. in Lee 2011, 1). The possibility and potential benefit of social media for threatened languages is also acknowledged by Cocq: "Twitter has indeed the potential for being a valuable instrument for small localized groups and endangered languages. It can increase language use and contribute to the visibility of languages that are not present in mainstream and traditional media" (2015, 283). Thus, without denying the warning given by Cormack, the potential to reclaim and repurpose (new social) media for the good of smaller, threatened languages seems clear. In the case of Zapotec, speakers are using Twitter for multiple, overlapping purposes:

as a place to use their language; a way to practice writing their language; a means to communicate with other Zapotec speakers; a venue to share their language, culture, and identity with non-Zapotec individuals; and as a form of resistance through digital language activism.

UNESCO's 2003 report on Language Vitality and Endangerment goes as far as to include how speech communities use new domains and media as one of the factors in determining the degree of endangerment of that language. The committee states that "if the [endangered language speech] communities do not meet the challenges of modernity with their language, it [the language] becomes increasingly irrelevant and stigmatized" (2003, 11). The "New Domains and Media" factor ranks languages that are used "in all new domains" as the least endangered with regard to this factor—one of nine factors—and languages that are "not used in any new domain" as the most endangered with regard to this factor. David Crystal echoes this sentiment in his book *Language Death*, in a section entitled "An endangered language will progress if its speakers can make use of electronic technology" (2000, 141). Crystal makes a connection between the use of digital media and a speech community's ability to create a "public profile" for their language:

> [T]he Internet . . . offers endangered languages . . . a fresh set of opportunities whose potential has hardly begun to be explored. The chief task presented by my first postulate above involved the need to give an endangered language a public profile. Traditionally, it is an expensive business: newspaper space, or radio and television time, does not come cheaply. Only the "better-off" languages could afford to make routine use of these media. But with the Internet, everyone is equal. The cost of a Web page is the same, whether the contributor is writing in English, Spanish, Welsh, or Navajo. It is perfectly possible for a minority language culture to make its presence felt on the Internet, and this has begun to happen. (2000, 142)

Crystal's emphasis on a "public profile" seems to address the more general vision of a language having a place in today's world. Too often, Indigenous languages are deemed things of the past, even in cases where the language continues to be used. This type of prejudice is extremely dangerous—the denial of a present for a language, culture, or people is a denial of the language itself, and this creates space for the abdication of responsibility to protect the linguistic rights of speakers of such a language. In such a scenario, the use of a threatened language in a modern digital domain can be an act of resistance—a claiming of space.[4] This sentiment is echoed by Cunliffe, who points out that new media has the potential to be a space of creation and a space of agency: "Minority cultures and languages should not be viewed simply as victims of the Internet or as passive recipients of Internet technology, services and content. Instead it should be recognised that they have the potential to be active shapers of this technology, able to create their own tools, adapt existing tools to the local needs and to create culturally authentic, Indigenous Internet media" (2007, 147).

Given these observations, then, it should not be surprising that many speakers of threatened languages are turning to social media, including Twitter, as a space to use their language. Table 9.1 shows the number of Indigenous languages used on Twitter in the years 2011, 2016, and 2017. As of October 2017, 184 Indigenous languages were listed on Indigenous Tweets (www.Indigenoustweets.com).

TABLE 9.1 Number of Indigenous Languages Used on Twitter 2011–2017

YEAR	NUMBER OF INDIGENOUS LANGUAGES USED ON TWITTER	SOURCE
2011	68	Lee (2011)
2016 (March)	170+	Lillehaugen (2016)
2017 (August)	184	Author, using IT (indigenoustweets.com)

This number is lower than the actual number of Indigenous languages used on Twitter for several reasons. First, of course, not all Indigenous languages are listed on the site. Secondly, many languages are grouped together—for example, all Zapotec languages are listed under "Zapoteco" and all Mixtec languages are listed under "Tu'un Sávi." The data, then, can be taken as a minimal number—at least 184 Indigenous languages are currently being used on Twitter.[5]

DIGITAL LANGUAGE ACTIVISM AND INDIGENOUS LATIN AMERICA

The use of Indigenous languages of Latin America on social media is part of a larger context of digital language activism, exemplified by workshops such as the Encuentro de activismo digital de lenguas indígenas that first took place in Oaxaca City in 2014 (Díaz Robles and Ávila 2014, fig. 9.1). Digital language activism goes beyond the use of language on social media, which is the focus of this chapter. Digital language activism includes a broad range of activities and results where language, activism, and the digital meet, such as the development of apps (such as the android app for the Teotitlán del Valle Zapotec Talking Dictionary, Dixza), the creation of instances of browsers in a particular language (such as the Miahuatlán Zapotec translation of Mozilla Firefox), and the use of language in a digital context, such as YouTube, blogs, and of course social media. Global Voices has created a network of Indigenous language digital activism in Latin America, available online at https://rising.globalvoices.org/lenguas. This website informs and connects participants in digital language activism projects with others doing similar work. Global Voices also offers micro grants, training, and community.

FIGURE 9.1. Publicity for the first Encuentro de activismo digital de lenguas indígenas. Image by Rodrigo Carús.

Speakers of Indigenous languages in Latin America are utilizing social media as platforms for language use. Some Twitter users will tweet multilingually, communicating in an Indigenous language and Spanish (and/or English) in a way that seems to desire understanding between the writer and a potentially monolingual Spanish reader. Such uses of Twitter invite a nonspeaker into the language being shared, as can be seen in the tweets of @Joel37M, who tweets in Nahuatl and Spanish, translating the Nahuatl for a Spanish-reading audience: "Ahmo motekipacho in motlahtol, no te apenas de tu idioma" (@Joel37M, October 7, 2017). Not all multilingual tweets contain translations or rephrasings. Given the level of multilingualism present in many Indigenous communities, it is perhaps unsurprising that many writers use multiple languages in a single tweet.

Table 9.2 lists several examples of social media accounts using Indigenous languages of Mesoamerica, organized by language family to show the range of languages being used in this region alone. Zapotec languages are addressed separately in table 9.3.

TABLE 9.2 Examples of Social Media Accounts Using Indigenous Languages of Mesoamerica

LANGUAGE (ORGANIZED BY FAMILY)		SOCIAL MEDIA ACCOUNTS
Arawakan		
	Garifuna	Twitter, GAHFU Noralez, @GAHFU
Chibchan		
	Ngäbere	Facebook, KÜGWE NGÄBERE AIBE (https://www.facebook.com/groups/852676718090681)
Mayan		
	Kaqchikel	Twitter, Kaqchikel Cholchi,' @KaqchikelCholch
	Yucatec Maya	Twitter, elChilamBalam, @elchilambalam (Llanes Ortiz 2016)
Mixe-Zoquean		
	Mixe	Twitter, Yásnaya Elena, @yasnayae
Otomanguean		
	Chatino	Twitter, Hilaria, @ChaqHilaria
	Mixtec	Twitter, cafe nu-yoo, @cafenu_yoo
	Triqui	Twitter, Lengua y Cultura Triqui, @LyC_Triqui; Misael Hdez M, @triquichicahuax
Uto-Aztecan		
	Nahuatl	Twitter, ticzalozque nahuatl, @Joel37M
	Nahuatl-Pipil	Facebook, Colectivo Tzunhejekat (https://www.facebook.com/Tzunhejekat) (Llanes Ortiz 2016)
Isolates		
	Purépecha	Twitter, Cultura P'urhépecha, @Purepecha_mx

Other uses of language on Twitter, as we will see throughout this chapter, include monolingual tweets in the language and tweets with images, links, or hashtags for additional context. Consider, for example, the tweet in figure 9.2, which shares a Triqui "Word of the Day." The hashtag #PalabraDelDía connects the tweets to a genre of other tweets, and the writer uses a SoundCloud link to provide audio so that the pronunciation of the word *xinaán-an* (*backstrap loom*) can be heard.

FIGURE 9.2. Tweet in Triqui and Spanish, @LyC_Triqui. Used with permission.

TWEETING IN ZAPOTEC

The remainder of this chapter will focus on the use of Zapotec languages on Twitter, in particular those associated with the hashtag #UsaTuVoz. I offer a brief introduction to the Zapotec language family and describe the Voces del Valle project and the #UsaTuVoz hashtag. It is worth noting that while Zapotec languages should be considered endangered because languages are losing more speakers than they are gaining, the Zapotec tweeters cited here are native speakers.[6]

Zapotec is a family of languages spoken primarily in the state of Oaxaca, Mexico, but also by large migrant communities in Mexico City and in the United States, especially the greater Los Angeles area. Zapotec languages belong to the Otomanguean stock. Based on speaker numbers provided in the *Ethnologue* (Simons and Fennig 2017), there are approximately 450,000 total speakers of Zapotec languages, though many language varieties have only hundreds of speakers and all are in danger of ceasing to be spoken within a few generations unless something changes.[7] All Zapotec languages have tonal contrasts, which comes into play as we discuss choices regarding how to write Zapotec. Most of the examples discussed in this chapter come from varieties of Western Tlacolula Valley Zapotec (ISO code [zab], Simons and Fennig 2017), though there are also examples from Isthmus Zapotec [zai].

VOCES DEL VALLE AND #USATUVOZ

There is a long-observed conundrum regarding the use of the Internet to pub-lish content in small languages. A UNESCO report identifies the core of this particular problem: the Internet facilitates easy and affordable publication, that is, the production of content, but it does not guarantee that content a readership: "The speakers of some regional and minority languages are using the WWW to publish in these languages and promote them. There is evidence that far more is published in this medium than in traditional print or in audiovisual. However, the extent of the readership is not at all clear. It may well be an activist led activity rather than response to general demand" (UNESCO 2004). Put more bluntly, people may be using the Internet to provide access to things written in threatened languages, but is anyone actually reading it?[8]

In the case of many threatened languages, and certainly in the case of most Zapotec languages, there is no (substantial) current readership, on- or offline. While Zapotec languages were written nonalphabetically in pre-Columbian times and had a strong alphabetic writing tradition that began during the colo-nial period, this practice of reading and writing Zapotec alphabetically almost ceased entirely with the onset of Mexican independence. Most Valley Zapotec speakers do not write their language today. In other areas there are more robust movements of written literature, particularly in Isthmus Zapotec, which boasts more than a handful of renowned Zapotec poets, including Macario Matus and the late Victor de la Cruz, as well as a vibrant new generation of Isthmus Zapotec poets: Natalia Toledo, Victor Cata, Victor Terán, and Irma Pineda, among others.

If it could be the case that a successful online community requires both writers and readers, what does this mean for communities where there is not currently a strong writing culture in the language? It is in this particularly chal-lenging set of circumstances that the Voces del Valle project is relevant. As described more fully in Lillehaugen (2016), Voces del Valle seeks to interrupt a vicious cycle: "Potential writers are reluctant or unmotivated to write in a lan-guage that no one can read. But at the same time, why learn to read a language for which there is nothing available to read? The writers wait for the readership, while the readers wait for material" (1). So if writers are waiting for a reader-ship and potential readers have nothing to read, we are stuck—and in the case of small, threatened languages, there is immense time pressure. The Voces del Valle project is a model that attempts to jump-start the production of writing in languages where there are willing potential writers but there may not be (a large) readership. Following a kind of "build it and they will come" model, an artificial readership is created to support a first wave of writers.

The readers were volunteers who, for the most part, did not speak any Zapotec. They committed to "reading" an assigned Zapotec writer's tweets and encouraging the Zapotec writer by asking about the tweet in a shared common language (English or Spanish). Although most readers couldn't understand the Zapotec, they were regularly attending to and interacting with the written text and the writer of that text. Readers often retweeted Zapotec writers' tweets, adding (partial) translations and hashtags. For example, figure 9.3 shows @mayhplumb interacting with @BnZunni's tweet by retweeting it and reframing it, focusing on the word *bzi* and its English translation, while also adding some new commentary regarding the deliciousness of squash blossoms in quesadillas. Within the Voces de Valle project, these retweets serve both to encourage the writer and to increase the potential readership of the original tweet. (Twitter account @linguistory has additional examples of supportive retweets.)

FIGURE 9.3. @mayhplumb retweeting @BnZunni's tweet. Used with permission.

Voces del Valle *began* in January 2016 and for the first six months most of the interactions between writers and readers on Twitter were of the types illustrated above. But by the end of the first year, other types of interaction started to become more common—namely interaction between Zapotec speakers in Zapotec. In one such conversation, @noelgarcia280 tweets in Zapotec, beginning, "This is how the houses of the ancient people are left, now they need repair . . ." and @DizhSa retweets the tweet, asking in Zapotec, "Who will fix them now?" We see something similar in figure 9.4 where @DizhSa tweets in

Zapotec, asking, "Hey, you guys! Do you like wrestling? Who is your favorite wrestler? Ever since I was little, I've liked how El Santo wrestles. And you?" In response to this, @nogarju retweets and answers in Zapotec, saying, "I remember El Santo and Blue Demon the most." We will return to these tweets when discussing choices made in spelling Zapotec below.

FIGURE 9.4. @nogarju retweeting @ DizhSa, with commentary in Zapotec. Used with permission.

The number of Zapotec speakers tweeting in their language has continued to grow since 2011, which is, as far as I am aware, when the first Twitter account was opened by a Zapotec speaker who tweeted in Zapotec. Table 9.3 lists more than twenty accounts that include tweets in Zapotec along with the year the account was opened. The Voces del Valle project continues and has grown organically to include writers who learned about the project through Twitter.[9] Writers of any small, threatened, or endangered language are welcome to join by tweeting in their language with the hashtag #UsaTuVoz.

TABLE 9.3 Accounts That Include Tweets in Zapotec

TWITTER HANDLE	TWITTER NAME (YEAR ACCOUNT OPENED)
@DizhSa	DizhSa (2011)
@noelgarcia380	Alex García (2015)
@YanethMolina99	Yaneth Molina (2016)
@BnZunni	Moisés García Guzmán (2013)
@JanChvzSanti	Jan Chvz (2012)
@nogarju	Noel Garcia Juarez (2016)
@Humbert92847371	hal (2016)

TABLE 9.3 *continued*

TWITTER HANDLE	TWITTER NAME (YEAR ACCOUNT OPENED)
@moralitos2197	Mayra Morales (2016)
@Isa_Antonio99	Martha Isabel (2016)
@la_na_angel	Angel Morales (2016)
@LeyrukLopez	Leyruk López (2012)
@ssamy_mtz	Sammy (2016)
@zandra_crUz36	Sandra CrUz (2016)
@chicoruiz1223	Chico Ruiz (2015)
@Ricardo01596181	Ricardo Santiago (2016)
@Juan_na1	Juan (2016)
@Nare_na_Juany	Nare La Juany (2016)
@vikisanlucas	Victoria Hernandez (2016)
@vane_g2118	valeria juan garcia (2016)
@Veronic24062527	Vero (2016)
@la_na_karina	Reyna K. Rodriguez (2016)
@AndyAEO13_12	Andy Hernandez (2016)
@NarenNa_Ni_Gaca	Droid Tec (2016)
@ClementinaLop13	Clementina Lopez (2016)

TWITTER AND LANGUAGE ACTIVISM

When linguists talk about language, they are careful to point out that the primary form of language is spoken or signed, not written. A language need not have a written form to be a language, and a speaker need not know how to write their language to be a native speaker. However, writing can be very useful and many people want to write their language. Within the context of endangered languages, writing can be an opportunity to use a language.[10] Writing and reading language on Twitter can have multiple intersecting roles for speakers, activists, and linguist allies. For example, writing on Twitter may be the first time speakers write their language, as is the case for many of the Zapotec participants in the Voces del Valle project (Lillehaugen 2016, 371). Zapotec writer @zandra_crUz36's first Tweet was also the first time she wrote in Zapotec: "Nde Na dac tëby dizhsa caküa #UsaTuVoz [This is the first time I am writing Zapotec]" (@zandra_crUz36, April 15, 2016).

As Cunliffe points out, through the use of the Internet, including social media, "new opportunities for language use can be created" (2007, 145). This has certainly been true in the corpus of Zapotec tweets. One salient example exists in a tweet written by @BnZunni, where he discusses how to translate "tweet" into Zapotec. He decides he will use *gal rú'uld*, which refers to the singing of a bird. This is an example of extending the vocabulary of a language to create terminology that applies to new technology: "I'm going to say: Gal Rú'uld, which refers to singing of a bird, or a 'tweet' sound . . ." (@BnZunni, February 21, 2014).

Cunliffe goes beyond the statement above, adding: "new opportunities for language use can be created, *even if they are limited to textual forms*" (2007, 145; emphasis added). Considering the corpus of Zapotec language tweets, impressionistically most are only text. But a significant number of them also contain images. It is also worth noting that Twitter allows videos to be attached to tweets, and Zapotec speakers have utilized this feature to tweet video that includes Zapotec language, such as figure 24 in Lillehaugen (2016, 377). These cases tend to be practiced performances, and thus are different from an everyday conversation, but they move beyond written text nonetheless. In addition, as we saw earlier, a writer can use the option to embed a link in a tweet to include access to sound alongside the text of a tweet.

DIVERSITY IN WRITING CHOICES (OR WRITING WITHOUT STANDARDIZATION)

Not only does social media create an opportunity to write and use language in new ways, perhaps creating new vocabulary, but it does so on a platform and in an environment that is viewed as casual and informal. This has been particularly helpful for speakers of Zapotec languages who want to write their language but worry about "doing it wrong." None of the Valley Zapotec languages used on Twitter have a widely accepted orthography, as far as I am aware. Few have any proposals of orthographic systems at all. Thus, there is in fact no way to "write the language wrong" in these cases. The informality of Twitter has eased new writers' anxieties about writing Zapotec languages for which no developed writing systems exist.[11]

For the most part, Zapotec writers using #UsaTuVoz on Twitter are applying their own writing strategies. In the Voces del Valle workshop, writers are offered some options for non-Spanish sounds and were encouraged to "just start writing, and not to worry about exactly how they were spelling things" (Lillehaugen 2016, 361). It became clear early on that for the Western Tlacolula Valley Zapotec language varieties, using personal writing systems did not impede one individual from understanding another individual's writing. It was not always easy, as there are grammatical differences between these language varieties as well, including differences in pronouns.[12]

Zapotec writers are not always making the same choices regarding how to spell certain sounds. Writer @noelgarcia380 uses both <c> and <k> for what appears to be the phoneme /k/, while @DizhSa only uses <c> to represent this sound in these two tweets, though elsewhere he also uses <qu>, following Spanish orthographic rules. Note that @DizhSa doesn't employ any apostrophes in his writing, while @noelgarcia380 uses an apostrophe after word initial <d> twice. Finally, note that @noelgarcia380 uses <sh>, which @DizhSa does not; he chooses to use <x> to represent the same sound.

The ability of native speakers to understand personal orthographic choices in Zapotec is consistent with what has been observed elsewhere in the literature. Cru (2015) finds that Maya speakers writing on Facebook do not necessarily follow normative writing practices, and this does not seem to hinder understanding. He references May's (2010) work, which found the same pattern in Maya written in other electronic media: "In Yucatán, May (2010) has looked at the use of written Maya in emails, text messages and chat. In his work, he describes the ways in which non-normative uses of orthographic signs . . . do not hinder intelligibility. The vague division between the spoken and written word, the use of Spanish borrowings, inconsistent spelling and non-standard spelling of Maya are all features that emerge in May's data and, similarly, in my own data below, which is based on Facebook posts" (Cru 2015, 286).[13] The Zapotec and Maya references above suggest that Twitter and other social media might be supportive places to write without standardization. This is important because standardization can create tension, where speakers of one variety claim their variety is the "prestige" variety, and thus should be the standard. As seen in these cases, social media has proven to be useful for writers of languages where standardization does not exist or is not desired. In many situations, there is no need to rush to create a writing system or standardize one.

CREATION OF CORPUS OF CONTENT

Often in language documentation projects, the linguist "expert" holds a gatekeeping position, making crucial decisions about what to record and document. As Eisenlohr points out: "[T]he processes of selection and collection in documenting 'endangered' languages in digital format often end up producing the 'heritage' of a people. . . . [I]n many instances, the linguist and ethnographer as expert may occupy a pivotal role in shaping credentials for ethnolinguistic recognition (Silverstein 2003). Experts' decisions of inclusion and exclusion of linguistic material in electronic artifacts intended for documentation of lesser-used languages therefore may have profound . . . consequences" (2004, 27). The Internet, and social media in particular, would seem to offer great promise in combatting the problems of having an expert gatekeeper—individuals can publish and contribute materials directly. Cocq expresses her view of social media as potentially empowering to speakers of Indigenous languages: "[F]olklore in social media not only opens new modes for the production of knowledge; participatory media also contributes to the continuity of expressive culture for Indigenous peoples. From this perspective . . . the vernacular dimension of participatory media enables revitalization and empowerment" (2015, 274).

Cunliffe, however, expresses worry that the Internet will decontextualize content, stating: "The transformation of a language to the Internet will typically decontextualize the language from its traditional cultural and physical context. It is one thing to bring a language to the Internet and quite another to bring a culture" (2007, 141). In addition to the dangers associated with the word "traditional," it is also important to point out that the same concerns Cunliffe expresses about language written online could be said about language written in a book—print media can decontextualize language from "traditional" culture and physical context as much as digital media can. The fact is, Indigenous writers are using social media to express their language and culture in very interesting and compelling ways. Rather than asking if language can be decontextualized in digital (or print) media (because of course it can), it is more interesting to ask how speakers of threatened languages are using digital media to express their language in context. What choices are they making and how are they creating space for local culture, context, and language in a global media?

In one tweet, Zapotec writer @BnZunni tweets an image of a cactus in bloom along with bilingual text in Zapotec and English talking about the implications of the blooming cactus—since many cactuses are blooming, there will be lots of (delicious, edible) cactus fruit. In another tweet, Zapotec writer @la_na_angel beautifully shares language in context in figure 9.5, when he provides an intimate and powerful image of women preparing a large amount of mole for a wedding. Complementing the Zapotec language text and the stunning photograph, he also uses emojis for further context—the fork and knife and the turkey leg. These seemingly playful additions are also cleverly appropriate. Turkeys are important in Zapotec culture and economy, and turkey is often eaten at ceremonial events, like weddings (Flores-Marcial 2015, 51, 85). The turkey leg emoji would likely be read and appreciated by Zapotec individuals as appropriate and in context. For outsiders, it allows a further connection to the meal preparation to be shared with us via the image and the Zapotec language. All in all, it is a superb example of Zapotec language and context being shared via digital media.

FIGURE 9.5. @la_na_angel, Language and Context. Photo by José Ángel Cruz. Used with permission.

Wilson et al. describe the use of social media as a type of reclamation: "Social media, however, is providing the means whereby Indigenous people can 'reterritorialize' and 'Indigenize' the information and communication space" (2017, 2). Rather than being out of proper context, these types of tweets claim context and space.

LANGUAGE VALORIZATION

One particularly insidious form of prejudice against Zapotec (and other Indigenous) language, culture, and people is the denial of a present and a confinement to the past.[14] Indeed, this is why we should be careful of such words as "tradition" and be sure not to use them in ways that exclude the possibility that, for example, a turkey leg emoji can be read as appropriate Zapotec context. Language and culture changes—and the absence of change—can be viewed as a reason to be alarmed.[15] Digital communication such as tweets or text messages have a "coolness" factor that may work to their benefit in language maintenance context, as Buszard-Welcher points out: "On the Web, new technology is always cool" (2001, 337). This "coolness" contrasts with what Eisenlohr refers to as "ideologies of contempt": "That is, the reindexing of such varieties by ideologically moving them away from peripheral, rural, and obsolete positions in space and time through the use of electronic mediation is a way to contest ideologies of contempt and to formulate alternative ways of ideologically mapping linguistic differentiation on time and space" (Eisenlohr 2004, 33). Here Eisenlohr is saying that one way to devalue Indigenous languages is to claim that they have no place in today's world, that they are "peripheral, rural, and obsolete." The use of these languages in a digital, modern, and public medium counters these misconceptions. The act of using language in these spaces, then, refutes this particular ideology of contempt and contributes to the public valorization of the language.

FIGURE 9.6. @YanethMolina99, language, culture, and pride. Photo by Yaneth Molina. Used with permission.

While all the examples of tweets presented so far are relevant to this point, the Zapotec selfie in figure 9.6 speaks to it in a particularly poignant way, as the content of the tweet, both in text and image, shine with pride. The writer is choosing to share her language, dress, and identity via social media because she values it and wants to share it with the global readership.

ARTICULATING INDIGENOUS IDENTITY

Zapotec speakers are using Twitter to articulate an Indigenous identity. The "oh-so-Zapotec" turkey leg emoji and the selfie in Isthmus huipil and braids in the figures discussed above demonstrate not only pride and valorization but also communicate a specifically Zapotec identity. While these tweets are global, they are also intensely local—the dress in each of these images and the form of Zapotec used expresses the pueblo of origin. While digital, these tweets also express the physical: cooking, eating, dancing, dressing up.[16] Cocq frames the use of a minoritized language in a digital space as a way of questioning power relationships: "More than a tool for communication, an Indigenous language functions as a symbol of identity, and its visibility in a majority society is part of revitalization efforts and a way of questioning minority/majority relations" (Cocq 2015, 274). Rather than contrast the use of language for communication in relation to its use as a symbol, I would rephrase this relationship as one of *both . . . and . . .* in terms of the use of Zapotec language use on Twitter. Zapotec speakers have used Twitter to announce events, thus clearly intending a communicative event, and at the same time the use of language is also a statement itself—a pushing back and a talking back in language.

Speaking Zapotec is a key component of Zapotec self-identification for many individuals. Few people living in Oaxaca would say they are Zapotec if they don't speak the language. Vincze and Moring emphasize ethnolinguistic identity as a motivational variable for use of a language in digital media. They state that "language is seen not only as a tool but also as an aim of media use" (2013, 48), and that ethnolinguistic identity is a particularly important element of language use in communities in which language is part of ethnic identification (2013, 47–48), as is the case among Zapotecs living in Oaxaca. This is consistent with the use of Zapotec on Twitter both expressing content and expressing identity.

CONNECTIONS: LOCAL AND TRANSNATIONAL

Speakers of Indigenous languages are using Twitter to establish, maintain, and strengthen transnational connections. Turin, speaking of diaspora communities, points out that "[t]hrough the Internet and mobile communications, people are reconnecting with fellow speakers using digital tools to revive languages on the endangered list" (2013, 1). In the case of Zapotec language speakers, this is particularly relevant because a large portion of the Zapotec community lives outside of Oaxaca, with particularly large and active communities in "Oaxacalifornia."

The use of the Internet, and social media in particular, to connect communities across distance is ubiquitous. Cru, cited earlier, continues his comments about the value of the use of Maya on Facebook by framing it as a way to connect speakers of Maya who live in the Yucatan and those who do not: "Undoubtedly, the visibility of Maya on Facebook has an ideological effect that accrues to its legitimacy from the ground up. . . . Furthermore, this deterritorialised use of Maya and its inclusion in a globalised and transnational context need also to be considered because it may encompass Maya speakers living outside of Yucatán" (2015, 292).[17] The tweets show the use of Twitter to connect across distance. In this tweet, we see two Zapotec writers talking about the importance of Zapotec language radio in their pueblo, though one of the writers does not currently live in the pueblo. Thus, we see here that Twitter can be a way of creating a speech community across geographic space: "Shtiusu cacuadiagu tsee ziguie, Shtiusu cacuau dish sa, sre na riquin yeniun te quet diun dish tixhun #UsaTuVoz" (@noelgarcia380, June 4, 2016). "Ca cuadigun dbenni ni cani len Tsae Xiguiae #UsaTuVoz @VocesValle @blillehaugen" (@TeotitlanDValle, June 4, 2016). Local connections can also be strengthened through Twitter, as already seen in several examples of Zapotec speakers responding to each other's tweets. In another example, @YanethMolina99 tweets about tamales, using images, Zapotec language, and the "oh-so-Mesoamerican" corn emoji. @noelgarcia380 replies, joking that he would like some of the tamales for tomorrow.

CONCLUSIONS

While the Internet and social media are not magic technological fixes for speakers who wish to maintain and increase the domain of use of their language, they have proven to be tools with significant potential. Dauenhauer and Dauen-hauer remind us that computers and technology—and the opportunities they provide—"are useful tools, and they greatly change the dimensions and possibilities for documentation and instruction, but they are no substitute for human desire and effort" (1998, 70). Throughout this chapter we have seen ways that speakers of threatened languages are taking advantage of these tools to write, share, and expand the domain of use of their languages.

Writing language on social media can be effective in taking (back) and making space for language in a variety of intersecting ways. Speakers of a language can be writers of their language in a low-stakes environment, and in the case of Zapotec Twitter, without the pressure of having to write their language "correctly." While most of the Zapotec speakers who tweet in their language seem to be younger, I am aware of several tweeters aged thirty-five and above, and I have observed quite a bit of interaction between Zapotec tweeters across generations. For instance, sometimes younger tweeters ask how to say something in Zapotec, and "older" tweeters reply with the sought-after vocabulary. I also notice that the tweeters over thirty-five seem to be particularly active both in their own writing and in their encouraging of the younger writers.

Zapotec speakers writing their language on Twitter make a range of choices about how to present their language—some always or usually tweet bilingually, some trilingually, others only in Zapotec. Their choices might be influenced by their perceived audience and/or by their intention. There is different power in presenting language with translation and presenting language untranslated, and Twitter and other social media allow these options.

It is also worthwhile to consider the audience of Zapotec language on Twitter. As seen above, we know that Zapotec speakers interact with each other on Twitter. We also saw examples of linguistics students responding to Zapotec tweets. But what does the audience of the Zapotec tweets look like overall? Impressionistically, I have noticed other linguists and anthropologists interacting with the tweets. I have also observed non-Zapotec speaking Oaxacans in both Oaxaca and California as part of the readership. In addition, other non-Zapotec Mexicans also interact with Zapotec tweets. A more in-depth look at the audience and the effect of seeing Zapotec on their Twitter feed would be interesting for future work.

Writing language on Twitter can be an effective and powerful way for speakers to make space for their language, creating new domains for language use. Speakers are choosing to write their language (often for the first time) on

Twitter, thereby creating new modalities of use. Quite compellingly, Twitter allows speakers to perform their language in a global, modern context, in direct resistance to discriminatory ideologies that assert that Zapotec has no place in the modern world or outside of the local context. Tweeting in Zapotec, then, can be language use, language documentation, language teaching, and language activism all at once.

ACKNOWLEDGMENTS

Thanks to Jennifer Gómez Menjívar and Gloria Chacón for organizing and editing this volume. Special thanks to Emily Drummond for her research and editorial support. I am indebted to all the collaborators on the Voces del Valle project, including Dr. Marco Antonio Pereyra Rito, Abisai Aparicio, Janet Chávez Santiago, Moisés García Guzmán, Dr. David A. Lopez Velasco, and especially Dr. Felipe H. Lopez. I also owe my thanks to Xochitl Flores-Marcial and K. David Harrison for their support and advice. Thanks to the Magill Library at Haverford College, the Center for Peace and Global Citizenship at Haverford College, the Haverford College Office of the Provost and the National Science Foundation REU Grant #1461056 (PI K. David Harrison) for support of this project. I should point out that all opinions, findings, conclusions, or recommendations expressed in this project do not necessarily represent those of the National Science Foundation. All errors are my own.

NOTES

1. See Hill 2002 regarding the publication of the Hopi Dictionary.
2. For example, Dixon 1991 lists "media pressure" as one of four factors contributing to language loss in Australia (236).
3. Cotter 2001 relates the use of entertaining Irish radio programming in the maintenance and expansion of the use of the Irish language. Cotter identifies this programming as an example of the "potential positive role of media in minority-language development" and further notes that the European Union's Bureau of Lesser-Used Languages endorses the inclusion of media in language preservation programs (301), which now, more than fifteen years later, might include social media.
4. In his discussion of the web presence of Asturian, a small and threatened Romance language, David Guardado 1997 points out that in addition to pragmatic aspects of using a language in a new domain, there are also creative aspects: "[The webpage] Austuria, and other similar initiatives, prove that a minority language is a valuable

means of expression in modern life. It also demonstrates how people involved in processes of language restoration belong, generally speaking, to the most dynamic sectors of society, are aware of the world we are living in, and propose imaginative and new approaches to economic and social development for depressed areas such as Asturies" (55).

5.   Twitter is being used as a tool by speakers of threatened languages worldwide, sometimes accompanied by hashtags associated with certain projects or movements, such as #SpeakGwichinToMe, which also exemplifies the multilingual nature of many tweets that include threatened languages.

6.   As such, the discussion may differ in important ways from cases where social media is being used by individuals who wish to learn a particular language.

7.   For an excellent and brief introduction to the linguistic features of the Zapotecan language family, I refer the reader to Beam de Azcona 2016.

8.   Cunliffe 2007 seems to claim that the answer to that question matters, arguing that "a successful online community requires both media producers and consumers" (134). The Voces de Valle project challenges this presumption.

9.   For more information on how Voces del Valle began, choices made in the early stages, and the development of the project, see Lillehaugen 2016.

10.   Wagner 2013 describes how writing on social media popularized the writing of Luxembourgish, which was a language typically used only in spoken form: "Until quite recently, Luxembourgish was rarely written. . . . Many people have felt insecure when writing Luxembourgish and have been worried about making mistakes. The use of written Luxembourgish came with the development of the new media. Within these media, Luxembourgish became a popular written form of language for text messages, blogs, emails and so on" (89). A similar result can be seen for the Frisian language, which, like Luxembougish, is a language that was used primarily in its spoken form, until recently: "64% of the Frisian population can speak it [Frisian] well, while only 12% indicate that they can write it well. However, in recent years Frisian contributions have frequently shown up on social media. . . . Although teenagers do not always follow its official spelling rules, Frisian has conquered a presence on social media. Social media thus seem to have introduced Frisian into the written domain for an extended group of people, which is a positive sign of the vitality of the Frisian language" (Jongbloed-Faber et al. 2016, 27).

11.   While I have not found any other literature on the use of Twitter for languages that do not have writing systems, there are cases where speakers are unaware of the writing systems, such as described by Wagner 2013 regarding Luxembourgish, who says the following regarding the high degree of variation in written Luxembourgish in new media: "[The variation] can be attributed to two factors: first, the fact that written language in the new media is highly variable in any language; second—and this I think is the more salient point in the case of Luxembourgish—the fact that writing Luxembourgish is not explicitly taught at school and hence many people are not aware of its orthography or grammar, and apply their own writing strategies" (90).

12. Another example can be found in Lillehaugen 2016, figure 8, 365.

13. The same phenomenon is reported regarding the writing of Welsh (Indo-European, Celtic; Cunliffe et al. 2013, 251) and Éton (Niger-Congo; Rivron 2012, 165) on Facebook groups. Rivron reports that standard writing practices for Éton are not necessarily used and that people still understand what others write: "There seems to be less hesitation to write in Eton in the "among friends" atmosphere of Facebook groups, where mutual understanding is postulated despite the absence of codification and official teaching of customary spelling. The inequality of language skills is evident in these exchanges, along with the diversity of resources mobilized to design graphic solutions" (2012, 165).

14. See n. 3, above. Cotter 2001 states that one of the motivations for creating the stations was "to enhance the status of the language via a modern discourse channel—the media—and in so doing show people that the language, generally associated with traditional activities, can be adjusted to modern life" (307). While this statement was made about Irish language and radio, it could just as well have been made about social media and threatened languages more generally.

15. K. David Harrison 2010 relates: "A Torres Straits' Islander in Australia told me: 'Our language is standing still, we need to make it relevant to today's society. We need to create new words, because right now we can't say *computer*'" (1). Harrison continues, "The lowly text message may lift obscure tongues to new levels of prestige. . . ."

16. This use of social media to express Indigenous identity aligns with the use of Facebook by Aboriginal Australians as described by Carlson 2013, who states that "Facebook is becoming a popular vehicle amongst Aboriginal people, to build, display, and perform Aboriginal identities" (147).

17. Outside of Latin America, De Falco and Cesarano 2016 describe how social networking connects members of the Lebu' Kulit linguistic community in disperse physical locations, stating that "a social network is able to dissolve geographical barriers" (63). Wilson et al. (2017, 1) discuss the use of social media by Māori to maintain kinship relationships and strengthen language and culture, citing O'Carroll, who refers to this use of social media as "the virtual *whanaungatanga* [a culturally specific process of attaining and maintaining relationships]" (O'Carroll 2013, 230). And lest we think that all types of connecting with community through social media are supportive, Carlson 2013 conveys a powerful personal experience in which connection to community through Facebook came along with inspection, judgment, and ultimately rejection (156–57).

REFERENCES

Arobba, Biagio, Robert E. McGrath, Joe Futrelle, and Alan B. Craig. 2010. "A Community-Based Social Media Approach for Preserving Endangered Languages and Culture." *Illinois Digital Environment for Access to Learning and Scholarship*, September 2, 2010. http://hdl.handle.net/2142/17078.

Beam de Azcona, Rosemary. 2016. "Zapotecan Languages." In *Oxford Research Encyclopedia of Linguistics*, edited by Julia Kostova and Mark Aronoff, n.p. New York: Oxford University Press. http://dx.doi.org/10.1093/acrefore/9780199384655.013.73.

Buszard-Welcher, Laura. 2001. "Can the Web Help Save My Language?" In *The Green Book of Language Revitalization in Practice: Towards a Sustainable World*, edited by Leanne Hinton and Kenneth Hale, 331–45. San Diego: Academic Press.

Carlson, Bronwyn. 2013. "The 'New Frontier': Emergent Indigenous Identities and Social Media." In *The Politics of Identity: Emerging Indigeneity*, edited by Michelle Harris, Martin Nakata, and Bronwyn Carlson, 125–46. Sydney: University of Technology Sydney E-Press.

Carroll, Kevin S. 2008. "Puerto Rican Language Use on MySpace.com." *Centro Journal* 10: 96–111.

Cocq, Coppélie. 2015. "Indigenous Voices on the Web: Folksonomies and Endangered Languages." *Journal of American Folklore* 128: 273–85.

Cormack, Mike. 2013. "Towards an Understanding of Media Impact on Minority Language Use." In *Social Media and Minority Languages: Convergence and the Creative Industries*, edited by Elin H. G. Jones and Enrique Uribe-Jongbloed, 225–65. Bristol: Multilingual Matters.

Cotter, Colleen. 2001. "Continuity and Vitality: Expanding Domains Through Irish-Language Radio." In *The Green Book of Language Revitalization in Practice: Towards a Sustainable World*, edited by Leanne Hinton and Kenneth Hale, 301–12. San Diego: Academic Press.

Cru, Josep. 2015. "Language Revitalisation from the Ground Up: Promoting Yucatec Maya on Facebook." *Journal of Multilingual and Multicultural Development* 36: 284–96.

Crystal, David. 2000. *Language Death*. Cambridge: Cambridge University Press.

Cunliffe, Daniel. 2007. "Minority Languages and the Internet: New Threats, New Opportunities." In *Minority Language Media: Concepts, Critiques, and Case Studies*, edited by Michael J. Cormack and Niamh Hourigan, 133–50. Clevedon: Multilingual Matters.

Cunliffe, Daniel, Delyth Morris, and Cynog Prys. 2013. "Young Bilinguals' Language Behaviour in Social Networking Sites: The Use of Welsh on Facebook." *Journal of Computer-Mediated Communication* 18: 339–61.

Dauenhauer, Nora M., and Richard Dauenhauer. 1998. "Technical, Emotional, and Ideological Issues in Reversing Language Shift: Examples from Southeast Alaska." In *Endangered Languages: Language Loss and Community Response*, edited by Lenore A. Grenoble and Lindsay J. Whaley, 57–98. Cambridge: Cambridge University Press.

Davies-Deacon, Merryn. 2018. "Facebook as a Potential Site for Non-Standard Breton." Presentation at the British Association for Applied Linguistics/Cambridge University Press Seminar on Minority Languages in New Media, Birmingham, U.K., April 28, 2018.

De Falco, Dario, and Alfonso Cesarano. 2016. "Endangered Languages in the Era of Social Media: The Case of the Kenya Lebu' Kulit Language." In *Linguapax Review*

2016: Digital Media and Language Revitalisation, edited by Josep Cru, 55–66. Barcelona: Linguapax International.

Díaz Robles, Tajëëw, and Eduardo Ávila. 2014. "Encuentro de activismo digital de lenguas indígenas." *FAHHO Fundación Alfredo Harp Helú Oaxaca*, November 11, 2014. http://fahho.mx/blog/2014/11/11/encuentro-de-activismo-digital-de-lenguas-indigenas.

Dixon, R. M. W. 1991. "The Endangered Languages of Australia, Indonesia and Oceania." In *Endangered Languages*, edited by Robert H. Robins and Eugenius M. Uhlenbeck, 229–56. Oxford: Berg Publishers.

Dorian, Nancy C. 1991. "Surviving the Broadcast Media in Small Language Communities." *Educational Media International* 28: 134–37.

Eisenlohr, Patrick. 2004. "Language Revitalization and New Technologies: Cultures of Electronic Mediation and the Refiguring of Communities." *Annual Review of Anthropology* 33: 21–45.

Flores-Marcial, Xochitl Marina. 2015. "A History of Guelaguetza in Zapotec Communities of the Central Valleys of Oaxaca, 16th Century to the Present." PhD diss. University of California, Los Angeles.

Guardado, David. 1997. "Asturia—A Head-Start for Asturian on the Internet." *Mercator Media Forum* 3: 52–59.

Harrison, K. David. 2010. "The Tragedy of Dying Languages." *BBC News*, February 5, 2010. http://news.bbc.co.uk/2/hi/8500108.stm.

Hill, Kenneth C. 2002. "On Publishing the Hopi Dictionary." In *Making Dictionaries: Preserving Indigenous Languages of the Americas*, edited by William Frawley, Kenneth C. Hill, and Pamela Munro, 299–311. Berkeley: University of California Press.

Honeycutt, Courtenay, and Daniel Cunliffe. 2008. "The Use of the Welsh Language on Facebook." *Information, Communication & Society* 13: 226–48.

Johnson, Ian. 2013. "Audience Design and Communication Accommodation Theory: Use of Twitter by Welsh-English Biliterates." In *Social Media and Minority Languages: Convergence and the Creative Industries*, edited by Elin H. G. Jones and Enrique Uribe-Jongbloed, 99–118. Bristol: Multilingual Matters.

Jongbloed-Faber, Lysbeth, Hans Van de Velde, Cor van der Meer, and Edwin Klinkenberg. 2016. "Language Use of Frisian Bilingual Teenagers on Social Media." *Treballs de Sociolingüística Catalana* 26: 27–54.

King, Lila, and Tim Berners-Lee. 2005. "Web Inventor: Online Life Will Produce More Creative Children." *CNN: Technology*, October 10, 2005. http://www.cnn.com/2005/TECH/Internet/08/30/tim.berners.lee.

Lee, Dave. 2011. "Micro-Blogging in a Mother Tongue on Twitter." *BBC News*, April 8, 2011. http://news.bbc.co.uk/2/hi/programmes/click_online/9450488.stm.

Lillehaugen, Brook Danielle. 2016. "Why Write in a Language That (Almost) No One Can Read? Twitter and the Development of Written Literature." *Language Documentation and Conservation* 10: 356–92.

May, Ismael M. 2010. "El maya escrito a través de los medios electrónicos de comunicación: localizando lo global." In *Etnia, lengua y territorio: El Sureste ante el globalización*, edited by Ricardo López Santillán, 211–35. Mérida: UNAM.

O'Carroll, Acushla Deanne. 2013. "Virtual Whanaungatanga: Māori Using Social Networking Sites to Attain and Maintain Relationships." *AlterNative: International Journal of Indigenous People* 9: 230–45.

Reershemius, Gertrud. 2016. "Autochthonous Heritage Languages and Social Media: Writing and Bilingual Practices in Low German on Facebook." *Journal of Multilingual and Multicultural Development* 38: 35–49.

Rivron, Vassili. 2012. "The Use of Facebook by the Eton of Cameroon." In *LANG: Towards the Multilingual Cyberspace*, edited by Laurent Vannini and Hervé Le Crosnier, 161–68. Caen: C&F Éditions.

Silverstein, Michael. 2003. "The Whens and Wheres—as Well as Hows—of Ethnolinguistic Recognition." *Public Culture* 15: 531–57.

Simons, Gary F., and Charles D. Fennig. 2017. *Ethnologue: Languages of the World, Twentieth Edition*. Dallas: SIL International. http://www.ethnologue.com.

Turin, Mark. 2013. "Globalization Helps Preserve Endangered Languages." *Yale Global Online*, December 3, 2013. New Haven: The Whitney and Betty MacMillan Center for International and Area Studies at Yale. http://yaleglobal.yale.edu/content/globalization-helps-preserve-endangered-languages.

UNESCO. 2003. "Language Vitality and Endangerment." Submitted to the International Expert Meeting on UNESCO Programme Safeguarding of Endangered Languages, Paris, March 10–12, 2003. https://ich.unesco.org/doc/src/00120-EN.pdf.

UNESCO. 2004. "UNESCO Sponsored Research Finds WWW Fracturing into Language Communities." UNESCO.org, November 2, 2004. http://www.unesco.org/new/en/brasilia/about-this-office/single-view/news/unesco_sponsored_research_finds_www_fracturing_into_language.

Vincze, Laszlo, and Tom Moring. 2013. "Towards Ethnolinguistic Identity Gratifications." In *Social Media and Minority Languages: Convergence and the Creative Industries*, edited by Elin H. G. Jones and Enrique Uribe-Jongbloed, 47–57. Bristol: Multilingual Matters.

Wagner, Mélanie. 2013. "Luxembourgish on Facebook." In *Social Media and Minority Languages: Convergence and the Creative Industries*, edited by Elin H. G. Jones and Enrique Uribe-Jongbloed, 87–98. Bristol: Multilingual Matters.

Wilson, Alex, Bronwyn Carlson, and Acushla Sciascia. 2017. "Reterritorialising Social Media: Indigenous People Rise Up." *Australasian Journal of Information Systems* 21: 1–4.

10

FROM FACEBOOK TO *IXAMOXTLI*

Nahua Activism through Social Networking

ADAM COON

Nahua artist Mardonio Carballo has a grueling schedule. In the summer of 2013 alone, he was responsible for presenting a nationally televised documentary series in Mexico, conducting another program of interviews on Internet television, giving weekly radio spots on Carmen Aristegui's news program and on the National University's radio station, and being the lead singer and composer for a progressive rock group. That same summer, he also gave a rock concert in an economically poor area of Mexico City, wrote a weekly news article, published a book/CD of poetry and experimental music, went on tour to present the volume, participated in protests denouncing the killing of news reporters, and created a bilingual Nahuatl-Spanish book for children. Faced with the question about his itineraries, he responds, "I sit a lot of the time and talk, and talk, but out in the cornfields my family does intense physical work. When I think of that, I can't complain."[1] The comparison of his projects with laboring in the cornfields is an apt metaphor for Carballo's own work, as he seeks to cultivate fields of music, literature, and mass media with Nahua and Indigenous voices, perspectives, and experiences—voices that are largely inaudible in mass media, and that among other things demand land rights to work the cornfields Carballo describes.

His work on social media constitutes a potent example of Indigenous strategies through recent technology. He is intensely active on Facebook, or *ixamoxtli*—literally *ix*, face, and *amoxtli*, book (fig. 10.1). Indeed, most Nahuas who live in urban areas are active on Facebook, as it allows them to stay in touch with rural communities and build kinship ties within places like Mexico City. This chapter focuses on Carballo and his collaborative book/CD/DVD *Las horas perdidas* (*The Lost Hours*, 2014), particularly the manner in which this work takes on new meanings and contexts through Carballo's posts. This is an invitation to look at *Las horas* beyond the narrative itself, and as part of a wider system in which social media serves as a key hub for Nahua activism. Such an approach reflects Carballo's own conceptualization of what a book should be—a multimedia work that reaches beyond the pages, networks with its readers, and challenges the conventional view of amoxtli as archaic and pre-Columbian.

FIGURE 10.1. Carballo's Facebook profile picture, November 2016. Used with permission.

Carballo created *Las horas perdidas* with his prog-rock group A²+C. C refers to Carballo and the A² to the Arreola brothers who play bass and drums. This work mixes genres—diary, poetry, rock, and documentary—and shifts fluidly between Nahuatl and Spanish, often in a mixed Spanahuatl or *nahuañol*. Crossing the borders of languages and genres, the work highlights the creative potential in breaking with traditional categorizations, particularly with stereotypical depictions of Indigenous nations. It recounts the travels of Carballo's band through Chiapas, Oaxaca, Veracruz, Morelos, and Mexico City from May to July 2014 (a trip also documented on Facebook). *Las horas perdidas* and its presence on Facebook point to new horizons in Nahua cultural production that fight the relegation of their perspectives and voices to the past and folklore through a diverse array of media. Although A²+C created *Las horas perdidas* before the disappearance of forty-three students, many of whom were Indigenous, from the rural teachers' college of Ayotzinapa in September 2014, and also before Article 230 in Mexico's Federal Telecommunications Law[2] that would have prohibited Indigenous languages on national media, Facebook becomes a platform for this text and the band's music to not only take part in protests against these two events but also to rally support and pressure the government for solutions. I argue that Carballo employs the Nahua kinship-based perspective of *nemilistli* ("way of life") on social media in a multifaceted struggle against the physical and epistemic violence signaled by Ayotzinapa and Article 230, using this medium to integrate *Las horas perdidas* into this movement.

A challenge that arises when working with Facebook, if we think of it as book, is how to study this perpetual text. In just two months, Carballo's Facebook wall amounted to more than two hundred pages in Word document form. While a traditional book has a clear first and last page, it is difficult to ascertain the length of a volume comprised of posts on social media. How does one, then, read denunciations of the disappearance of forty-three students from Ayotzinapa followed by a post in which Carballo describes what he had for breakfast? What might at first blush appear to be cat-meme-like posts about a meal are in fact elements of a carefully crafted text on his wall. They are well-planned publications that aim to strengthen Nahua and Indigenous kinship ties in Mexico City, strengthen Nahuatl, and protest social injustices. This *post*-modern mix makes this ixamoxtli/ face-book a challenge to read, and at the same time all the more dynamic. Rhizomatic in nature, one link or post can send a reader down a different string of publications and users. There is no single center, and, by studying Carballo's use of Facebook, visitors become familiar with many other Nahuas and Indigenous activists using this medium.[3] By concentrating specifically on *Las horas perdidas*, one can see Nahua activism on Facebook brought into focus.

This chapter identifies the wider significance of Carballo's use of social media and brings closer attention to publications that tend only to receive ephemeral attention contingent upon a continued flurry of likes for a couple weeks at most. It highlights the particular value of Nahua participation on social media. Who are Nahuas and why study their use of Facebook? What is unique about that, when nearly two billion people use it today? Nahuatl, popularly known as the language of the Mexica or Aztecs, is often relegated to a distant past. Many are unaware that today there are more than three million Nahuas (a term generally used to refer to people who speak the Nahuatl language).[4] While the majority resides in Mexico, there are also numerous communities in the United States and other countries. Carballo's *Las horas perdidas* represents Indigenous peoples as part of social networks (in the sense of kinship as well as electronic media like Facebook) that move well beyond their communities—beyond the common depiction of them as relegated to rural areas—and rather underscores a relevance of their perspectives throughout Mexico and on an international scale.

A Nahua *comunalidad* or kinship-centered approach, encapsulated in nemilistli, frames my analysis of Carballo's works.[5] With its emphasis on transit, nemilistli displaces the depiction of Nahuas as somehow stuck in place or time. The root *nemi* can signify walking, living, feeling, being, thinking, and philosophy. It is a philosophy based on personal experiences and an affective connection with one's knowledge production—a way of life key to healthy kinship and communities. Nahua nemilistli encompasses the following perspectives, which by no means is an exhaustive list: 1. *Ixtlamatilistli* ("knowledge with the face") values knowledges gained from personal experiences. It proposes a different view of who constitutes an intellectual, can offer solutions to problems, and serve in community *cargos* or community positions. In Nahuatl, an intellectual is not someone removed from the context with an objective view but rather someone who is personally involved—"one who knows with the face";[6] 2. *Tlaixpan* ("that which is in front") references the past as in front of the subject in a dynamic present and future. Tlaixpan is the word for "altar," made for festivities like the Day of the Dead. On these altars are placed pictures of deceased relatives, and they like the past are in front. They constitute what is known and help guide into an unpredictable future; 3. *Yoltlajlamikilistli* ("knowledge with the heart") underscores an affective intelligence in which cognition is viewed as conjugated with emotions. This view underlies the affective space of kinship ties and practices such as reciprocity and community festivities, of seeing these practices as knowledge production as opposed to folklore. What is unique about Carballo's use of Facebook is his continued use of these perspectives throughout his works and posts (both in the sense of Facebook and *cargos*). He employs the concepts connected to nemilistli within *Las horas perdidas* and Facebook to highlight contemporary Nahua knowledge production and community formation against the backdrop of Ayotzinapa and Article 230.

CARBALLO INEMILIS/CARBALLO'S PATH

Carballo is from northern Veracruz, the Huasteca, where there is the largest Nahua population. He has nonetheless spent most of his life outside of this region. In his teens, he moved to Mexico City to complete his high school studies and has lived there since, joining a large pan-Indigenous urban population. Among the most innovative artists of contemporary Indigenous cultural production, Carballo works with many types of media, including radio, poetry, documentary, short stories, television, and progressive rock. He uproots stereotypical and patriarchal re-presentations of First Peoples. This is evident in *Las horas* with its vying for an affective space in which the gender of the poetic voice and their lover is ambivalent, and on Facebook with Carballo's participation in LGBTQ movements. Acceptance of a gender spectrum connects with the work's aim to defend linguistic diversity against Article 230 and convene large groups in street protests against social injustices like Ayotzinapa.

Carballo traces his activism and media strategies back to the 1994 Zapatista uprising.[7] The Zapatistas' demand for tangible rights and respect through a successful online media campaign captured Carballo's interest and inspired him to take pride in his Nahua upbringing. The perspectives of the Ejército Zapatista de Liberación Nacional (EZLN) are a common theme in his works, and there are allusions to EZLN symbols such as *conchas* (conche shells) and *ceiba* trees in *Las horas*. For Carballo, this movement underscored the need to go beyond the state-sponsored defense of "Indigenous culture," and instead demanded concrete rights and representation (Mardonio Carballo's wall, Facebook, December 21, 2012). In a similar vein, underscoring the presence of Nahua perspectives in *Las horas*, he explains that "Nahuatl is one more language, an instrument of creation, independent from all the cosmogony that circumscribes it. I always make texts in Spanish with a completely Indigenous universe, fully Nahua, even though the Nahuatl language is not present explicitly or implicitly" (Actividades Culturales Mardonio Carballo wall, Facebook, September 19, 2012).[8] This comment goes against the tendency to portray the Nahuatl language as exotic, and it also challenges the idea that one has to speak Nahuatl to be Nahua. A key point in Carballo's later quest against Article 230, as well as denunciations of the disappearance of the forty-three students, is that Nahuas and Indigenous nations should be seen as people, and not as pristine informants relegated to the past.

Band members Alonso and José María Arreola met Carballo in March 2011 at the event "Poesía en voz alta" ("Poetry Outloud") on the campus of the Universidad Nacional Autónoma de México (UNAM). From there they began a collaboration of Carballo's poetry with the Arreola brothers' musical compositions, which first resulted in the song "Ezo" (Blood) for Arreola's album *Trilogía cruento* (2011). They then embarked on a wider project in 2012 that would become *Las horas perdidas*. A²+C had their first official performance together at SXSW in Austin, Texas, that same year. This gradual coming together is represented on Facebook and reflects the creation of kinship ties and alliances across borders and among Indigenous and non-Indigenous allies. As Carballo was composing these songs, he posted the criticism regarding the desire to defend "Indigenous culture." Rather than attempt to preserve "Indigenous culture," he defends any group that has become a target of discrimination.

Las horas perdidas is organized into two parts. The first is a diary that tells of the band's travels throughout Mexico. The second part contains the lyrics to the songs, written by Carballo. One of the main themes in the songs is remembrance of those who have disappeared, in a number of senses: first, of people disappeared during the "War on Drug Trafficking"; second, the displacement of people—their disappearance from towns—due to transnational companies taking over their lands; and third, the disappearance—the inaudibility and invisibility—of contemporary Nahuas and their language within mass media. The same themes are present in Carballo's postings on Facebook and encompass these three remembrances. The DVD documents the band's travels throughout Mexico and their interviews with those who have lost relatives. It emphasizes dynamic movement, from the city to other spaces, and the networks of kinship among rural and metropolitan spaces—and this network extends to social media such as Facebook. Evoking the Nahua concept nemilistli through these movements underscores the need to become closely familiar with the people in these communities, of walking with them and being personally involved in the context.

Shortly after submitting *Las horas perdidas* for publication,[9] forty-three students from Ayotzinapa went missing on September 26, 2014.[10] The subsequent protests not only put faces on the forty-three missing students but has since become a symbol of the many who have lost their lives in what some have called the "War on Drug Trafficking" (2006–present).[11] This is a main objective of *Las horas perdidas* and Carballo's Facebook wall: to put names on the ever-increasing statistic of those disappeared. This effort ties into the perspective of *yoltlajlamikistli*, knowledge with the heart, an intelligent affectivity that feels this loss. Also in 2014, Aleida Calleja, from the nonprofit organization Fundación Libertis, informed Carballo that the federal legislature was attempting to pass Article 230 in the Law of Telecommunications. That article would have prohibited broadcasting in an Indigenous language unless the station or channel were specifically categorized as Indigenous, which in effect would have prohibited some of Carballo's own programs mentioned at the beginning of this chapter.

Carballo took to Facebook to denounce both the disappearance of the forty-three students and Article 230's attempt to erase Indigenous languages. *Las horas perdidas* took on a new critical voice with these current events. For example, within a Facebook post containing the link to Carballo's interview with Carmen Aristegui on her radio program November 20, 2014, he spoke about the book and connected the publication with the recent events at Ayotzinapa. Even though the group had composed the songs three years earlier, he sadly reflected on "el México que estamos viviendo ahora . . . de lo mismo de hace tres años" (figs. 10.2 and 10.3). The image on the book's cover, posted along with the link to the interview with Aristegui, is from the group's visit to La Ventosa, Oaxaca, with its more than one hundred wind turbines. Foreign companies bought up land to construct these turbines without the required consultation of Zapotecs in the area.[12] The image is a metaphor within *Las horas perdidas* for the importance of listening to those in the communities and confronting, like Don Quijote, transnational and government giants in a denouncement of injustices.

FIGURE 10.2. Cover of Carballo's *Las horas perdidas.*

FIGURE 10.3. Facebook post announcing the release of *Las horas perdidas* and its connection to Ayotzinapa on Aristegui´s news program, November 24, 2014. Used with permission.

The diary at the beginning documents travels across Mexico and corresponding posts appear in status updates on the band members' Facebook pages. To give a summary, the DVD begins with the group's journey to Chiapas. There they play the first two songs, "Vete de mí" (Leave Me) and "Las horas perdidas" (The Lost Hours), emphasizing an ambivalent longing for a lost love that relates back to the theme of disappearances. Images of Afro-Cuban singer Ignacio Jacinto Villa Fernández, better known as "Bola de Nieve," are projected directly on the group as they play. Indigenous voices, with a Nahuatl version of the song "Las horas perdidas," are positioned in solidarity with Afrodescendants.

The band continues on its journey to Oaxaca, where they meet with Zapotec poet Irma Pineda. Pineda and her mother Cándida share their testimonies regarding the military's disappearance of Irma's father, activist Víctor Pineda Henestrosa. The intense affect emphasized in the first two songs of their journey is now transposed into a catharsis of feeling in coping with the disappearance of friends and family. They play the third song, "Desaparecidos" (The Missing), for the Pineda family. Like the protests over the disappearance of the forty-three students from Ayotzinapa, the band seeks to give name and personal stories to the many disappeared and murdered. From Oaxaca they move on to Xalapa, Veracruz, where they sing the fifth song, "¿Cuánto pesan los muertos?" (How Much Do the Dead Weigh?), for Mexican poet Esther Hernández, whose daughter Irene was brutally slain in 2010. The song asks the listener to reflect on the worth of each of the tens of thousands of individuals who has died in the "War on Drug Trafficking." From Veracruz, they travel to a Nahua community in Morelos and sing the sixth song, "Mitote," which emphasizes dance as a way to overcome biases. They play the final song "Sabotage" in Mexico City, which is fitting as the capital serves as a main hub in Carballo's activism and his work highlights the large Indigenous communities within the metropolis. This space, the central location of the federal government, is also significant as the closing lyrics stress the importance of speaking up and questioning governmental discourse. A²+C uploaded performances of these songs to Facebook.[13] In the following sections I analyze how the *nemistli* approach is reflected particularly within the images and songs "Las horas perdidas," "¿Cuánto pesan los muertos?" and "Sabotage," and how *Las horas perdidas* has taken on new life within social media. Carballo's posts and comments from other Indigenous activists underscore the potency of their networking to project *Las horas* onto a wider movement that seeks to effect change against the backdrop of Ayotzinapa and Article 230.

THE DISCOVERED STEPS AMONG THE LOST HOURS

The main text and the Spanish version of the second poem/song have the same title, "Las horas perdidas." This title plays on the name of Cuban writer Alejo Carpentier's 1953 novel *Los pasos perdidos*, in which a musicologist travels to a remote Indigenous village in search of special musical instruments. With its own exploration of alternative soundscapes, *Las horas perdidas* breaks with the exoticized gaze of Carpentier's "real maravilloso" (marvelous realism). Unlike the *othered* depiction in that novel, Carballo represents Indigenous perspectives as necessary for solutions to present challenges—not in a romanticized sense but rather as equally valid knowledge production with which people need to engage. The song "Las horas perdidas" represents the poetic voice waiting at night for a lover to return and begins with the entreatment "Vuelve esta tarde" (return this afternoon/evening; 45). That love is not requited, and the poetic voice continues to search for their lost lover, who very well might be one of the disappeared described explicitly in the other songs. On a symbolic level, the song/poem/video contends for an affective space away from the violence that has enveloped Mexico.[14] These references to a search for a missing person relate to the network of connections made tangible through A²+C's travels to the homes of those who have suffered such losses, as described in the book's preface: "These are *The Lost Hours* we encountered ambling through some parts of the world, searching for paths with less blood and less violence" (6).[15] These travels appear in Facebook, forging a remarkable interplay between various media but ultimately providing access to a wider audience.

Through this journey, A²+C and their Facebook followers re-create kinship connections that cross national, ethnic, and linguistic borders. The concept of yoltlajlamikistli is crucial to nemilistli and its emphasis on kinship relationships. This is reflected in a post dated November 11, 2014, and in a video trailer for "Las horas perdidas" posted the following day (fig. 10.4). The trailer shows them performing this same song at the base of the wind turbines on the cover. Those who comment, share, and like these postings vary from Indigenous intellectuals throughout Mexico, such as Ayuuk linguist Yásnaya Elena Aguilar Gil, Maya literary critic Genner Llanes Ortiz, and Nahua writer Martín Tonalmeyotl, to non-Indigenous artists both inside and outside Mexico. These artists also form part of the movement "Artistas contra la discriminación lingüística" ("Artists Against Linguistic Discrimination," the name of Carballo's campaign against Article 230) as well as a campaign against the killing of news reporters and protestors. Two years later in November 2016, these movements came together during the performance of A²+C at the Feria Internacional de Libro (FIL) in Guadalajara, Mexico, from which Carballo posted a performance of "Las horas perdidas." There, the band members wore black shirts in solidarity with the disappeared.

"Las horas perdidas" emphasizes close observation of surroundings, evident in the first stanza, in which the sun is described as a "Sun-Bird" that "furrows" across the horizon, with its "last feathers" representing the sunset. The description of the feathers "surcando" (furrowing) alludes to the corn crop, the prime metaphor in Nahuatl poetics. The cyclical nature of the crop connects with the concept of tlaixpan, that those who have been lost still are a part of the present and future. Like the corn crop that lives and then dies to give sustenance, deceased or lost loved ones also return. The third stanza underscores this imagery when the poetic voice states that "he robado un poco de sol en la punta de una cera" (45). Candles are placed out during Xantolo (Day of the Dead) to help

FIGURE 10.4. Carballo sharing *Las horas* on Facebook, November 13, 2014. Used with permission.

guide deceased relatives back to their homes. The importance of the agricultural cycles and Xantolo is also reflected within Carballo's postings on Facebook, as shall be seen in more detail later when addressing posts with food from Café de Raíz, his family's restaurant.

There are significant differences between the versions of "Las horas perdidas" in Spanish and Nahuatl. The song is entitled "Las horas perdidas (Cielo mar)" (The Lost Hours [Sky Sea]) in Spanish, but only "Iljuikatl-ueipuyekatl" (Sky-Sea) in Nahuatl.[16] Carballo's "Las horas perdidas" alludes to the lost hours of those who have been killed and disappeared, imagining a different space—an "imaginary sea"—in which those tragedies cease. In tandem with this text, through his participations on Facebook, he attempts to create that (cyber)space for remembering the dead or missing—Ayotzinapa serving as a metonym for those tens of thousands of absences and Article 230 for the continual attempts at erasing Indigenous languages—and challenging colonial practices that misrepresent those lives and languages as expendable.

The poetic voice of "Las horas perdidas" invites, both in *Las horas* and on Facebook ("A lo lejos se escucha . . . ," Facebook post on Mardonio Carballo's wall, December 28, 2014), the absent lovers to put their ears up to the conch shell, so that they can hear "akualantika," angry like water. This fiery water, a Nahua metaphor for war, represents a defense against injustices. The poetic voice states that they cannot see it but "imagínalo"—imagine this utopic space. There is another key Maya metaphor employed by the EZLN in the line "to sleep above in a mythic *ceiba*" (46).[17] This oneiric space imagines a more just world in which one recognizes the connection with surroundings and the common origins of humanity in the mythical ceiba tree. The ceiba also constitutes a metaphor in letters from EZLN members for a place from which they can closely observe their surroundings. According to Carballo, it constitutes a stellar map in which the tree represents reality, between the stars and the *inframundo* (the alternate title "sky-sea" refers to this cosmogonic mapping). In his community, boys were taught to hug this tree's thorned trunk to prepare them for a painful life (Carballo, 2017). Similarly, Carballo through *Las horas perdidas* acknowledges the harsh reality in Mexico, and in doing so he seeks the strength to tackle those challenges. The heights of the ceiba contrast with the wind turbines of Oaxaca, and on the DVD the band plays this song at the base of the turbines. The apostrophic structure of the poem/song also allows it to be an invitation to the reader/listener to imagine a world, as described by EZLN, "in which many worlds fit."[18] This song forms part of Carballo's effort on Facebook to create a network among the band itself, and alliances among both Indigenous and non-Indigenous communities. While the turbines create immense wattage exported to non-Indigenous regions, the band produces music at the base of these behemoths for locals and listens to their struggles. The question begs who is truly losing hours.

There is a one-verse stanza: "Silencio" in Spanish and "Axtlen tij kakin" (We hear nothing) in Nahuatl. That lover has not returned and it grieves the poetic voice. The use of the first-person plural expands that grief to not only their situation but beyond as part of a shared community of suffering. The text attempts in a sense to silence that silence, to speak out and make that loss known. In the song's performance, Carballo pauses before this line and then yells "silence!" in a strident tone reminiscent of heavy metal to signal oppression. The battle against censorship is a common theme throughout Carballo's postings on Facebook with the hashtags #noalsilencio and #nonoscallarán and ties into his denunciation of Ayotzinapa and Article 230.

In the final verses the previous stanza is repeated, cyclical in nature like the corn crop to which they allude. The poetic voice ends by stating, "It is a shame that it cannot be real and finally drown the memory of you and your eyes" (46).[19] The sting of the lost lover still pains the poetic voice, in spite of attempting to imagine a different space. This same pain is represented in Facebook, as Carballo seeks to put names to faces and documents this travel of *Las horas perdidas*, and fills cyberspace with Nahuatl to fight Article 230. The word *mar* plays on its resemblance to *amar* and vies for an affective space and yoltlajlamikilistli in which those feelings are valued. It is one in which this oneiric space is not considered "horas perdidas." The work and Carballo's postings constitute an attempt to imagine that (cyber)space in which "many worlds fit," although doing so may sound quixotic. It is one in which Ayotzinapa and Article 230 are replaced by an affective sensibility to each individual and the acceptance of linguistic and epistemological diversity. The poem ends hoping that these imaginings of a different world can swallow up the absence of the lost love, and the poetic voice laments that such a world has not materialized.

HOW MUCH DO THE DEAD WEIGH?: KNOWLEDGE WITH THE HEART

In this section I analyze the fifth song, "¿Cuánto pesan los muertos?" Unlike the other compositions in *Las horas perdidas*, there is no version of this poem in Nahuatl. The question "How much do the dead weigh?" refers to how much they weigh upon our conscience. The poem consists of thirteen stanzas, which vary in length from between one and seven lines written in free verse. It begins with a sampling from Gil Scott Heron's "The Revolution Will Not Be Televised" (originally played at the beginning of earlier versions of the song "Las horas perdidas"), which is fitting in its message that mass media excludes Afrodescendant and Indigenous perspectives that challenge the status quo. Heron's line is echoed in the poetic voice's repetition of "¿Cuánto pesan los muertos?"—death being the ultimate silencing of dissonant voices. The sampling common to hip-hop and rap functions as a contact zone for moving beyond expected borders to the creation of a solidarity network among dissonant voices.

The first line begins: "A short time ago we found out that in the so-called War on Drug Trafficking / there have been more than 90 thousand killed" (2014, 57).[20] The song then challenges the effectiveness of this ever-increasing statistic. It goes on to ask, "What are the codes that a human being must break to kill another / who is their equal?" (57).[21] A loss of the affective connection described in the previous songs, of not seeing other people as equals, helps permit such violence. The song invites us to leave the statistics that reduce individuals to numbers in order to feel each loss, with yoltlajlamikilistli or knowledge of the heart.

Instead of statistics, the final two verses of the first stanza stress materiality, stating, "There is a ritual that is premonition, poem, and omen that people make / before they die: they retrace their steps" (57).[22] In the second stanza the poetic voice goes on to describe this practice, which consists of a person retracing their steps before they die, in Nahuatl literally to gather one's feet, as Carballo codeswitches into Nahuatl: *moijxipejpena* (*ijxi* or *ikxi*, "feet," and *pejpena*, to "collect" or "choose").[23] This code-switching emphasizes the perspective of nemilistli and being personally connected and familiar with one's surroundings: "mo ijxipe-jpena, mo ijxipejpentinemi" (they collect their feet, they go around collecting their feet; 57). The suffix–*tinemi* consists of the root *nemi*—from which the word nemilistli is derived—and signifies going around doing something. The band describes *Las horas perdidas* as "un disco al revés" (a backward CD), of a dynamic revisiting of origins—such as the Nahuatl language itself—and these memories form part of a dynamic creation, rather than "holding them back" in time as so often depicted in misrepresentations of Indigenous cultural production. This depiction of the past is a common theme within Carballo's Facebook posts. It connects with the concept of tlaixpan (literally "that which is in front"): the past is in front instead of behind, as "past" and "pasado" suggest in English and Spanish. Carballo reposted this song on Facebook in October 2014, two weeks after Ayotzinapa ("¿Cuánto pesan los muertos," post on Mardonio Carballo's wall, October 14, 2014). "¿Cuánto pesan los muertos?" has become one of the most shared from this work, and @mardoniocarbalo, @mardoniocarballo, #PlumasdelaSerpiente, and #cuantopesaunmuerto are @tags and hashtags for speaking of Ayotzinapa and the tens of thousands murdered in the "War on Drug Trafficking."

The tenth stanza is key to the poem and consists of only one verse: "Un muerto nos bastaba" (One dead was already too much; 58). We should be just as affected if one person dies as if many lose their lives, recognizing the individual worth of each person—moving beyond what Seneca literary critic Mishuana Goeman calls the "mode of statistics" toward the power of individual stories (Goeman 2014, n.p.). The final stanza, also consisting of one verse, is a translation of Heron's song, "La Revolución no será televisada," and emphasizes that this affective connection, these Nahua perspectives, the recognition of the worth of each individual are for the most part not being televised and not being remembered and, as Carballo denounced in his campaign against Article 230, are being actively suppressed (fig. 10.5). He emphasizes an affective space as part of a revolution—this *moikxipejpena*—as the word "revolution" itself means a return, a rolling back, a retracing of steps. Through his art, Carballo seeks to retrace the steps of Nahua knowledges and perspectives and underscore their importance in a dynamic present and future.

How does one read protests against Ayotzinapa followed by what Carballo had for breakfast ("Mandan decir del Café de Raíz," Facebook posting, October 31, 2014)? While many Facebook users post cat videos and recipes, his use of the

FIGURE 10.5. Facebook post of episode from *Las plumas de la serpiente*, November 1, 2014. Used with permission.

social network—and that of other Nahuas—is different. They post food from their hometowns, carrying a greater significance; these dishes are placed on the altar in remembrance of ancestors and in honor of corn. Food is sacred. It reminds one of a connection with the fields, which in turn becomes a key metaphor for life, nemilistli, one's way of life in general as well as artistic production. The restaurant run by his family in Mexico City constitutes an attempt to carve out a space for this Huastecan food, as well as a meeting space for Indigenous and non-Indigenous allies to form kinships within Mexico City.[24] A subtext to these posts is that they are eating Huastecan food, as opposed to eating at transnational chains such as Starbucks or McDonald's (and in this sense ties into the protests against the wind turbines in Oaxaca on the cover of *Las horas perdidas*). It underscores the importance of festivities such as the Day of the Dead. Such festivities are an opportunity to create and solidify kinship ties. As mentioned earlier, the perspective of tlaixpan, "that which is in front," is the word used to refer to altars on which images of deceased relatives are placed and point to a kinship with the deceased. So it is not whimsical to post a denunciation of a massacre, followed by an invitation to eat *zacahuil* or another Huastecan dish; instead it forms part of the process of mourning and remembrance of those lost and described in songs such as "¿Cuánto pesan los muertos?"—this food, especially in Mexico City where it is uncommon, becomes a continual mnemonic device for community, ancestors, language (many of these dishes have no translation into Spanish or else are Hispanicized loanwords from Nahuatl), and untimely deaths.

In response to Article 230—230 being another number that could be added to that fictional "national lottery of democracy" he describes—Carballo particularly started organizing events in December 2015. His use of Facebook allows him to resist the monochrome of numbers and promote yoltlajlamikilistli with media (images) and songs (sound) that challenge visual and acoustic colonialism. He began posting images to Facebook that championed linguistic diversity, one of the most frequent being of two people with long snake-like twisted tongues that spell out "Contra la discriminación lingüística" (fig. 10.6). Similar to the ever-increasing number of the disappeared without personal names or stories, the federal legislature perhaps hoped that Article 230 would go unnoticed—this was Article 230 buried within a more expansive law. In addressing such incursions within mediascapes, Luis Cárcamo-Huechante's work goes beyond what is traditionally thought of as "colonialism," the takeover of land, to more broadly speaking of media colonialism (2013, 50–51),[25] the domination of mass media and control over what sounds and images circulate. Carballo has fought that media colonialism. He organized an event in December 2015 to denounce language discrimination with Indigenous rap and hip-hop artists. His own work, *Las horas perdidas*, and the use of Nahuatl in many of the songs have been included in these protests. His use of Nahuatl in the songs and Nahua concepts such as moikxipejpena (retracing one's steps) constitute a performance against the languages that Article 230 proposed to prohibit and silence.

Carballo took on a position similar to a *cargo* (community position) within the new government of Mexico City[26] on the Asamblea de Constituyentes (Constitutional Assembly) to ensure that Indigenous communities were not left out of the constitution. Carballo represented the view of *ixtlamatiliztli*, "knowledge with the face," as one who is able to offer effective knowledges because he is personally involved. While still holding this cargo or position, he spoke in November 2016 regarding his representation of Indigenous voices in a meeting with representatives from the United Nations: "Lamentablemente este no es el rostro de México. Esto solamente es una parte del rostro de México porque si habláramos del rostro de México, tendríamos que hablar de que nos faltan 43 rostros de los 43 estudiantes mayoritariamente indígenas desaparecidos . . . si esto fuera el rostro de México, tendríamos derecho a estar en los medios de comunicación con todas nuestras lenguas" ("Mi participación en la Reunión de

A continuación va info delicada e importante.

El artículo 230 de la ley de telecomunicaciones aprobada el año pasado prohíbe de facto el uso de las lenguas indígenas en cualquier punto del espacio radioeléctrico mexicano que no sea de uso social indígena. Bajo esta lógica todo el trabajo que venimos realizando, el de posicionar a las lenguas indígenas en los medios de comunicación masivos, es ilegal. Ante esta alerta nos pusimos a trabajar de manera jurídica y vía amparo estamos luchando por el que se reconozca la inconstitucionalidad de este artículo ante La Suprema Corte de Justicia de la Nación que se resolverá en el mes de enero de 2016. Para pagar los honorarios de los abogados que han y están llevando nuestro caso -han trabajado 19 meses sin recibir un quinto- hicimos una carpeta de grabados de edición limitada. Gabriel Macotela, Demián Flores, Antonio Gritón, Gustavo Monroy y Jesús Miranda -artistas plásticos de generoso y bien ganado prestigio-, se unieron a esta empresa que, de ganar resultará en una victoria que beneficiará a todas las lenguas indígenas de nuestro país. Esta carpeta que consta de 5 grabados de 25 x 35 (Linóleo sobre papel de algodón) consta de una Edición Limitada de 25 ejemplares firmados por sus autores, quitando pruebas de autor y el respectivo ejemplar para imprenta y artistas a la venta sólo saldrán 15, cada una de ellas cuesta $15, 000.00 (Quince mil pesos). La impresión de ella ha sido financiada por nuestra casa productora Nauyaka Producciones y Ediciones y El Taller Gráfico La Cebada, maravilloso proyecto de Demián Flores, sin auspicio institucional (a pesar de tener un Instituto Nacional de Lenguas Indígenas que, se supone es el encargado de velar por el bien de las lenguas originarias mexicanas y su desarrollo). Una buena inversión para estas navidades. Informes por mail o inBox: oficinamardoniocarballo@gmail.com Abrazos siempre y gratitudes.

FIGURE 10.6. Carballo's post on Article 230 on Facebook, December 14, 2015. Used with permission.

la Relatora Especial." Post on Mardonio Carballo's wall, Facebook, November 8, 2016). He referred to the importance of the face of Mexico and the incompleteness of that face because of the disappearance of the forty-three students and the attempt by Article 230 to disappear Indigenous languages also. Carballo's participation in mass media constitutes an attempt to fight against those erasures. He not only fights for Indigenous presence on mass and social media but also demands Indigenous land rights within Mexico City. It is a demand for a virtual space as well as a call for geographic spaces for Indigenous communities within urban areas. He resigned his position on the Constitutional Assembly in December 2016, as he explained on Facebook, because his Indigenous presence was treated more as tokenism than valuation of an Indigenous perspective. In contrast with this political landscape, Carballo has found within Facebook, his family's restaurant, and his artistic production the (a/e)ffective depth to address injustices such as Ayotzinapa and Article 230, similar to what Françoise Lionnet and Emmanuel Bruno Jean-François describes as the "human interest stories that pull us into the concrete lives of individual migrants and their families" (2016, 1223). Nonetheless, by leaving the Constitutional Assembly and denouncing the racism within it, he brought visibility to the issue and in the end, no one voted against the proposals he introduced defending Indigenous rights within Mexico City (interview August 31, 2017).[27] His activism pushed for a real presence of Indigenous voices and knowledges within mass media and decisions made within politics and society at large.

SYNCRETIC SAMPLING: "SABOTAGE"

This final poem of the collection code-switches from Spanish to Nahuatl in the final verses, and the version in Nahuatl code-switches from Nahuatl to Spanish. The title of the song in both languages is the English word "Sabotage." The title references the Beastie Boys's hardcore punk composition of the same title, released in January 1994, the same year and month as the Zapatista uprising. The title in English reflects the goal of putting Nahuatl in unexpected places and emphasizes a dialogue among different cultural products, rather than the provincial re-presentation of Nahua cultural production. This is a key goal with Carballo's use of Nahuatl throughout social and mass media.

In its seventh verse, the poem shifts to apostrophe, speaking to a "tú" who has long hair. From the context of *Las horas perdidas* as a whole, it is clear that the poetic voice could be speaking to the many who have lost relatives. The social network on Facebook enabled this song to take part in discussions surrounding Ayotzinapa and Article 230, as the band continued to tour after the production and circulation of *Las horas perdidas*. The official discourse demands "you will not speak out, you will be quiet."[28] The poetic voice criticizes that "you": "You will only want to wear new things."[29] The focus is on the new material objects that are produced and distract from social problems. It also ties back into two different ideas of what a "revolution" is: that revisiting of the past in dynamic present and future, versus the idea of "modern" in the sense of an industrial and technological revolution. In the context of the latter sense, the poetic voice states, "Y no podrás ver a los que padecen" (63). This alienation from the modes of production distracts from those who suffer, in this case those who have been killed or disappeared. Here the word in Nahuatl for "padecen," *majseua*, plays on the word for "Indigenous" in Nahuatl: *maseuali*. The poetic voice states that "you" could "gritar con todo tu corazón" (63). The "you" to whom the poetic voice speaks could resist what "they" state and control their voice, as well as choose to remain silent (as opposed to being silenced). "They" "tienen miedo cuando gritas," and "se atemorizan ante tu silencio" (63). Those who allow themselves to be silenced, "Han cerrado ya la casa de su corazón" (63). They lack that knowledge with the heart that allows one to see those who suffer.

The same lines repeat from the beginning, but then the poem code-switches from Spanish to Nahuatl in the final verses. This shift underscores the importance of the Nahuatl language, and how the poem can also be interpreted as having the ability to speak that language, but then giving up due to peer pressure and ceasing to use it. By singing in the two languages, the song is performative in challenging the displacement of Nahuatl—in both resisting that suppression by switching to Nahuatl at the end of the Spanish version, as well as symbolically losing the language at the end of the Nahuatl version. This is not to suggest that this code-switching occurs because of language activism, but rather that it defies the stigma aimed against such mixing—a stigma especially salient in Nahuatl studies and publications.[30] In that sense the song ties into Carballo's campaign through Facebook to denounce Article 230. This is made explicit in the recording from the performance at the Museo Universitario del Chopo and posted on November 23, 2014, with the words "Justicia Ayotzinapa. Arreola + Carballo." The video shows the band members have traded their habitual blue T-shirts with their initials for black clothing. In the background they project images of the forty-three disappeared students and their families. Carballo interrupts the lyrics to count from 1 to 43. Through the rhizomatic movement on Facebook, the shares and likes within posts like this one connect to an activist network of many other Indigenous writers and artists such as Zapotec activist Héctor Pineda Santiago and artist Érika Karina Jiménez Flores (Akire Huauhtli).

RETRACING REVOLUTIONARY STEPS

This chapter has shown that Carballo's ixamoxtli or Facebook interplay with *Las horas perdidas* represents one of the most innovative developments in contemporary Nahua cultural production and the creation of kinship ties in urban areas such as Mexico City. The concept of nemilistli and the corresponding perspectives of ixtlamatilistli, yoltlajlamikilistli, and tlaixpan have helped me explore how these multiple texts displace colonial practices in mass media, the taking over of airwaves and cyberspace—both in his writing and directly within courts and constitutions. The genres of rap, hip-hop, rock, and heavy metal attract many Indigenous artists due to these genres' unabashed quest to expose hypocrisy, rather than, according to these artists' descriptions, singing of a nonexistent idyllic space that the privileged class and official government discourse attempt to inculcate. They resemble more the perspective of nemilistli ("way of life"/"philosophy" rooted in personal experiences), focused on actual, lived experiences on the ground instead of official discourse. Indigenous compositions in these genres, like *Las horas perdidas*, subvert numerous stereotypes tied to their languages, among them the idea that they are not "modern." Through his untiring work to have Nahua perspectives present throughout all media, Carballo seeks to displace colonial practices and have this revolution—in the deeper sense of moikxipejpena—televised, and sung, and shared.

Carballo's Facebook profile pictures parody well-known film shots by Russian filmmaker Sergei Eisenstein in the early 1930s, entitled *Que viva México* ("Long Live Mexico"). Those famous side profiles highlight what is popularly viewed as a "Mesoamerican nose." Carballo's photographs and Facebook posts denounce repeated depictions of Nahuas as frozen in the past like the stones by restaging these. Such misrepresentations are a target of Carballo's criticism in *Las horas perdidas* and his posts on Facebook. He seeks to represent Nahuas with voices and faces in the present. Carballo has succeeded in telling the stories of many of the disappeared—his voice along with numerous others has helped keep the memory of Ayotzinapa alive—and he won the case to have Article 230 struck down as unconstitutional in 2016. His efforts made international news and were described in social media as Quijote having gone up against the giants and triumphed. The perspectives tied to nemilistli have helped make these victories possible, as well as many future successful movements and campaigns through his works and social media that are sure to come.

ACKNOWLEDGMENTS

The research for this article was supported by a University of Minnesota Imagine Fund Grant, University of Minnesota Faculty Research Enhancement Funds, and the MacArthur Lecture Series at the University of California Merced.

NOTES

1. Personal interview conducted in Spanish: "Paso todo el día sentado, y hablo, y hablo, pero mi familia trabaja duro en el campo. Cuando pienso en eso, no puedo quejarme." In a more recent interview, Carballo reiterated this inspiration for his work and added that the work in the cornfields, "eso sí es trabajo." Personal interviews, June 9, 2013, and August 30, 2017.

2. Proposed by the executive branch under President Enrique Peña Nieto, the Ley de Telecomunicaciones was enacted on July 14, 2014 (Secretaría de Comunicaciones y Transportes 2014). Article 230 is contained within a more expansive law with the expressed goal of improving media communications and competitiveness. Carballo successfully had the article struck down as unconstitutional on June 1, 2016 (see Secretaría de Comunicaciones y Transportes 2016). See LXIII Legislatura, "LEY federal" n.d., for access to all changes made to this law.

3. Numerous Nahua and other Indigenous nations' artists and activists in Mexico City and beyond it comment on Carballo's posts, such as: Yásnaya Elena Aguilar Gil (Ayuuk), Genner Llanes Ortiz (Maya), Natalia Toledo (Zapoteca), Martín Tonalmeyotl (Nahua), Enriqueta Lunez (Tzotzil), Isaac Carrillo (Maya), Leticia Aparicio-Soriano (Nahua), Victoriano Tepoxteco (Nahua), Irma Pineda (Zapoteca), Hubert Matiúwàa (Mè'phàà), Martín Tonalmeyotl (Nahua), Mikeas Sánchez (Zoque), and Juan Gregorio Regino (Mazateco). The power of this Indigenous network on social media was recently apparent when earthquakes struck southern and central Mexico on September 8, 2017, and September 19, 2017. Carballo organized relief efforts through Facebook. There are similar examples of Indigenous activism and social networking throughout Abiayala, among them: Cortamortaja; Comunicación Redes A.C.; Ojo de Agua Comunicación; Renamur-Red Nacional Mujeres Rurales; Casa de la Mujer Indígena; Pueblos Indígenas; Renji Jóvenes Indígenas; Comunalidad; Servicios del Pueblo Mixe A.C.; Nayuujk; Idle No More; Grupo de Acción Abya Yala NAISA; Sacred Stone Camp; Native Lives Matter. For additional studies of this activism through social media, see: Cru 2015; Doncel de la Colina et al. 2017; Grandia 2017; Gilio-Whitaker 2015; Samira 2016; Wood 2015; and Tupper 2014. Regarding activism in general on social media, see: Dahlgren 2014; Cohen et al. 2012; Kandiyoti 2014; Lievrouw 2012; Velasquez and LaRose 2015; Petray 2011; and Burke and Şen 2018.

4. The official census of the Mexican federal government calculates approximately 1.5 million. I use the figure of at least three million from Nahua author Natalio Hernández (personal interview 2012). He argues that in the census many—especially those in urban areas—avoid stating that they are Nahua due to discrimination. Moreover, the Mexican census does not take into account the tens of thousands who live outside of Mexico or those who identify as Nahua but do not speak the Nahuatl language. See INEGI n.d.

5. A key concept that helps in understanding Nahua kinship ties is the Ayuj (Mixe) and Zapotec concept *comunalidad* ("communality"), which Zapotec anthropologist Alejandra Aquino 2013 identifies as a grassroots theoretical approach to community creation in rural or urban areas (8). Comunalidad constitutes a community-centered approach to life based on reciprocity and participation in institutions such as *la Asamblea* (Assembly), *el Tequio* (altruistic action taken on behalf of the community), and *el sistema de cargos* (a system of community posts and tasks). The use of comunalidad as a methodology in studying a Nahua text would be problematic since the principle proponents of this concept, Ayuj sociologist Floriberto Díaz

Gómez and Zapotec Serrano anthropologist Jaime Martínez Luna, emphasized specificities—it was not meant to describe all Indigenous communities. Nonetheless, comunalidad is an excellent starting point to begin conceptualizing Nahua kinship as there are numerous similarities.

6. For a more in depth discussion of ixtlamatilistli (also spelled ixtlamatiliztli), see McDonough 2014, 15; Coon 2015, 33–39.

7. Personal interviews, June 9, 2013, and September 30, 2017.

8. Original in Spanish: "El náhuatl es un lenguaje más, es un instrumento de creación, independientemente de todo el asunto cosmogónico que lo circunscribe. Siempre hago textos en español con un universo totalmente campesino, totalmente náhuatl, aunque no esté la presencia de la lengua implícita o explícita."

9. The band completed the book mid-2014, and it was printed in November 2014 with a run of one thousand copies.

10. These students, many of them Indigenous, commandeered commercial buses near Iguala, Guerrero, to participate in a protest commemorating the October 2, 1969, Tlatelolco Student Massacre. Iguala's mayor ordered their arrest and disappearance, and there have been continual debates over how complicit the federal government was in this. For a more in-depth analysis of Ayotzinapa, see Maldonado 2015; "Caso Ayotzinapa" 2017; Forensic Architecture n.d.

11. For a detailed investigation of the effects of Ayotzinapa at the local level, see Maldonado 2015.

12. For more information regarding the conflict over these turbines, see Juárez-Hernández and León 2014.

13. The band began posting performances of their compositions in progress from its inception. For example, on Mardonio Carballo's page: "Vete de mí" on September 15, 2012 (Plaza Condesa), October 9, 2012 (Casa de Lago), April 24, 2014 (Montevideo-Zitarrosa), March 16, 2013 (Foro del Tejedor, Festival Latino); "Las horas perdidas," which Carballo changed from the original title "Cielo mar" in response to his public: September 21, 2012, December 4, 2012 (Casa del Lago), March 20, 2013 (Vive Latino), November 11, 2014, November 29, 2016 (Feria Internacional del Libro, Guadalajara); "Desaparecidos" on March 26, 2013 (Vive Latino 13), July 26, 2016 (Xalapa, Veracruz); "¿Cuánto pesan los muertos?" on March 11, 2013 (UNAM, Casa del Lago), October 14, 2014 (reposted performance at UNAM, Casa del Lago); "Mitote" on March 19, 2013 (Vive Latino 2013), October 2, 2013, September 5, 2014 (WOMAD Fest, England); "Sabotage" on July 4, 2012, December 14, 2012, March 10, 2013, March 15, 2013, November 23, 2014 (Museo Universitario del Chopo).

14. The poem/song in Spanish is written in free verse, with lines varying in length from three to twenty-six syllables. It imitates the shape of a bird with its wings extended to suggest rising up through this affective space. Original: "Vuelve esta tarde / cuando las plumas últimas del Sol-Ave surquen con doradas líneas el cielo, / cuando las primeras notas de la Luna-Música inunden los oídos de los cometas / y en vertiginosa danza las estrellas caigan hasta el fondo del mar / y den a luz una

estrella nueva. / Son ya las horas perdidas, la madrugada. / Las personas se han cerrado, duermen, tienen miedo de perder la cordura. / Son ya las horas perdidas, la madrugada. / Tendido en sacrificio a la mitad de la mesa" (45). My translation: Return this evening / when the last feathers of the Sun-Bird furrow across the sky with gold lines, / when the first notes of the Moon-Music flood the comets' ears / and the stars fall in a vertiginous dance into the depths of the sea / and give light to a new star. / It is already the lost hours, the early morning. / The people have locked up, they sleep, they are afraid of losing their sanity. / It is already the lost hours, the early morning. / Laying in sacrifice in the middle of the table.

15. Original in Spanish: "Estas son, pues, *Las horas perdidas* que nos encontramos andando por algunas partes del mundo, buscando rutas con menos sangre y menos violencia."

16. Original in Nahuatl, "Iljuikatl-ueipuyekatl": "Xi uala katiotlak / keman ne tonalto-totl i ijuio koxtikpepetlakaz pan iljuikatl / keman meztli itlatzotzonali kakiztiz pan citlamen i nakaz uan peuazen mijtotizen / uan mo achomonitin pan ueipuyekatl / Uan mo nextiz ze iankuik citlalueipuyekatl. / Son ya las horas perdidas / Panojka tlajkoioal / Nochi kaltzakuakenya, iajken kochiton / Tlamakazin / Ax ki nekin mo kuapolozen / Son ya las horas perdidas / Nij tlamana no tlakayotl, ni mitz chia, ni mo kuezojtok" (47).

17. Original in Spanish: "a dormir arriba de una mítica ceiba." In Maya cosmogony, the ceiba sustains life throughout the world. It is also a key symbol in the writings of EZLN figure "Don Durito": http://enlacezapatista.ezln.org.mx/1996/09/18/el-amor-y-el-calendario. He climbs to the top of a ceiba tree to observe and see things more clearly. In personal interviews, Carballo quoted long portions of EZLN declarations from memory. See also Ejército Zapatista de Liberación Nacional 1994, 368–71.

18. See Ejército Zapatista de Liberación Nacional 1996.

19. Original in Spanish: "Es una lástima que no pueda ser real y ahogar al fin el recuerdo de ti y de tus ojos."

20. Original in Spanish: "Hace poco nos enteramos que en la llamada Guerra Contra el Narcotráfico ha / habido más de 90 mil muertos."

21. Original in Spanish: "¿Cuáles son los códigos que tiene que romper el ser humano para matar a otro / que es su par?"

22. Original in Spanish: "Hay un ritual que es premonición, poema y augurio que hacen las personas / antes de morir: recorren sus pasos."

23. The word *pejpena* as a loanword in Spanish, *pepenar*, has negative connotations—to scavenge for trash—that are absent in the original language. In Nahuatl, *pejpena* refers to the gathering precious corn kernels from off the ground.

24. I first met Mardonio Carballo at Café de Raíz in summer 2010. That same day he had taken part in protests against the persecution of newsreporters, and they all met together at the café afterward. This space could be described as Carballo's main headquarters for his activism and kinship formation in Mexico City.

25. In his article, "Indigenous Interference" (2013), Cárcamo Huechante develops the concept "acoustic colonialism." Cárcamo Huechante also spoke of "visual colonial-

ism" in the Fall 2017 Mellon-Sawyer Faculty Seminar at the University of Texas at Austin.

26. In January 2016, Mexico City became a federal entity (*entidad federal*) like Mexico's other thirty-one states. As part of the transition from federal district to entity, a constitutional assembly was formed to draft the Mexico City Constitution. See Gaceta oficial de la Ciudad de México n.d.

27. Among other demands, the constitution for Mexico City assures that Indigenous communities "tienen derecho a establecer sus propios medios de comunicación en sus lenguas. Las autoridades establecerán condiciones para que los pueblos y las comunidades indígenas puedan adquirir, operar y administrar medios de comunicaciones en los términos que la ley de la materia determine."

28. Original in Spanish: "no gritarás, / guardarás silencio."

29. Original in Spanish: "Sólo novedades querrás vestirte."

30. See Coon 2013. The purist stigma against loanwords and code-switching often leads youth to cease speaking the Nahuatl language. These youth are left with the sense that they do not speak "correctly," and instead only know "un náhuatl cuatrapeado" (a corrupted/ruined Nahuatl).

REFERENCES

Aquino, Alejandra. 2013. "La comunalidad como epistemología del Sur. Aportes y retos." *Cuadernos del Sur* 73: 7–19.

Burke, Barbara Ruth, and Ayşe Fulya Şen. 2018. "Social Media Choices and Uses: Comparing Turkish and American Young-Adults' Social Media Activism." *Palgrave Communications* 4 (1): 40.

Carballo, Mardonio. n.d. "Facebook Profile Picture." *Facebook* (blog). Accessed November 30, 2016.

Carballo, Mardonio. 2013. Personal interview.

Carballo, Mardonio. 2016. Personal interview.

Carballo, Mardonio. 2017. Personal interview.

Carballo, Mardonio, José María Arreola, and Alonso Arreola. 2014. *Las horas perdidas*. Mexico City: CONACULTA.

Cárcamo-Huechante, Luis E. 2013. "Indigenous Interference: Mapuche Use of Radio in Times of Acoustic Colonialism." *Latin American Research Review* 48: 50–68.

"Caso Ayotzinapa." 2017. *El País*, October 2017. https://elpais.com/tag/matanza _estudiantes_normalistas_iguala/a.

Cohen, Cathy J., and Joseph Kahne. 2012. "Participatory Politics: New Media and Youth Political Action." DML Research Hub, May 31, 2012. https://dmlhub.net/ publications/participatory-politics-new-media-and-youth-political-action-6ca85d2f -2387-4529-a282-1b198f6457d1.

Coon, Adam W. 2013. "To In or Not to In: The Politics Behind the Usage or Disavowal of Classical Nahuatl within Contemporary Nahua Literature." Revitalizing Endangered Languages (website), October 19, 2013. http://www.revitalization.al.uw.edu.pl/eng/Nahuatl/31/studies.

Coon, Adam W. 2015. "Iajki Estados Onidos / She Went to the U.S.: Nahua Identities in Migration within Contemporary Nahua Literature, 1985–2014." PhD diss. University of Texas.

Cru, Josep. 2015. "Language Revitalisation from the Ground Up: Promoting Yucatec Maya on Facebook." *Journal of Multilingual and Multicultural Development* 36 (3): 284–96.

Dahlgren, Peter. 2014. "Social Media and Political Participation: Discourse and Deflection." In *Critique, Social Media and the Information Society*, edited by Christian Fuchs and Marisol Sandoval, 191–202. New York: Routledge.

Doncel de la Colina, Juan Antonio, and Emmanuel Talancón Leal. 2017. "El Rap Indígena: Activismo Artístico Para La Reivindicación Del Origen Étnico En Un Contexto Urbano." *Andamios* 14 (34): 87–111.

Ejército Zapatista de Liberación Nacional. 1994. *EZLN: Documentos y comunicados, 15 de agosto de 1994–29 de septiembre de 1995*. Vol. 2. Mexico City: Ediciones Era.

Ejército Zapatista de Liberación Nacional. 1996. "Cuarta Declaración de La Selva Lacandona." http://palabra.ezln.org.mx/comunicados/1996/1996_01_01_a.htm.

Forensic Architecture. n.d. "The Ayotzinapa Case: A Cartography of Violence." Accessed October 7, 2017. http://www.forensic-architecture.org/case/ayotzinapa.

Gaceta oficial de la Ciudad de México. n.d. "Constitución Políitca de la Ciudad de México." Accessed September 1, 2017. http://www.cdmx.gob.mx/constitucion.

Gilio-Whitaker, Dina. 2015. "Idle No More and Fourth World Social Movements in the New Millennium." *South Atlantic Quarterly* 114 (4): 866–77.

Goeman, Mishuana. 2014. "Heteronormative Constructions of Electric Lights and Tourist Sights in Niagara Falls." Paper presented at the Annual Meeting of the Native American and Indigenous Studies Association, Austin, Texas, May 2014.

Grandia, Liza. 2017. "Sacred Maize against a Legal Maze: The Diversity of Resistance to Guatemala's 'Monsanto Law.'" *Journal for the Study of Religion, Nature & Culture* 11 (1): 56–85.

Hernández, Natalio. 2012. Personal interview.

INEGI. n.d. "Lenguas Indígenas En México y Hablantes (de 3 Años y Más) Del 2015." Accessed October 6, 2017. http://cuentame.inegi.org.mx/hipertexto/todas_lenguas.htm.

Juárez-Hernández, Sergio, and Gabriel León. 2014. "Wind Energy in the Isthmus of Tehuantepec: Development, Actors and Social Opposition." *Problemas del desarrollo: Revista latinoamericnaa de economía* 45: 178. http://www.probdes.iiec.unam.mx/en/revistas/v45n178/body/v45n178a6_1.php.

Kandiyoti, Deniz. 2014. "Contesting Patriarchy-as-Governance: Lessons from Youth-Led Activism." *OpenDemocracy*, March 7, 2014. http://www.opendemocracy.net.

Kreps, Daniel. 2014. "Beastie Boys Deny Arnold Schwarzenegger Use of 'Sabotage.'" *Rolling Stone*, June 3, 2014.

Lievrouw, Leah A. 2012. "Alternative and Activist New Media: A Genre Framework." In *Media and Cultural Studies: Keyworks*, edited by Meenakshi Gigi Durhama and Douglas M. Kellner, 2nd ed., 471–91. West Sussex: Wiley-Blackwell.

Lionnet, Françoise, and Emmanuel Bruno Jean-François. 2016. "Literary Routes: Migration, Islands, and the Creative Economy." *PMLA* 131 (5): 1222–38.

Maldonado, Tryno. 2015. *Ayotzinapa: El Rostro de Los Desaparecidos*. Mexico City: Planeta Mexicana.

McDonough, Kelly. 2014. *The Learned Ones: Nahua Intellectuals in Postconquest Mexico*. Tucson: University of Arizona Press.

Ordorika, Imanol, and Adolfo Gilly. 2014. "Ayotzinapa, crimen de Estado." *La jornada*, October 6, 2014. http://www.jornada.unam.mx/2014/10/06/politica/007a1pol.

Petray, Theresa Lynn. 2011. "Protest 2.0: Online Interactions and Aboriginal Activists." *Media, Culture & Society* 33 (6): 923–40.

Samira, Samaro. 2016. "Unsettling Spaces: Grassroots Responses to Canada's Missing and Murdered Indigenous Women During the Harper Government Years." *Comparative American Studies* 14 (3–4): 204–20.

Secretaría de Comunicaciones y Transportes. 2014. "Ley Federal de Telecomunicaciones y Radiodifusión," July 14, 2014. http://www.diputados.gob.mx/LeyesBiblio/ref/lftr/LFTR_orig_14jul14.pdf.

Secretaría de Comunicaciones y Transportes. 2016. "Decreto por el que se reforma el artículo 230 de la Ley Federal de Telecomunciaciones y Radiodifusión." *Diario Oficial*, June 1, 2016, sec. Primera sección.

LXIII Legislatura. n.d. "LEY Federal de Telecomunicaciones y Radiodifusión." Accessed September 2, 2017. http://www.diputados.gob.mx/LeyesBiblio/ref/lftr.htm.

Tupper, Jennifer. 2014. "Social Media and the Idle No More Movement: Citizenship, Activism and Dissent in Canada." *Journal of Social Science Education* 13 (4): 87–94.

Velasquez, Alcides, and Robert LaRose. 2015. "Youth Collective Activism through Social Media: The Role of Collective Efficacy." *New Media and Society* 17 (6): 899–918.

Wood, Lesley J. 2015. "Idle No More, Facebook and Diffusion." *Social Movement Studies* 14 (5): 615–21.

CONTRIBUTORS

Arturo Arias is John D. and Catherine T. MacArthur Foundation Professor in the Humanities at the University of California, Merced. He has published *Recovering Lost Footprints: Contemporary Maya Narratives, Volume 1* (2017), *Taking their Word: Literature and the Signs of Central America* (2007), *The Rigoberta Menchú Controversy* (2000), *The Identity of the Word: Guatemalan Literature in Light of the New Century* (1998), and *Ceremonial Gestures: Central American Fiction 1960–1990* (1998), as well as a critical edition of Miguel Angel Asturias's *Mulata* (2000). In 2018 he published volume 2 of *Recovering Lost Footprints: Contemporary Maya Narratives*, which analyzes contemporary Yucatecan and Chiapanecan Maya texts.

Debra A. Castillo is Stephen H. Weiss Presidential Fellow, Emerson Hinchliff Professor of Hispanic Studies, professor of Comparative Literature, and director of the Latina/o Studies Program at Cornell University. She is past president of the international Latin American Studies Association. She specializes in contemporary narrative and performance from the Spanish-speaking world (including the United States), gender studies, comparative border studies, and cultural theory. Her most recent books include *Mexican Public Intellectuals* (with Stuart Day, 2014), *Despite all Adversities: Spanish American Queer Cinema* (with Andrés Lema Hincapié, 2015), *Theorizing Fieldwork in the Humanities* (with Shalini Puri, 2016), and *South of the Future:*

Speculative Biotechnologies and Care Markets in South Asia and Latin America (with Anindita Banerjee, forthcoming).

Gloria Elizabeth Chacón is an associate professor in the Literature Department at the University of California, San Diego. The author of *Indigenous Cosmolectics: Kab'awil and the Making of Maya and Zapotec Literatures* (University of North Carolina Press, 2018), Chacón is also co-editor of a special issue of *Diálogo*, "The Five Cardinal Points in Contemporary Indigenous Literature" (Spring 2016). Her scholarly articles have appeared in anthologies and journals such as the *Routledge History of Latin American Culture*, *Latino Studies*, *Cuadernos de Literatura*, and *Revista Canadiense de Estudios Hispánicos*. Chacón is working on her second book, tentatively titled "Metamestizaje, Indigeneity, and Diasporas: New Cartographies."

Adam Coon is an assistant professor at the University of Minnesota, Morris. He specializes in contemporary Nahua cultural production, contemporary Indigenous literatures, and language revitalization. His current project is entitled *Iahqui Estados Onidos: The Articulation of Identities in Migration within Contemporary Nahua Literature and Media, 1985–2015*. He analyzes contemporary Nahua cultural production in order to explore how these texts disarticulate the narrative frame of vanquished Indians as exemplified in Mexican national discourse and its championing of "modernity."

Emiliana Cruz is originally from San Juan Quiahije, Oaxaca. She received her PhD in Linguistic Anthropology from the University of Texas Austin in 2011. She specializes in social and linguistic anthropology. Her work focuses mainly on the application of anthropological methods for the documentation and preservation of languages now approaching extinction. In particular, she works with Chatino communities in Oaxaca using participatory research methods in which she works directly with communities and creates with them pedagogical materials for the preservation of language and culture. Her areas of interest in anthropology are education, decolonization, social movements, language revitalization, mobility, autonomy and territory, linguistic rights, and material culture. Cruz currently works at CIESAS-DF, where she has organized workshops for both the elaboration of pedagogical grammars and tones for speakers of otomangue languages. She is a native speaker of Chatino and founder of the Chatino Language Documentation Project.

Mauricio Espinoza, from Costa Rica, is Assistant Professor of Spanish and Latin American Cultural Studies at the University of Cincinnati. He holds a PhD in Latin American Literatures and Cultures from The Ohio State University. His research and publications focus on Latin American/Latino comics and film, Central American migration narrative and poetry, and Latin American immigrant communities. He has translated the work of Costa Rican poet Eunice Odio into English. His book *Respiración de piedras* won the 2015 University of Costa Rica Press Poetry Prize. His poetry also appears in *The Wandering Song: Central American Writing in the United States* (Tía Chucha Press, 2017).

Alicia Ivonne Estrada is a professor in the Chicana/o Studies Department at California State University at Northridge. She has published on the Maya and Guatemalan diaspora in the United States as well as on contemporary Maya literature, film, and radio. Estrada is coeditor of the anthology *U.S. Central Americans: Reconstructing Memories, Struggles and Communities of Resistance* (University of Arizona Press, 2017). Her work has appeared in *Romance Notes*, *Latino Studies*, and *Revista Canadiense de Estudios Hispánicos*, among other journals and anthologies. Estrada's current book project is on the Maya diaspora in Los Angeles. Since 2006, she has actively collaborated with the Maya radio program *Contacto Ancestral*. The show has been on the airwaves for more than a decade on the Southern California community radio station KPFK and on the World Wide Web.

Jennifer Gómez Menjívar is an associate professor of Spanish and Latin American studies at the University of Minnesota Duluth. Gómez Menjívar's publications have appeared in *Mesoamérica*, *NAIS: Native American and Indigenous Studies*, *Chasqui*, *Diálogo*, *Alter/nativas*, *A contracorriente*, *Applied Linguistics*, and the *Journal of Pidgin and Creole Languages*, among others. She is co-author of *Tropical Tongues: Language Ideologies, Endangerment, and Minority Languages in Belize* (2018), the inaugural volume in the Studies in Latin America series distributed by the University of North Carolina Press. Her current book project explores the authority of print and digital mediums on Indigenous and Black legacies in Central America, focusing on their contours in the bicoastal and highland topographic zones of the isthmus.

Sue P. Haglund, a Dule poet and scholar native of Panama, received her doctorate from the Department of Political Science at the University of Hawai'i at

Mānoa. Her article "Dule Urwed and Boxing: The Production of Dule Knowledge via Baby San Blas" was published in York University's *InTensions Journal* (2014), and her poem "Conversaciones con mi abuelo" was published in the first anthology of Dule poetry, *Antología de Poetas Kunas* (Panama City, Panama, 2015). Among other publications, she coauthored with Monisha Das Gupta an article titled "Mexican Migration to Hawai'i and US Settler Colonialism," which was published in the journal *Latino Studies* (2015).

Brook Danielle Lillehaugen is a linguist at Haverford College who specializes in Indigenous languages of Mexico. She received her PhD in linguistics in 2006 from the University of California, Los Angeles and has been learning from Zapotec speakers since 1999. Lillehaugen's research profile includes technical grammatical description as well as collaborative language documentation and revitalization projects. She publishes on the grammar of Zapotec languages in both their modern and historical forms. She has found combining linguistic fieldwork with tools from the digital humanities to be a productive way to collaborate with both Zapotec speaking communities and undergraduate students. She is codirector of *Ticha*, a digital text explorer for colonial Zapotec texts and leads several teams in developing online talking dictionaries for Zapotec languages.

Paul Joseph López Oro (Garifuna) is a doctoral candidate in the Department of African and African Diaspora Studies and a 2017–2018 dissertation fellow in the Department of Mexican American and Latina/o Studies at The University of Texas at Austin. His dissertation project "Queering Garifuna: The Diasporic Politics of Black Indigeneity in New York City" is an ethnographic and archival study on how gender and sexuality shapes the ways in which Garifuna New Yorkers negotiate and perform their multiple subjectivities as Black, Indigenous, Latinx. His subject position is as a Garifuna Brooklynite of Honduran descent. He is a 2018–2020 predoctoral fellow at the Carter G. Woodson Institute for African American and African Studies at the University of Virginia.

Rita M. Palacios is a professor of Liberal Studies at Conestoga College Institute of Technology and Advanced Learning in Kitchener, Ontario, Canada. She holds a doctorate in Latin American Literature from the University of Toronto, and her research examines contemporary Maya literature from a cultural and gender studies perspective. Her work has appeared in *Apuntes Hispánicos*, *Diálogo*, *Hispania*, and *Revista Canadiense de Estudios Hispánicos*, among others. Her book with Paul Worley, *Unwriting Maya Literature*, is forthcoming in 2019 from the University of Arizona Press.

Tajëëw Robles is Mixe, from Tlahuitoltepec. She majored in social anthropology with an emphasis in legal policy at CIESAS-Oaxaca. She is a member of the Colmix collective, whose goal includes the dissemination of the linguistic diversity of the Mixe language. Through the Juan de Córdova Research Library, she organized a conference for digital activism of Indigenous languages.

Gabriela Spears-Rico is a cultural anthropologist and Assistant Professor of Chicanx Latinx Studies with a joint appointment in American Indian Studies at the University of Minnesota. Her work examines manifestations of consumption and cultural appropriation in touristic transactions between mestizos and Indigenous people in Mexico. Gabriela has had a fifteen-year ethnographic relationship with P'urhépecha communities in Michoacan. Having examined the Days of the Dead in Patzcuaro, she critically engages with the mestiza/o desire to tour and inhabit Mexican Indigenous communities. Her forthcoming book *Mestiza/o Melancholia and the Legacy of Conquest in Michoacán* will explore how gendered violence has framed the racialization of Indigenous people and the manufacturing of mestizaje in Mexico. She hails from Uruetaro and Charo, Michoacan, and identifies as both P'urhépecha and Matlatzinca.

Paul M. Worley is Associate Professor of Global Literature at Western Carolina University. He published *Telling and Being Told: Storytelling and Cultural Control in Contemporary Yucatec Maya* (2013) and has recently published articles in *A contracorriente*, *Studies in American Indian Literatures*, and *Latin American Caribbean Ethnic Studies*. Stories recorded as part of his research on Maya literatures are available at tsikbalichmaya.org.

INDEX